2002-2003 Prices

An Overview of
Homer Laughlin
Dinnerware

by
Mark Gonzalez

Published by:
L-W BOOK SALES
PO Box 69
Gas City, IN 46933

ISBN #: 0-89538-118-4

In Memory of: **SEPTEMBER 11, 2001**

Published by: L-W BOOK SALES
PO Box 69
Gas City, IN 46933

Please write for our free catalog of books on Antiques

Table of Contents

**Fiesta® is a registered trademark
of the Homer Laughlin China Company**

Acknowledgments

Without the help of those listed below, this book would not have been possible. Some took the time to take pictures, and others actually shipped large quantities of HLC ware to be photographed. Words cannot express the appreciation I have for the collectors and the staff and management at the Homer Laughlin China Company who aided in this project.

Steve Beals	Dottie Payne
Candy Fagerlin	Delida Pederson
Pete Fagerlin	Steve Sfakis
Susan Gonzalez	Fran and Carl Stone
Bill & Donna Gray	Judith Stout
Sharon Lincks	Becky Turner
Fred Mutchler	Matthew Whalen
Bradley Payne & Sara Gatza	Brenda Wood

Staff of Robbins Nest at www.robbinsnest.com
Bill Mackall of Tudordane Antiques in Chester, West Virginia
Linda Wilson of the Company Store in Negley, Ohio
Anastasia Sfakis and The Museum of Ceramics of East Liverpool, Ohio

And extra special thanks to those from the Homer Laughlin China Company:

Judi Noble	Joseph Geisse	Pat Shreve	Mary Ann Dunn

Introduction

When I first told a friend that I was working on a book on Homer Laughlin dinnerware, his response was, "Great! But, isn't that a crowded field?" This is the type of reaction I have gotten from several people over the past year. The Homer Laughlin China Company (HLC) has been in continuous operation for 130 years. They have made millions of pieces of dinnerware using dozens of shapes and thousands of different treatments. The fact of the matter is fifty people could write books on Homer Laughlin. While there would almost certainly be overlap with the most common shapes and patterns, HLC has produced such a volume and diversity of products that each book would be distinct with unique items. No one book (or even a series of books) could ever fully document the wares that have come out of HLC's doors.

With that said, how is the book different from others? This work will cover a wide range of dates. Most books on HLC cover the "golden age" of dinnerware which lasted from the 1920s until the late 1960s. Many references come to a halt after such shapes as Cavalier, Rhythm and Charm House. This is not at all surprising since there is very little demand for dinnerware made after 1960, so why write about it? There were some interesting shapes that came out of this era such as Victoria, Orbit, Granada, Hearthside, Challenger, White Dover and a slew of Ironstone shapes. The only problem with these lines is, with the exception of most flatware, pieces are unmarked. There are thousands of pieces of dinnerware on the open market and many collectors aren't aware they were made by Homer Laughlin.

Will 60s and 70s dinnerware ever become popular? It's hard to say. Ten years ago, the 30s and 40s shapes such as Century and Virginia Rose were very inexpensive, but today there are collectors who try to collect every type of decal on each shape. It may be hard for today's collector to think of dinnerware from the 60s and 70s as being "old" or valuable, but shapes from that era are now 30 to 40 years old. Consider the famous line of Fiesta. When the first books on Fiesta were being published, the oldest pieces from that line were 37 years old. So, one never knows what will or will not become valuable.

Covering 60s, 70s and even some 80s shapes is one of two objectives of this book. The second concerns the more popular lines from the 30s, 40s, and 50s. The Art Department at Homer Laughlin was gracious enough to allow me to go through old records, modeling logs and journals. Frederick Rhead, art director from 1927 to 1942, kept extensive journals for most of his time at HLC. From these the development of many vintage HLC lines can be pieced together. For the most part, there were no problems with creating new shapes, glazes or treatments, but it is interesting to know how a line evolves from original concept to a finished product.

Throughout the book, there are sketches taken from the modeling log as well as entries cited from Rhead's journals. Rhead makes numerous mention of "JMW" who is Joseph M. Wells, general manager at HLC during most of Rhead's tenure. Wells followed the creation of each shape, treatment and glaze very closely so his name will appear throughout the text with regard to the development of popular 30s and 40s shapes.

Besides discussing various dinnerware lines, there are sections on markings, children's sets, special order items, distributors and decorators. As the title states, this book is an overview so there is a little bit of everything! Hopefully the reader will consider this work a satisfactory addition to their growing library on Homer Laughlin.

The Homer Laughlin China Company

In the mid 1800s, pottery making was done primarily with stoneware. Dinnerware production was not much of an industry in the United States at this time. Potters generally had small operations and would sell their wares by going town to town. Towards the 1880s, larger companies started to emerge in the Ohio River Valley area. This was prime ground as not only was there a rich supply of clay and natural resources, but the Ohio River served as an excellent shipping route.

At this time, potteries were still making utilitarian ware such as mixing bowls and crocks out of crude clay bodies – commonly called "yellow ware" due to the color of the body. There were some early potteries which would take white clay "slip" and pour it over a stoneware piece giving it the appearance of a white body. In 1871, brothers Homer and Shakespeare Laughlin started a pottery in East Liverpool, Ohio. The following year, the people of East Liverpool offered a prize of $5,000.00 to the pottery that could make white ware instead of the old yellow wares. The brothers won the award and in 1873, the first plant of what would become known as the Homer Laughlin China Company was erected. In 1877 Shakespeare left the business and in 1897 Homer Laughlin sold the plant to Louis Aaron and William E. Wells.

Victor Teapot

Examples of early HLC wares:

Shakespeare Sauceboat

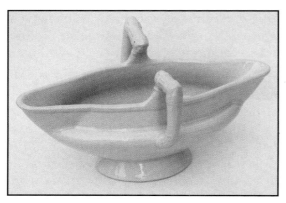
Victor Double Handled Sauceboat

Victor Handled Urn

Toilet set brush holders – often confused for small vases   Early HLC covered soap dish

During these early years, HLC was making several dinnerware shapes and toilet wares. These pieces usually have the famous eagle-over-lion backstamp symbolizing the American dominance over British wares. In 1897 and 1899, plants 2 and 3 were constructed respectively. In the early 1900s, there began a practice of copying French china shapes and patterns. (See section on Hudson for more.)

More plants were constructed across the river from East Liverpool in Newell, West Virginia. Newell, West Virginia plants and dates in which they opened:

Plant 4 – 1906   Plant 6 – 1923
Plant 5 – 1914   Plant 7 – 1927
Plant 8 – 1929   (the old East Liverpool plants closed at this time)

Vintage postcard showing the decorating shop at HLC's then new plant number 5.

By 1910 there were hundreds of potteries all over the country. Homer Laughlin soon found itself in a very crowded market. From 1912 to 1914, HLC went on an advertising blitz featuring ads in various magazines including *The Ladies Home Journal* and *Cosmopolitan*. Such ads advised housewives to check the backstamp on dinnerware to make sure they were getting a Homer Laughlin product. A June 1912 ad gives some important basic information on the company:

The Greatest China Factory In The World . . . Not in England, or France, or Germany, but at Newell, West Virginia, U.S.A., is located the pottery of the Homer Laughlin China Co., the largest in the world. To make the 45,000,000 pieces of Homer Laughlin China annually produced requires the work of 1,800 people; 15 acres of floor space is necessary; and for decorating, $50,000 worth of gold alone is used annually. These figures indicate the popularity of Homer Laughlin China. In addition to its beauty and refinement of design and decoration, Homer Laughlin China gives splendid service. It is "as good as it looks." In buying, see that trade-mark name "Homer Laughlin" appears on the underside of each piece of sufficient size.

An important change occurred in dinnerware in the mid 1920s. Many companies started to design their own wares and treatments instead of purchasing molds and importing decals. By 1930, potteries started to have assortments that were no longer copies of popular British and French wares. Instead, each U.S. company developed its own style resulting in a divergence of shapes and patterns. It was during this time American dinnerware truly came into its own. U.S. potters were no longer copying foreign wares – they were now copying each other!

HLC hired Frederick Hurten Rhead as art director in 1927. He was no stranger to the pottery industry having worked at two Ohio art potteries, Weller and Roseville. From '27 until his death in 1942, Rhead created what many collectors consider HLC's greatest shapes and designs. He was responsible for such popular lines as Virginia Rose, OvenServe, Harlequin, Century and of course, Fiesta. His death in 1942 foreshadowed the end of the "golden age" of American dinnerware. With the United States involvement in W.W.II, Americans had more important concerns than purchasing dinnerware.

This Rhead creation is from the very late 1920s. The rim features a very detailed etched design.

From the end of 1942 until 1948, Homer Laughlin did not introduce any lines – the longest the company has ever gone in not creating a new product. After WWII, there was a rebirth in the dinnerware industry. A new demand emerged for clean and uncluttered shapes. Most potteries responded to this by creating simple coupe or plain rim shapes. Homer Laughlin's contributions were Jubilee, Charm House, Rhythm, Cavalier, Epicure and Kenilworth which were designed by Don Shrekengost who served as art director from 1945 to 1960. Gone from these new shapes were floral embossings, scallops and ring pattern so popular in the 30s and 40s. It was also during the 1950s that two eggshell lines, Georgian Eggshell and Nautilus Eggshell, which were developed in the late 30s, became very big sellers for HLC.

Some HLC Eggshell lines featured in a 1950s montgomery Wards catalog.

In the early 1960s, many of the big names in American dinnerware closed their doors. Crooksville closed in 1959, Universal Potteries and Salem in 1960, Paden City in 1963, Knowles in 1964 and others cut back production dramatically. There were several reasons for this change. Americans had been introduced to Melmac and similar products in the early to mid 1950s and by the early 60s, dinnerware made of pottery could not compete with the guarantee of indestructibility put forth by Melmac. Another factor was the flood of Japanese imports which also started in the 1950s. There was a certain appeal to the "Fine China" made from overseas and American products took a back seat. Surviving U.S. companies responded to the Fine China imports by creating wares using the same type of translucent clay. In Homer Laughlin's case, at least two Fine China lines were made; Triumph and Triumph Snow White.

Another reason so many potteries closed in the 1960s is that many were producing similar products. Every manufacturer had a plain round coupe shape and almost identical stylized treatments. With so many companies producing identical products, it's not a wonder many couldn't stay open. Many of the "old" standards were finally discontinued in the 1960s. Republic, Virginia Rose and Harlequin were all gone by the end of the 1960s.

Homer Laughlin had been producing utilitarian ware and hotel ware since its earliest days. In 1960, with the general dinnerware market in a state of flux, HLC turned attention to expanding their hotel and restaurant ware shapes. New lines were created and all were sold under the name, "Best China." Those potteries that didn't make the transition into the hotel/restaurant ware trade had to shut down; Red Wing in 1967, Harker in 1972, Taylor Smith & Taylor in 1981, Royal China in 1986.

From the end of the 1960s and into the 1970s, Homer Laughlin continued to make dinnerware for supermarkets and various distributors. These shapes and treatments have the earth-tone colors typical of the 1970s; orange, gold, brown, and olive green. Today, most collectors overlook these pieces, but they do reflect the tastes of the time. In 1979, HLC reissued the Harlequin line in a limited assortment for Woolworth's which would continue to be produced until 1983.

There weren't too many retail dinnerware lines produced in the mid 1980s. By this time, the majority of HLC's operations were geared towards the hotel/restaurant wares. In 1984, Jonathan Parry became art director and in 1986, oversaw the reissuing of Fiesta at the request of Bloomingdales. This has grown from a limited assortment in five colors to a hot collectible in today's market. It's still being produced with new shapes and colors being offered from time to time.

Today Homer Laughlin continues to make new shapes and treatments. Art Director Judi Noble and Senior Modeler Joseph Geisse create new and innovative designs to fill special orders as well as expand the ever popular Fiesta line. Just some of the various shapes offered by HLC today are shown here:

The Milford backstamp has "Lead Free" in its backstamp. In 1992, HLC started to guarantee that all materials used in production are lead free. Milford is a restaurant shape that has been in production since 1996.

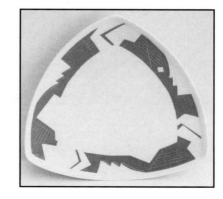

This Milford plate is called a "Triangle Salad." The purple treatment highlights the triple saw tooth embossing at the rim.

Seville covered soup tureen.

Gothic plate.

Pristine charger with casino rim embossings with a small handled bowl.

Royale plate.

Rolled Edge in various solid colors.

Rolled Edge in various solid colors.

Rolled Edge in speckled glazes.

To see all of the current HLC shapes and more designs, be sure to visit their site at www.hlchina.com

Star soup bowl – one of several new "geo" shapes.

Markings

The Homer Laughlin China Company has used over 250 different types of backstamps in their 130 year history. Most are geared to a specific line or treatment. Wells, Coronet, Fiesta, Kraft Blue, Kraft Pink, the Eggshell lines, Rhythm, Epicure and many others had their own backstamps. There were also many special lines and promotional items that made use of special markings. Just a few examples include Quaker Oats promotions such as Harvest, Pastoral, Wild Rose and Tudor Rose. Historical America and Early American Homes were also given special backstamps.

Backstamps are commonly called, "inkstamps" but this implies the use of ink in the markings. Backstamps are really made up of a colored glaze which is formulated to withstand high firing temperatures. While most products received special markings, HLC has made use of general backstamps throughout the years. These marks don't make reference to any particular line and many times have a date code.

Its generally accepted that the horseshoe mark was one of the first markings used by the Laughlin brothers.

The "lion-over-eagle" mark was first used in the late 1880s. British dinnerware was typically considered to be of much higher quality in the 19th Century, but when Homer Laughlin started producing high quality ware of their own, the lion-over-eagle mark was adopted signifying the American dominance over British wares.

There are several versions of this mark. Some have the name Laughlin in script, but this was soon changed to, "Homer Laughlin" in upper case letters. It may be the case that the change occurred when Shakespeare left the pottery. Expect this general mark to make reference to products being "Semi-Vitreous" or "Premium Stone China." Certain early shapes may also be named in conjunction with the lion-over-eagle mark such as American Beauty, Colonial, and King Charles.

In 1912 the common type of backstamp using the logo of the intertwined letters HLC and the Homer Laughlin name written out below was used. This version either came plain or with names of specific shapes: The Angelus, Empress, Hudson, Niagara or Genesee.

These marks have the "N" and "L" as the last letter. The "N" stands for Newell and the "L" for East Liverpool. Starting in the late 1920s, a number was placed after the Newell marks to designate the plant numbers as in N4, N5, N6, N7, or N8. The first symbol in the dates shown are letters, but numbers were used as well. These represent the month and the second single digit represents the year from 1911 to 1919. For example, "3 4 N" would mean March 1914 in Newell and "B 5 L" would stand for February 1915 in East Liverpool.

Starting in 1920, the backstamp recorded the month and year in digits. As shown, the year 1921 is expressed as "21" but in the mid 1920s, HLC started to use letters to represent the month and went back to the method of using single digits for the years. This causes a lot of confusion among collectors. For example, the Yellowstone shape was released in 1926 and almost every piece from the 20s will have a single year for the marking. A piece may be marked, "A7N6." This would mean January 1927 at plant 6. Almost every collector makes the mistake in interpreting the date in the example as 1917.

In 1930, a double digit was used. The first letter still represented the month and the last was now just the letter N. These marks may or may not have a final digit (4, 5, 6, 7, or 8) to denote the plant number in Newell.

For some reason, HLC went back to the old method of one digit for the year after 1930. The first letter was month. The number following either a "1" or a "2" stood for 1931 and 1932 respectively.

How can such date codes be differentiated from 1921 and 1922? Shape can be very helpful. The marking shown comes from a piece of Ravenna – a line first offered in 1932. Keep in mind that Yellowstone, Wells, Century, Jade, Ravenna, Trellis and Newell were available in '31, '32 or both, but not in the early 1920s.

The "Second Selection" marking is a gold stamp applied over the glaze. This was done to less than perfect specimens to indicate they had some small defect either with the glaze or the body of the ware. Special decals were placed on seconds and sold at a lower rate than pieces of first quality. Second Section markings were used mainly in the early 1930s.

At the end of 1932, Homer Laughlin went back to two digits for the year. Everything else, letter for the month and "N" with a number for the plant, stayed the same. This general mark would last until the end of 1967.

Here is another example of the general marking used from 1932-1967. Notice the letter "M" used for the month – the *13th* letter of the alphabet. Apparently, HLC didn't use the letter "I" so the order of months without the letter I becomes:

A: January	E: May	J: September
B: February	F: June	K: October
C: March	G: July	L: November
D: April	H: August	M: December

Some collectors maintain the letter "I" was used. If this is so, then it must have been used for only a short period of time and then abandoned.

In 1968, Homer Laughlin started expressing the date with the standard four digits. This "explicit" marking was used until around 1983.

HLC went back to the two digit year around 1981. This marking was used concurrently with the explicit marking until '83. The two digit year backstamp was used primarily in the 1980s only.

Today's markings have a bold HLC logo with the shape name and a date code which originated in 1960 with their restaurant were called, "Best China." For an explanation of the letters with these codes, see the section on Best China in the appendix.

All lines from 1992 to present, including reissue Fiesta, will have the words, "LEAD FREE" in the backstamp.

Cunningham & Picket

There are several marks used by Cunningham and Pickett of Alliance, Ohio. Lehner describes the company in her book on marks (see bibliography) as, "... a series of jobber or retail agencies in Alliance, Ohio." They would commonly stamp a special name in gold to products purchased from potteries in the Ohio River Valley area. Most of Homer Laughlin's decaled shapes received C&P markings over the years until the late 1960s.

One of the greatest advantages to pieces with a C&P or related marking is the inclusion of a treatment name. Even the smallest items such as fruit cups and saucers, which ordinarily wouldn't receive an HLC marking, were given the special C&P backstamp.

This handled platter has a C&P marking, but the piece was not made by Homer Laughlin. It's from Universal's Ballerina shape. It's important to note that usually the pottery's mark isn't included. If a piece is found with a C&P marking, that doesn't automatically mean it came from HLC.

Sheffield & Coventry

Homer Laughlin had made dinnerware for distributors for many years, and beginning in the late 1960s, they made lines for two in particular, J&H International of Wilmette, Illinois and Coventry Ware, Inc. of Barberton, Ohio. These two are being singled out for several reasons:

(1) Pieces which are marked, dinner plates, chop plates and platters, have no mention of Homer Laughlin in the backstamp. For lines made for J&H International, the marking consists of the trade name, SHEFFIELD with a Fleur-de-lis symbol, pattern name, and mention that the line was, "MADE IN U.S.A." Some markings will include guarantees of: Detergent-proof, Oven-proof and Dishwasher safe, but ALL markings have the three common factors of Sheffield, symbol and USA.

Here is a listing of some of the lines made by Homer Laughlin with the Sheffield marks:

LINE	SHAPE
Sheffield Amberstone	Fiesta (modified)
Sheffield Imperial Blue Dresden	Virginia Rose (modified)
Sheffield Bone White	Victoria
Sheffield Granada	Granada
Sheffield Sunset	Granada
Sheffield Serenade	Regency
Sheffield Bravado	Hearthside
Sheffield Provincial	Provincial

There are fewer lines for Coventry. The easiest to find are: Coventry Casualstone (modified Fiesta) and Coventry Castilian (Granada shape). Both are in a rich gold glaze and flatware has a black stamp decoration. The symbol commonly used for Coventry is a lion in a shield.

(2) All Sheffield and Coventry lines have handled trays a.k.a. tidbit or snack trays. This wasn't a standard item in the shapes of the day and seem to have been made special order for both companies. They were assembled at the HLC plant, though the metal handle was made outside the factory.

(3) Sheffield and Coventry pieces are very easy to find today.

One final note on Sheffield and Coventry markings: If you find a piece of dinnerware with either mark, it does not automatically mean it is a piece of Homer Laughlin. There were other companies which produced wares for both distributors, but HLC's seem to be the most available. You may also find Sheffield Bone White made by a Japanese pottery.

Examples of Sheffield and Coventry lines can be seen in the appropriate shape sections.

Shapes and Treatments

With any piece of dinnerware (HLC or otherwise) there are at least two names involved in identification: the **shape** and the **treatment**. The "shape" is the blank or the bare piece of pottery without any decoration of any kind. Fiesta, Jade, Rhythm, Harlequin, Nautilus, Cavalier and Epicure are examples of shapes. Each shape has distinctive characteristics. Fiesta is a round ringed shape, Jade is a square rim shape, Rhythm is a plain round coup shape. Each shape is made up of an **assortment** of items.

Treatments are the decorative elements applied to shapes. These include: decals, handpainted work, trim, gold or silver stamps, solid colors, silk screen or even special methods such as Applique and Dura-Print. Many beginning collectors and dealers who don't normally sell dinnerware get names of shapes confused with treatments. This happens mainly with pieces which are marked with the shape name which are misinterpreted as the decoration.

Homer Laughlin has used thousands of treatments and it would be next to impossible to catalog them all. Most of the treatments used are decals. Sometimes these were imported from other countries (see Hudson) but starting in the 1920s, HLC and other companies in the Ohio River Valley area would acquire their decals in the same way. First, a sketch would be made. This could be anything from florals to people to animals – realistic or stylized. These would then be turned over to a company which would make decal sheets, usually Decal Products of East Liverpool, Ohio. Many other area potteries used these same companies. Since there were so many potteries using the same decal and stamp makers, a lot of decals ended up not being exclusive to one company.

There is also the fact that two area potteries would sometimes share in the production of a large order. In other cases, one company might start out making a line for a particular buyer, but another would step in to either help or take over completely. This results in the same decoration appearing on different shapes.

The oval baker is Homer Laughlin's Nautilus shape, but the 8" plate is the "Conversation" shape made by Taylor Smith and Taylor. They are being shown together to demonstrate that decals were not always "exclusive" property of a pottery company.

In this case, the rose decal was used by almost every pottery company in operation in the 1950s. A complete listing would be a who's who in ceramics: HLC, TS & T, Hall, Universal, Crooksville, W.S. George, Salem, Harker and several others.

The rose decal is often called, "Rhythm Rose" no matter what the shape. It can be found on Rhythm and Kitchen Kraft (as "Rhythm Rose") as well as Virginia Rose, Marigold and Nautilus.

The fruit cup in the center is "Mexicana" on the Century shape. HLC also used this decal on Eggshell Nautilus, Virginia Rose and Marigold. The teacups are wearing smaller versions of the Mexicana decal, but they were made by other potteries. To the left is W.S. George's Lido shape and on the right is Taylor Smith & Taylor's Empire/Laurel shape.

Treatment Numbers

It was not common practice for a pottery to give a proper name to every decoration. Rather, they would assign them designations made up of numbers and letters. This was the only way to keep track of the volume of treatments which would have been made difficult had they used names instead. Each pottery had their own codes. Taylor Smith and Taylor often used a four or three digit code and would stamp the numbers on the undersides of creamers. In Harker's case, it was done on the undersides of sugars.

Throughout the rest of this book, many official numbers are given. Most of the time, an official number is found stamped over the glaze on the underside of oval bakers (or nappies if a line lacked bakers) and the undersides of casserole lids. There have been instances of Wells and Century where decoration numbers are found on the underside of sugar lids. Treatment numbers will have a shape name, but not always. Some reflect a particular buyer such as SR for Sears & Roebuck or VM for Vogue Mercantile. A brief listing of letters used with official treatment numbers is given on the next page.

A – Applique
B – Brittany
C – Century
CO – Coronet
CV – Cavalier
D – Debutante
DC – Daisy Chain
E – Empress
G – Georgian
H – Hudson
HA – Handy Andy
HLS – Skytone
J – Jade
K – Kwaker

KK – Kitchen Kraft
L – Liberty
M – Marigold
MF – Modern Farmer
N – Newell or Nautilus
O – Orleans
OR – Old Roman
P – Piccadilly
R – Republic
Reg – Regency
RV – Ravenna
RY – Rhythm
S – Swing
T – Trellis

TH – Theme
V – Victoria
VR – Virginia Rose
W – Wells
Y – Yellowstone

Distributors/Retailers
CP – Cunningham & Picket
JJ – J.J. Newberry's
SR – Sears & Roebuck
VM – Vogue Mercantile
W – F. W. Woolworth's

Examples of date codes AND official treatment numbers. Treatment numbers will usually be in gold and below the backstamp.

Here is just one example of a treatment that was given several names over the years. For several successive editions of Sharon and Bob Huxford's book, *The Collector's Encyclopedia of Fiesta*, the colorful decal on Liberty has been called, "Dogwood." In the 1950s, this line was offered by several wholesalers. In one ad, it was called, "Magnolia" and in an Altman's catalog from the early 1950s, it was given the name, "Apple Blossom." The treatment really depicts a type of Magnolia, but collectors have gotten in the habit of calling it Dogwood.

While there have been several names applied to the treatment, HLC only had one designation: L-613. The "L" is for the shape, in this case, Liberty and the 613 is the particular treatment complete with gold trim. If a treatment originated on one shape but was later used on another, then it was given a new designation to reflect the new shape. The magnolia decal shown was also used on Rhythm, but HLC referred to that line as RY-106. The decals were also used on Georgian Eggshell and Virginia Rose and have appropriate "G-" and "VR-" numbers.

Glazes

A glaze is basically a glassy layer that is fired onto dinnerware. It serves to protect the body of the ware and can be either clear or solid color. Beginning in the 1920s, Homer Laughlin and other potteries began work on perfecting white and ivory glazes that would be clean and even with no runs or crazing. Throughout the years HLC has produced various "neutral" solid color glazes that have been used for the decaled lines. One of the first was an ivory glaze that collectors would call white today. It was developed around 1926 and first used on the Yellowstone and Kwaker shapes, and sets in the new color were priced slightly higher than the "white body ware."

In the late 1920s, HLC created a light yellow glaze. The Trellis soup bowl in the picture – right foreground – has this special color. This transparent glaze was of very poor quality and often "pools" in deep areas of hollowware and verges of flatware. Light yellow was used on mainly Trellis, Newell, Old Roman, and to a lesser degree, Wells. It was basically phased out with the development of Vellum and the OvenServe glaze.

Shown in Vellum is the Yellowstone plate – left background. This special matte glaze was created for the Century shape (see section on Century) but was also used on Wells, Jade and Fiesta.

Behind the Yellowstone plate is a Virginia Rose 9" plate with an ivory glaze that was developed for OvenServe. It was also used on the embossed shapes, Marigold and Republic.

One glaze not shown is a white color originally made for Georgian/Craftsman. After Vellum, it was HLC's best neutral color to date being virtually craze proof. It was also used on Nautilus, Kwaker, Empress and other wares calling for white bodies.

The last piece in the photo – left foreground – is a Swing/Andover Eggshell shape 6" plate with the "Star & Ribbon" treatment. Because of the light weight body of Eggshell lines, a special white glaze was developed. Rhead often referred to this glaze as the "Swing glaze." It was used on all the Eggshell lines; Nautilus, Georgian, Swing, Andover, Theme and Cavalier.

These are the basic neutral glazes. They underwent slight changes over the years and if examples from a particular line were gathered together, there would be slight differences in tones. This is also true for the solid color glazes used with Fiesta, Harlequin, etc. but is of little consequence to collectors.

Pick-Up Pieces

Once in a while, a piece from one line will be used in another. The Nautilus teacup is a good example. Having originated with the regular and Eggshell Nautilus lines, it was used with the Rhythm and Cavalier shapes in many of the "Lifetime China" sets. For the most part, if you find a large set of dinnerware, all the pieces will belong to one specific line. This means that if you find a large set of dinnerware using the Republic shape, then every piece will probably be Republic without any Virginia Rose, Marigold or other similar shapes.

However, there are some exceptions. Pick-up pieces are those which started out in one line, but would eventually become "generic" shapes used with others. The four most common of these versatile shapes are: the Cable egg cup (shown), the Jade butter dish, the Swing shakers and Jubilee shakers.

Ironically, if you encounter a Jade shape butter dish, chances are is wasn't used with the actual Jade line. Jade was in production for only a few years, but the butter dish would span almost 20 years. Solid colored butters were used with Harlequin and Riviera and decaled versions can be found in sets of Virginia Rose, Nautilus Eggshell and Marigold.

Values

Throughout the rest of this book are current estimated values. Values are given for items in PERFECT condition. Whether damage occurred at the factory or after it left the factory doesn't matter. There are some unscrupulous dealers who may make the claim that the damage from the factory shouldn't and doesn't effect values. Such imperfections would include the following: a chip under the glaze, a glaze rub, kiln dirt, mold cracks. It's up to the buyer whether he or she wants to include such pieces in a Homer Laughlin collection. Consider two Virginia Rose 10" plates with the popular VR-128 "Fluffy Rose" decal. One has no imperfections and the other has no other damage except for a small chip that occurred during production and was glazed over. Should the plates be worth the same? Of course not. Any collector would choose the perfect example over the one with a factory flaw (commonly called, "Seconds") and the values should reflect that.

Post production flaws – those types of damage that occur at home effect values dramatically. A chip or crack can cut the value of an item almost in half. One of the most common questions collectors ask, especially beginners, is: "How much should I pay for a damaged piece?" It's important to take several factors into consideration:

> – How bad is the damage?
> – Is the damage visible?
> – Can the piece still be used?

The worse the damage, the less a collector should pay. Setting guidelines on how much a piece should be reduced in price isn't practical. There are pieces which are rather hard to find and some collectors are willing to live with a little bit of damage. For example, a Marigold casserole with an unusual decal was auctioned off on eBay not to long ago. Even though it had a chip on its foot, it sold for over $40.00 which is close to the estimated value for one in perfect condition. In that case, the buyer could live with the imperfection.

There is one important piece of advice I give to all new collectors: BE PATIENT. Vintage HLC dinnerware has many pieces which are hard to find, but there really aren't too many truly one-of-a-kind items. Don't rush into buying a lot of HLC dinnerware at any price and in any condition. Because HLC produced so many dishes over such a long period of time, any collector can afford to sit back and make rational decisions.

No matter what advice other collectors and dealers give on buying dinnerware it all boils down to this: If you like it, can afford it, and can live with it, then buy it.

Crazing

One of the most common misconceptions regarding crazing is that it is a result of age. When dinnerware is made, the glaze must be formulated properly so that as the body expands and contracts, the glaze does so at the same rate. When the glaze and body contract at different rates, the glaze becomes crackled or crazed. This process is almost immediate and does not occur over several decades. In fact, there are some decals that HLC would only use on pieces of crazed dinnerware. These "bottom shelf" treatments were reserved for less than perfect specimens.

Many pieces of dinnerware made prior to the 1940s (not only by HLC but other companies) are often found crazed, not because they are old, but because potteries had a hard time perfecting glazes. In the early 1930s, the ivory Vellum and white glaze developed for Georgian/Craftsman were the first two neutral glazes produced that almost never crazed.

Is crazing damage? Its definitely a manufacture's flaw and not damage in the traditional sense as a chip or crack. Its much more desirable to have a piece with a nice clean and even glaze rather than one that is crazed. Again, this is something that has to be left up to the individual collector.

The biggest problem with crazing is the buildup of dirt due to use. Shown are two pictures of a Homer Laughlin Piccadilly casserole base. The first shows the base as it was purchased in an antiques mall. The second is of the same piece but after a 24-hour hydrogen peroxide bath. There are still some brown spots, but repeated baths should clear up any remaining stains.

There are several home remedies to clean up the dirt in crazing. Most involve the use of hydrogen peroxide – as either a 30% or 40% solution that can be purchased from beauty salon shops. Some collectors advise diluting the peroxide with water – 50% water to 50% peroxide. Others say to use it straight. Completely submerge the piece in the peroxide bath, cover and leave over night. Take it out the next day and allow it to dry out for two to three days. If the staining is still obvious, repeat the process again. Many advise not leaving an item in a peroxide bath for extended periods of time.

If you choose to clean your ware with peroxide, try out some test pieces first. There are some decorations which are not well protected and may be effected. Try to avoid using peroxide on pieces with over-the-glaze red trim and many collectors try not to soak pieces with gold trim. There are conflicting reports on how long a piece should remain in a peroxide bath. Some say no more than two or three days and others will keep it in for weeks. Experiment or conduct your own research on how to clean crazing. No doubt you will find dozens of variations and helpful hints along the way.

HOMER LAUGHLIN DINNERWARE

Brittany

This plain round rim shape started out as a very limited line. The first pieces were modeled in November of 1935: 8" nappy, fruit cup, saucer, teacup, 6", 9", 10", 13" plates, sugar and creamer. Most of these pieces underwent revisions in January of 1936 and the 7", 8" plates and a deep plate were added. Two sizes of platters; 11" and 13" as well as a 7" nappy were also created.

In mid 1938, the sugar and creamer were put into production. Several more shapes were modeled and released into production for the first time in February 1939; and A.D. cup and saucer, sauceboat, and the sauceboat stand. In April of that year, the oatmeal (a.k.a. 36s) bowl was also modeled, and in May, both the 8" and 9" nappies were offered simultaneously.

The biggest change to Brittany occurred in June of 1939 when several different models of sugars and creamers were considered to replace the original versions.

Here are eight sketches of Brittany shapes that appear in the modeling log. The piece on the top row and to the left is a covered gravy fast stand. There is no indication these were ever put into production but if they had, they would have been slightly larger than the original sugar. To the right is a Brittany creamer with a ringed foot. The second row shows sugars which have identical bodies but they have different applied handles. The third row is of the 15.25 oz. creamer and the 17.25 oz. sugar. And finally, the forth row shows a 13.8 oz. cream and 15.25 oz. sugar. These last two sets of sugars and creamers are the basic shapes used for the final product. In July 1939, the standard Brittany creamer and sugar that is most often seen, replaced the original and smaller versions. It was also during this time that the covers for the nappies were restyled to match the lids of the sugars.

There were several pick-up pieces such as the cable egg cup and a cream soup cup. No major changes would occur with this line until the early 1950s when the handles of the sauceboat, sugar and creamer were made smaller, and a teapot was introduced.

Expect pieces of Brittany to have a generic HLC backstamp with date code. Since there were no oval bakers with this line, treatment numbers may often be found on the round nappies and the undersides of the casserole lids, which, by the way, will have nappy bases. Often a Brittany casserole is found with the official treatment number on its lid and the base.

The maroon/floral border treatments are the most common and the most collected. "Majestic", made up of a specific maroon border and floral sprigs, is very popular, but there were so many other similar decorations made by HLC on the Brittany shape that even the most experienced collectors have trouble telling them all apart.

Brittany is still in production today in a heavy restaurant body. Over the years, the number of items in the assortment has decreased. The sauceboat, sauceboat stand, A.D. cup and saucer, teapot and casserole were no longer in use by late 1965. The Brittany currently in production is called, "Diplomat." While this line has the familiar shapes of the teacup, creamer and sugar, most of the flatware looks as if it comes from the wider rim shape Cavalier. While the original Brittany had no shakers, Diplomat has been made in recent years with the Jubilee shakers.

The name of this treatment is commonly back-stamped in silver along with the general HLC marking. Known as "Royal Splendor," its official treatment number is B-1346.

Sown on Brittany, "Colonial Blue" is common on Eggshell Nautilus. On Nautilus, however, the floral sprigs may or may not be with the blue border.

Shown are the first style sugar and creamer for Brittany. This style was made for only a year or so being replaced with larger bodies and handles.

Second style creamer. Notice how the body is wider than the first version towards its base. Also handle stretches much higher than the first version.

To the untrained eye, the three pieces in this photo might seem to have identical treatments. The key with Brittany is to look at the ends of the borders. The rim soup has the most common treatment, "Majestic." The creamer is the second style used in the Brittany line. The treatment on the fruit cup is B-1315.

The teapot was added to the assortment in late 1952. Unfortunately, many popular treatments from the 30s and 40s were discontinued by then. The pattern shown is "Hemlock" in maroon. You will also find other colors of this pattern – one color which is particularly easy to find is turquoise.

In back of the teapot is a 9" Brittany plate with a blue laurel treatment.

Another Brittany teapot; this time with a pink and gray decoration.

This is the original style casserole which is basically the round serving bowl with a lid. The casserole, along with the sugar and creamer, was later restyled. In the case of the casserole, the lid was changed while the base remained the same. The decoration shown is B-1323.

Another view of the lid and base of the B-1323 casserole.

Here is the revised casserole which replaced the older style within the first few years of production. The only major change involves the lid. It has a solid finial which is part of the lid; older lids had applied "open" finials.

This particular casserole shown was decorated by an outside company with floral sprigs, gold filigree and cobalt trim.

The focus in this picture is on the sauce-boat. It is the standard Brittany body (dated 1953) but with a shorter-than-normal handle. In the early 1950s, HLC produced a limited line which used Brittany hollowware with exterior solid colors and decaled flatware. All of the handled pieces: sugar, creamer, sauce-boat and teacup have small handles. This sauceboat with a gray exterior is shown with a 'second style' creamer for handle comparison.

A pair of Brittany serving bowls.

The cup in the photo is a hard to find A.D. cup. It has the same Majestic style border, but this time it's in cobalt. Shown for size comparison is a 7" plate.

In the early 1980s, Brittany hollowware was used with Cavalier flatware. Three patterns are shown in this ad and use Cavalier prefixes in their treatment numbers; Solitude CV-197, Sterling CV-178, Millbrook CV-198.

A Millbrook plate with a Christmas decal dated 1983.

The Brittany shapes are still in use today. HLC has produced a line called "Diplomat" for a number of years using the old hollowware and the Jubilee shakers. Shown is a Diplomat cup and saucer. The basic design of the Brittany teacup has remained largely unchanged for the past 60+ years.

Brittany Assortment and Values:

13" Chop Plate	$15-18		Covered Sugar, first version	$18-20
10" Plate	8-10		Covered Sugar, later versions	7- 9
9" Plate	6- 8		Creamer, first version	12-15
8" Plate	8-10		Creamer, later versions	4- 6
7" Plate	4- 5		Round Serving Bowl, any size	6- 8
6" Plate	2- 3		Serving Bowl lid, first version	15-20
Teacup	5- 6		Serving Bowl lid, later version	10-12
Saucer	1- 2		Teapot	20-25
AD Cup	15-18		Sauceboat	8-10
AD Saucer	8-10		Fruit Cup	2- 3
Pickle	5- 7		36s Bowl	8-10
11½" Platter	6- 8		Oatmeal Bowl	4- 6
13" Platter	7- 9		Rim Soup	5- 8
15" Platter	10-12		Cream Soup Cup	10-12
Eggcup, Cable	12-15		Cream Soup liner	10-12

Piccadilly

Backstamp

The Piccadilly shape is made up of Brittany flatware – plates, platters, bowls and teacup saucer – and five specially modeled pieces of hollowware. These special pieces are cylindrical with flattop handles and a slight foot. They are the covered sugar, creamer, covered casserole, teacup and sauceboat. All five were modeled in December of 1939 and were immediately released into production. Before the name "Piccadilly" was applied to this line, it was referred to as, "New Brittany."

The treatments between Brittany and Piccadilly might look very similar with the maroon, cobalt, pink or light blue borders with floral sprigs, but most collectors have noted that treatments between Brittany and Piccadilly are not shared.

Piccadilly hollowware is marked with a special backstamp with its name and more often than not, with a date code. Flatware is often marked in the same manner as Brittany flatware; with a general HLC backstamp.

Looking at the five pieces of hollowware, the sugar, creamer and teacup are the easiest to find followed by the casserole and sauceboat.

The line continued to be produced until the early 1950s. There are mold notes regarding size changes to the sugar and a modification to the lid of the casserole, but from beginning to end, Piccadilly remained largely unchanged.

This covered casserole is partially treated. In general, it should have floral sprigs and gold or silver trim, but was given a partial treatment because it was a factory second.

The Piccadilly sugar and creamer received a partial treatment at HLC with a maroon border, but was decorated by Royal China with heavy gold trim and filigree.

Piccadilly Assortment and Values: for flatware, use Brittany Values

Teacup	$ 5-6
Sugar	$ 7-9
Creamer	$ 5-7
Casserole	$15-18
Sauceboat	$12-15

Cavalier

One of the first Cavalier entries in the modeling log occurs on November 26, 1951: CUP FOR FLAT RIM EGGSHELL SHAPE. For the rest of the year and for all of 1952, the Cavalier shape was developed. This new shape had formal lines and curves with elegant handles and finials and pronounced feet. This was a sharp contrast to the more casual lines offered in the early 50s such as Rhythm, Charm House and Jubilee.

Cavalier had several pick up pieces. The shakers and the demitasse cup body are from Jubilee. Records indicate a special A.D. handle for the Jubilee body was made on November 4, 1952. The cereal bowl is from Charm House and has the distinctive mushroom type base.

Unlike other shapes created in the 1950s, Cavalier was never made in solid colors but instead received a large array of decals. The majority of treatments used on Cavalier are realistic floral treatments.

Cavalier became a great seller almost immediately and was a favorite with Lifetime China (Cunningham and Pickett) of Alliance, Ohio. (For more on this company, see section on Markings.) Lifetime commonly would mix Cavalier with Rhythm flatware and Nautilus teacups resulting in more casual lines. Montgomery Wards carried several patterns in the eggshell weight, but not all Cavalier was made in this special clay.

HLC continued to produce Cavalier into the late 1960s, though the number of treatments became very limited. The flatware was also used in the early 1980s with Brittany hollowware to create a new line.

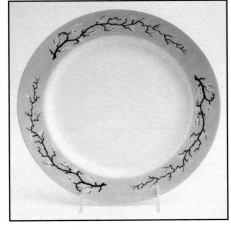

A common treatment on Cavalier Eggshell: CV-116.

Cavalier teapot, sugar and creamer with green trim.

The Cavalier pieces shown here come from a set with a gold and blue wheat decal called, "Somerset." The official number is: CV-87.

Pink floral treatment on Cavalier.

"Pink Radiance" was described in one ad as, "...a pink and charcoal spray, bordered within solid pink." A 16 piece starter set cost $4.89. While almost all the pieces which come from this line are from Cavalier, the teacup is the Nautilus shape.

Kennedy Plate. It's marking indicates the plate was made in 1957, but the decal treatment must have been applied to the blank after 1963 since it has JFK's dates of birth and death.

Cavalier sugar and creamer sets.

"Crinoline" Sauceboat.

These next two photos show the different styles of cups used in Cavalier sets. First, with the wheat decal, is the regular Cavalier shape cup and saucer. The second picture is of a Nautilus shape cup with a Cavalier saucer. This set comes from a line called Lynwood.

10" plate	$6- 8		teapot	$12-15
9" plate	4- 5		covered sugar	7- 9
8" sq. plate	6- 8		creamer	5- 6
7" plate	3- 4		covered casserole	12-15
6" plate	1- 2		shakers	4- 5
teacup	2- 3		rim soup	3- 4
saucer	1- 2		fruit cup	1- 2
AD cup	7- 9		round vegetable	5- 7
AD saucer	2- 3		cereal	3- 4
15" platter	8-10			
13" platter	6- 8			
11" platter	5- 7			
9" pickle	5- 7			

Century & Riviera

The earliest known journal kept by Rhead starts on February 2, 1931. Unfortunately, the Century shape had already been developed so piecing its early history is next to impossible. But, the first journal entry on February 2nd makes reference to Century: *Finished modeling Century Square shape with Vellum glaze. Samples shown at Pittsburgh show in January.*

For the next two months, work proceeded on developing decals and silver stamps on the Century shape. Rhead notes the use of black stamps and decals that were used on older shapes being applied to the new Century line. It was also during this time the very popular English Garden (C-4) treatment was designed.

In March, there were problems with the Vellum glaze. Rhead notes on March 3rd: ....*Type of Uranium used effects browns stains on glazed edges.* Any glaze that has uranium in its mixture (such as ivory or red glazes) is very difficult to manage. Its not uncommon for such staining to occur during firing if the kiln temperature is too high. One solution was to take examples already fired and decorate with ivory trim. But, on the 5th, Rhead notes that the special ivory trim wasn't working in covering up the brown staining. It would take more trials to get the new vellum glaze perfected. After being shown at Pittsburgh in January and at the Cleveland exhibit at the end of February, Century was put into production.

In July 1931, two replacement items were ordered for Century: an individual creamer and sugar. The only specification listed with these pieces is that they have a "straight foot" to replace the original flared foot type. Both styles are very hard to find so they must have been in production for a very short period.

Century is rather easy to find. It was a major HLC decal shape from its introduction in '31 until it was phased out around 1948. Some items were discontinued early such as the covered butter, A.D. sugar, A.D. creamer, A.D. cup and saucer, utility bowl and cream soup cup and its liner. These have become "key" pieces for Century collectors and when found in ivory with no decoration, they become very desirable to Riviera collectors. Century is usually marked with the multicolored Wells peacock mark or with a general backstamp. The square shape received just about every type of decoration available at the time such as decals, silver and gold stamps, silk screen, and of course, solid colors.

A Century dinner plate with the "Mexicana" treatment, C-228. This particular plate has red trim, which is by far the most common. If you're lucky enough, you may encounter trims in different colors. Mexicana can also be found on Kitchen Kraft and Eggshell Nautilus and is very rare on Marigold, Liberty and Virginia Rose.

Mexicana fruit cup with rare yellow trim and a 36s bowl.

The "Hacienda" (C-237) cup and saucer has a feature which is somewhat common on HLC cups which come from the mid to late 30s: the "front" of the cup will have the standard decal for a given treatment, while the "back" has a smaller "sprig" which is in step with the overall theme. Hacienda on the Century shape was sold through Woolworth's.

Here is a 15" platter with pastel stylized flowers. I've seen two vintage ads featuring this treatment and in both cases, the sets are referred to as "Century Pattern." Of course they are making reference to the shape and not the treatment, so this may not have any given retail name. Its official number has been identified as C-2. According to the company records, C-2 was no longer offered by 1937. It can also be found on Yellowstone, but is more common on Century.

In the front are the very rare second style Century AD creamer and sugar. See the text for more on the A.D. Century sugars and creamers.

In the background are two other pieces that are hard to find (though not nearly as difficult as the AD creamer and sugar). To the left is the batter jug and the right is the scaled down syrup. All pieces in the photo are in vellum with the Black Tulip decal treatment.

"English Garden" is one of the most popular treatments on Century.

This "square" platter has the English Garden treatment and a combination of green and platinum trim.

The Garland treatment, C-132, is among the most common. The gold stamp decoration originated on the Yellowstone shape as Y-56, and besides being found on Century, it was also used on Virginia Rose in both silver and gold form.

10" Nappy with the colorful C-3 treatment.

Century covered butter with gold trim.

Century Assortment and Values:

10" plate	$15-18		Milk Jug	$30-40
9" plate	7- 9		Batter Jug (open)	25-30
8" plate	10-12		Batter Jug with lid	65+
7" plate	6- 8		Syrup with lid	55-60
6" plate	4- 5		7" Baker	7- 9
teacup	6- 8		8" Baker	6- 8
saucer	2- 3		9" Baker	6- 8
AD Cup	18-20		7" Nappy	10-12
AD Saucer	7- 9		8" Nappy	7- 9
Covered Sugar	8-12		9" Nappy	8-10
AD sugar (either style)	UND		Fruit Cup	4- 5
Creamer	6- 7		Oatmeal Bowl	6- 8
AD creamer (either style)	UND		Deep Plate	8-10
Sauceboat	8-10		Cream of Soup liner	18-20
Gravy Fast Stand	20-25		Cream soup liner	12-15
Teapot	75+		36s Bowls	18-20
Casserole	25-30		9" Platter	6- 8
Onion Soup	18-20		11" Platter	8-10
Round Butter	75+		13" Platter	12-15
Butter, Jade shape	40-45		15" Platter	20-25
			Square Platter	35-40

Riviera

Riviera was a special line which used Century shapes in solid colors. It started out in 1938 with two colors from Fiesta: red and light green, and two colors from Harlequin: mauve blue and Harlequin yellow. Ivory was picked up after 1943 when red was no longer used by HLC. Riviera was not exclusive to any one retailer and was carried by The Murphy Co., J.J. Newberry, and was even in various wholesale catalogs throughout the years. Not only do retailers apply names to decaled dinnerware, but also to solid color. While most of the Riviera vintage ads do refer to the line as, "Riviera," at least one 1939 wholesale catalog called the line, "Bohemia."

Several of the Century pieces were selected for Riviera and shakers were picked up from another solid color line, Tango. This line had mauve blue, red and Harlequin yellow so shakers found in those colors could belong to either Riviera or Tango. But, maroon and spruce were never used with Riviera and hence shakers in those colors belong to Tango only. Conversely, light green and ivory shakers are Riviera.

Since the Century shapes and various solid color glazes were already in production, there wasn't much for the Art Department at HLC to work on in developing the Riviera line. One of the first times Rhead mentions the lines in his journals is on December 15, 1938 when a sauceboat and oatmeal were added to Riviera. There were also "new" items added to Riviera which had not appeared in Century – most of which started out as exclusives.

The first involves the "Newberry tumbler" or simply, the "handled tumbler." On January 21, 1939, Rhead notes the specifications for this piece: *Take Harlequin tumbler, lines taken off, add handle to match Riviera.* On February 2nd trials of the new Newberry tumbler were made with and without the Harlequin rings. By the end of March, the Riviera handled tumbler (or a Rhead called it, "Newberry Handled Tankard") was released into production.

Later that same year, on July 10th, Rhead mentions a "Juice set premium." The pieces were to be the same as Fiesta's with the following specifications: "Tumbler same capacity, change lines. Jug same capacity, mouth type." This set was listed in Riviera colors. It may be the case that the jug was Harlequin yellow – as they are commonly found – and the tumblers were various combinations of the four standard glazes. In May 31, 1940, another Riviera juice set is ordered, this time with the jug in "Riviera blue" and tumblers in, "Riviera blue, yellow, red, Fiesta turquoise, ivory and Riviera (light) green." This set was intended as a Murphy Co. exclusive, however, Riviera juice sets in the same colors were sent to Newberry in August the same year.

On July 19th, more items were added to Riviera. Rhead lists these as: "42s Riviera covered jug in red; 24s jug covers in green." Rhead commonly used trade sizes when listing entries for pitchers. Here the 42s jug refers to the syrup and the 24s jug is the batter jug. The open batter jug was a standard item, but the cover (only in light green) didn't come about until July 1939. Furthermore, the syrup, used in the older Century line, wasn't a standard Riviera piece either. The entry explains why today batter jug lids are only found in light green (save some rare exceptions in red) and why syrups are only found in red. Perhaps this was a special order, but the retailer isn't mentioned.

On December 27, 1939, the next new shape for Riviera is ordered. Rhead notes: "...to model Riviera Butter Dish after glass sample." These were later modeled, approved and released into production. He writes on one occasion making these for J.J. Newberry.

The last shapes modeled for Riviera didn't go into production; a compartment plate and the console set. A memo dated July 17, 1940 discusses the compartment plate:

> *We have discussed with Mr. J.M. Wells the possibility of making a Riviera compartment plates. Mr. Feuchtwanter* [of the Chicago office] *has a customer who can use a large quantity of these if we can supply them with the right item.*
>
> *Would suggest you have modeled a Riviera compartment plate that would have approximately the same size and outside design of the* [10"] *Riviera plate. Then cut down the rim of the plate considerably and make 3 compartments. The partitions between the compartments should be fairly low so there would be no trouble about jiggering the item.*

The first Riviera compartment plates came out of the kilns on September 9, but had to be remodeled. Rhead never mentions the compartment plate again so its safe to assume they were never released into production. There is one known to exist and it's pictured in Sharon and Bob Huxford's book, *The Collector's Encyclopedia of Fiesta.*

Riviera was produced until 1948 – the same time the Century shape was discontinued. Many older square and embossed shapes were being taken out of production to be replaced by "cleaner" coupe lines. Riviera was never meant to be marked, but some are found with an HLC USA stamp. Its believed such pieces were marked for export to Canada. There is one point to note about ivory Riviera and markings. If you find a piece of ivory Century and its backstamped, then it's basically a Century piece which didn't receive a decoration. However, unmarked ivory pieces are Riviera. This is a technicality and most Riviera collectors are willing to add any ivory pieces to their collection: Riviera or Century.

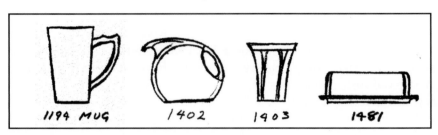

Modeling log sketches for Riviera. From left to right: handled tumbler, juice pitcher, juice tumbler, covered butter.

1194 MUG   1402   1903   1481

SQUARE
"BOHEMIA" WARE
24-PC. SET—4 COLORS

As discussed in the section on Decorations, it was common practice for a retailer or wholesaler to name a decal treatment. Here is a vintage ad from a 1940s catalog where the wholesaler took it upon himself to apply a different name to the Riviera line. Labeled as "Bohemia" ware, this Riviera set was offered as a service for four in the four original Riviera colors. Another interesting feature with this ad is that the sugar from this particular source was offered as an "open sugar."

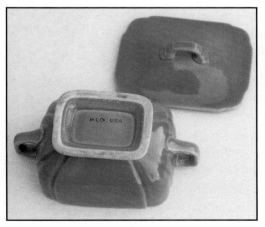

The green Riviera sugar has the same HLC USA marking commonly found on pieces of Fiesta which weren't normally marked. It has been surmised by collectors over the years that HLC used this marking for pieces that were exported to Canada. It's not surprising then that this Riviera sugar was purchased from a Canadian seller through eBay.

Riviera casserole in green, covered sugar in ivory, creamer in Harlequin yellow.

This Century shape teapot has no backstamp which would indicate that its part of the Riviera line and not just an "untreated blank."

Cobalt pieces of Riviera are hard to find. To date, there is at least one of each of the following known in the dark blue color: covered casserole, deep plate, covered sugar and creamer. The Jade shape butter, platter with oval well and 7" plate are easier to find in cobalt.

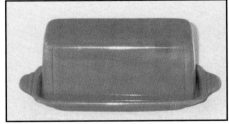

The ¼-pound butter, shown in red, was used only with Riviera and not Century.

To the left is the Harlequin tumbler in blue. The design for the Riviera version, shown on the right, was based on the Harlequin shape. The rings were removed and a special handle was added.

Since the handled tumbler is included in the listing along with the color red, these brochures must come from between February 1939 (when the tumbler was modeled) and 1943 (when red was discontinued).

Riviera Assortment and Values:

10" Plate	$40-50	Nappy	$8-10
9" Plate	10-12	Baker	7- 9
7" Plate	6- 8	Creamer	6- 8
6" Plate	4- 5	Sugar	10-12
Fruit Cup	6- 8	Sauceboat	7- 9
Oatmeal Bowl	10-12	Teapot	125+
Teacup	10-12	Handled Tumbler	85-95
Saucer	3- 4	Shakers (Tango), pr	8-10
Covered Syrup	125+	11" Platter	10-12
Juice Pitcher (yellow)	125+	11" lug Platter	10-12
Juice Tumbler	35-40	12" lug Platter	12-15
1/2 lb. Butter	85-95	13" lug Platter	15-18
1/4 lb. Butter	125-150	15" lug Platter	20-25
Deep Plate	8-10	Covered Casserole	55-65
Open Batter Jug	65-75		
Batter Jug Lid	50+ (green or ivory)		

Challenger & International

The Challenger and International shapes were both introduced in the 1970s. They are two separate lines, but are put together here since International made use of Challenger hollowware.

Challenger, modeled in mid 1973, was first. Originally, it was a limited line consisting of only the most basic pieces: 12", 10" and 7" plates, cup, saucer, creamer, sugar, vegetable and coffee server. All of the shapes were round and cylindrical and because of its unique flared rim design, many pieces underwent several revisions. Challenger was released into production sometime in late 1973. According to the modeling log, the following pieces were added in January and February 1976: sauceboat, handled mug, sauceboat stand, shakers, butter bottom and cover, covered casserole.

In comparison to HLC's other 70s shapes, Challenger was in production for a short amount of time and its rather difficult to find. When gathering material for this book, examples of the hollowware modeled in 1976 could not be located. On the other hand, flatware was much easier to find.

International was first produced in mid 1977. Like Challenger, it started out with a very limited assortment. While hollowware was created for the new shape, it made use of sugars, creamers, cups and other shapes from lines already in production. The Challenger sugar and creamer were used in several instances. True International hollowware is cylindrical, but not as wide and flared as Challenger's. Another major difference is in the lids. International's sugar finials are raised and Challenger's are recessed knobs.

The flatware used in all International lines is easily recognizable. The narrow rim is "framed" with an outer and inner beaded edge. At some point the inner bead was softened considerably resulting in a slight bump just above the verge.

International became a workhorse of sorts for HLC. Multiple treatments using the International flatware with various forms of hollowware were offered in ads as the "International Group." Both Challenger and International flatware will have general HLC backstamps. There are a few treatments used on the International shape that are marked as the "Country-Inn Collection." This refers to a specific group of decorations and is not a shape or specific decal name. When it comes to hollowware, pieces are either unmarked or will have an impressed MADE IN U.S.A. marking.

Both Challenger and International were discontinued in the 1980s. Since they are relative unknowns, values are very low. Expect most examples to have decal decorations, but there are several solid colors, including the reissue Harlequin yellow glaze, that was used on International.

Challenger Examples:

10" Dinner plates. The yellow example is decorated in a richly textured mustard color glaze. This color was also used on the White Dover shape. Note the flared rim – a feature only found on Challenger flatware.

This Challenger dinner plate has a special decoration. According to the backstamp, it was made for International Silver.

Challenger hollowware will have the same type of flared rims found on the flatware. The Challenger sugar shown comes from a line which uses Internationl flatware. This spatter effect decoration also comes in blue. Both blue and brown versions were produced in the early 1980s.

International Examples:

This ad from "Dutch Pantry" shows the International shape covered sugar and creamer.

This treatment was offered in the early 1980s and is called, "Schooldaze" or IN-259. As you can see in the photo, different shapes had different treatments.

The International 12½" chop plate in the yellow glaze used in the reissue Harlequin line.

Another International chop plate – this time in a rich beige glaze. The dinner plate comes from 1979 and is decorated with a peach decal.

Only plates from this "Country Manor" line will have the decoration shown. All other pieces will be in a rich ivory glaze with a brown band. The official number for Country Manor is IN-174.

This plate has a decal from the "Country Inn Collection" and was made in the early 80s. Matching International shape hollowware

can be found with solid brown exteriors.

The International plate is in a sky blue glaze. Pieces from this line aren't terribly hard to find and will have the general HLC backstamp used in the early 1980s.

Most International is marked with a generic HLC backstamp except for a special set of floral decals from HLC's Country Inn Collection.

Challenger and International Assortment and values:

For piece of flatware (saucers, plates and bowls) – $1-2
Sugars, Creamers, sauceboats – $3-5
Larger items, coffeepots, casseroles, etc. – $5-10

Charm House

Charm House is one of the most complicated subjects since it was used in so many different ways. It was made with two new types of decorations in the 50s: Applique and Dura-Print, and it received decal treatments. There were at least six distinct uses of the Charm House shapes:

1. Decaled for China and Glass (CG) Distributors
2. Decaled for Lady Stratford and Lady Greenbrier lines
3. Solid colors for Dura-Print
4. Applique
5. Solid colors for decaled Rhythm
6. With decaled Ironstone

Before going into a discussion on the various uses of Charm House, the shapes themselves should be examined. Of all the items in the modeling log, only two are referred to as Charm House. The others are all listed as, "Fry." This is in reference to Ed Fry, a buyer for Montgomery Wards. From this it can be assumed that Charm House was modeled due to Montgomery Wards' request for a new shape. Several "Fry" cups were modeled in 1947, but at that time, most of the Art Department's attention was placed on finishing the Jubilee shape. In the summer of 1948, with the Jubilee shape complete, more "Fry" pieces were crafted, but it wasn't until March 1949 that the familiar Charm House pieces were modeled. From then until October 1950, over 40 shapes were created or revised for the new line.

Except for the sugar, there are no modeling log drawings for Charm House. One of the biggest questions in the log concerns the flatware: plates, platters and bowls. When Charm House is used with various treatments, the flatware is generally picked up from other shapes such as Rhythm or Brittany. The original Charm House flatware was a rim shape. It's very similar to Brittany, but the Charm House rim is wider and not as flat and Charm House flatware was used in only one instance, for CG Distributors.

Some other items in the listing are of importance: the sauceboat fast stand, AD cup, AD saucer and the cream soup cup. The gravy fast stand has been found with several decals, and what is listed as a cream soup cup may be the little cereal/soup often used with Dura-Print and Rhythm. As for the A.D. cup and saucer, none have been found so far.

Charm House hollowware is very distinctive. It has mushroom like bodies with dome type lids. Casseroles and sugars are handleless. Finials and handles are very simple with no ornamentation which was typical for the casual shapes of the 1950s.

C. & G. Distributors

The first use of Charm House, for China & Glass Distributors, Inc., is the decaled version. According to *Lehner's Encyclopedia of U.S. Marks on Pottery, Porcelain & Clay,* by Lois Lehner, C.G. used several types of markings including, "The Pantry Parade" by Cronin China and HLC's "Charm House." It seems reasonable to conclude that this is where the name Charm House originates. There are at least two known treatments sold by C.G. Charm House: Lotus Hai and Magnolia. It is with these two lines that the rare gravy fast stand is found. With every other instance involving Charm House hollowware, the fast stand is dropped in favor of the Rhythm sauceboat.

C.G. Charm House marks make no mention of Homer Laughlin. Other companies produced wares for C.G. but the HLC Charm House hollowware should be unmistakable.

Charm House marking

Charm house "Lotus Hai" 10" Plate, 7" Plate, cup and saucer. The 10" and 7" plates are both rim shapes, but the saucer is a plain round coupe shape.

Covered sugar and creamer with the Charm House "Lotus Hai" treatment.

The rare Charm House gravy fast stand.

Lady Stafford & Lady Greenbriar

Another use of Charm House occurs with two popular treatments, Lady Stafford and Lady Greenbriar. Both shapes use Nautilus flatware, a Nautilus Eggshell teapot, Charm House sugar, creamer, teacups and casseroles and a Rhythm sauce boat. Lady Stratford is decorated with a thick maroon band, gold filigree and a rose decal. With Lady Greenbriar, the band is dark green and the decal is of a yellow rose.

Of the Charm House hollowware, only the casserole has the decal with the band and filigree. The other pieces of hollowware will have filigree and colored band only. Both lines were offered in the early 1950s and Charm House pieces will have a general HLC backstamp.

This Charm House creamer, with a 1952 backstamp, belongs to the Lady Greenbriar line.

Dura-Print

Dura-Print is a line that makes use of a special decorating technique from the 1950s. Colors were applied to pieces of flatware from a bladder that would expand with air. The decoration was "stamped" onto the flatware and then given a clear glaze. This could only be done to flatware and the Rhythm shape was best suited for this technique. Hollowware was primarily solid color Charm House, but other shapes were used.

Treatments consist of either one color or combinations of two colors. The plaid treatments are by far the most plentiful followed by the brown rooster design. One problem with all Dura-Print lines is the hollowware often gets separated from the flatware. Its not uncommon to find stacks of plates and saucers but without cups, sugars and creamers.

Colors used for the Charm House hollowware include: turquoise, brown, forest green, Harlequin yellow, cobalt, pink, maroon and black. Chartreuse Charm House was used with a decaled version of Rhythm. The most often found examples of hollowware are cups, sugars and creamers followed by shakers and Rhythm shape sauceboats. Teapots and covered casseroles in colors other than yellow and dark green are hard to find.

Dura-Print has its own backstamp and according to the date codes, the line was made from 1953 until circa 1960.

This treatment has had several names depending on the source. In Homer Laughlin brochures, it was sold as, "Break of Day" and in Montgomery Wards catalogs of the 1950s, it was called, "Chanticleer" (the French word for Rooster). In both cases, it was sold with brown Charm House hollowware. Some rooster plates and platters are found trimmed in gold and marked "California Provincial."

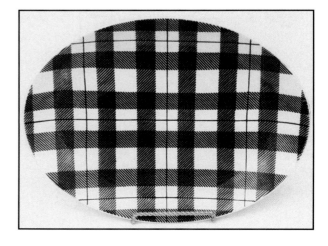

This Dura-Print plaid treatment takes black Charm House hollowware.

The "American Wheat" pattern was made in the mid 1950s and makes use of dark green Charm House. Unlike other Dura-Print lines, the plates and platters for American Wheat have a special backstamp.

In a 1955 ad, this line was offered as , "SOMETHING BLUE...clear blue Snow Blossoms." The hollowware was advertised as, "Color-matched solid Blue cups, vegetable and soup bowls, sugar and creamer offer a daring touch." The soup and vegetable wasn't shown in the ad, but can it be assumed there are Rhythm shape nappies and soups in solid blue glazes? With other Dura-Print treatments these two shapes receive the prints and not the solid colors. The solid blue glaze is not the same as the cobalt used in Fiesta.

Charm House creamer and sauceboats in solid color glazes. These pieces are often found in Rhythm collections, but their colors indicate they belong to Charm House.

The Charm House casserole in dark green. These, along with the teapot, are the hardest pieces to find in solid colored glazes.

A covered sugar in maroon.

Not all Dura-Print lines have Charm House hollowware. There are several cases where other shapes were used. Once in a while a set of Dura-Print is found in its original box with solid color a Harlequin hollowware. Shown in the picture are three Dura-Print lines offered by Montgomery Wards in the 1950s. The Chanticleer and Confetti (black polka-dot) both have Charm House in appropriate solid colors, but the third line, Calypso, Dura-Print treatment of black and yellow swirls, makes use of Rhythm hollowware.

Besides the use of solid color Charm House, Harlequin and Rhythm, a new shape was made in 1957 called, "Studio." This round deep shape was used mainly with Pink Magnolia. The Dura-Print treatment is a combination of pink and gray and the Studio hollowware has solid color interiors.

The Studio shape creamer and sugar set shown here has a gray and yellow Dura-Print wheat pattern on their exteriors. Lines using Studio hollowware make use of the Brittany sauceboat.

This bowl is marked with the Dura-Print backstamp and has a green floral design. What's unusual is that its the Liberty shape. Ordinarily, the Rhythm shape was used with Dura-Print treatments, but as this example shows, others were given the all-over decoration as well. These are also found in blue.

Applique

The majority of "Applique" lines consist of flatware from Brittany, and the hollowware, save the Rhythm sauceboat, from Charm House. There are a few treatments that make use of Brittany flatware and hollowware.

When Applique was released in the 1950s, it was described as, "Homer Laughlin's new, exclusive decorating technique, perfected after years of research to develop designs resistant to acids and dishwashing detergents."

This "new technique" was described as resulting in a "colorful raised enamel effect." If you encounter a piece of Applique, the treatments (of which there are very few) will indeed feel raised as compared to decal or silk screen treatments. Two of the most common treatments are "Yellow Daisy" and "Wild Cherries" but others can be found such as apples and strawberries. The known Applique treatments are combinations of red, yellow, chartreuse, dark green and brown colors. Perhaps other colors can be found in the future.

Pieces are marked with a general HLC backstamp and dates indicate production primarily from 1953-1955.

Yellow Daisy 10" plate, teacup and saucer. Here we see two shapes of Applique together: a Charm House cup and Brittany flatware.

Provincial, A-102, dinner plate.

This Applique treatment of Apples uses Brittany hollowware.

Assortment and Values: Use the higher end for solid color Charm House. For lines that use flatware from other shapes, see appropriate sections. The flatware listed below is the rim shape used for C & G Distributors.

Charm House flatware:		Charm House hollowware:	
(C&G Distributors only)		(C&G, Dura-Print, Applique, etc.)	
10" Plate	$4-5	Cup	$2-3
9" Plate	$2-3	Sugar	$6-8
7" Plate	$1-2	Cream	$4-5
6" Plate	$1-2	Soup/Cereal	$4-5
Rim Soup	$3-4	Sauceboat (Rhythm)	$6-8
Fruit Cup	$1-2	Casserole	$15-18
13" Oval Platter	$5-7	Teapot	$20+
11" Oval Platter	$4-5	Shakers	$8-10
Saucer	$1-2	Gravy Fast stand	
Nappy	$4-5	(C&G only)	$12-15

Other Uses of Charm House

There is at least one instance where solid color Charm House is used with decaled Rhythm. The 50s treatment is called, Desert Flower – a chartreuse, yellow and dark green floral treatment on Rhythm flatware with Charm House hollowware glazed in Chartreuse. Desert Flower is somewhat common. See the section on Rhythm for an example of the Desert Flower treatment.

In the early 1960s, Charm House hollowware was used for the last time with some "Serenade" lines – not to be confused with the pastel colored line from the late 30s and early 40s. For more, see section on Ironstone.

Charm House sugar and creamer with fruit decals.

Coronet

At the end of September 1934, Rhead worked on several fluted plates. The first were 9" plates with various types of flutes as well as versions with floral embossings on the verge. J.M. Wells approved the fluted plate with the floral embossing on October 5, 1934 and ordered development to commence. Rhead was very optimistic about this shape stating, *New shape is different from anything on the market.* Potteries were producing shapes with embossing and shapes with flutes, but there wasn't anything quite like the Coronet shape.

Modeling the rest of the Coronet shape was put on hold for several weeks while the Art Department worked on expanding the Marigold line which had recently been put into production, as well as some oven ware pieces for Royal Metal. At the end of November, work began on what was then called the "fluted" or "paneled" shape. It wasn't until the first week of December that Rhead starts to call the line, "Coronet." He notes special backstamp drawings for both Coronet and Royal Metal being delivered to The Quality Stamp Company (producers of backstamps for many potteries in the area) on December 4, 1934.

By the end of January, most of the Coronet pieces were finished. There was only one "problem" item: the handled soup bowl. The original plan was to make a cream soup cup – basically a low bowl with handles at either side. However, this was changed to an onion soup. Onion soups are usually taller than a cream soup and have lug handles. The onion soup was modeled in December 1934, but on January 1, 1935, Rhead notes trying a replacement. It involved taking the onion soup, cutting off the lugs and applying the sugar bowl handles. Rhead never mentions this version again, and its safe to assume it was never accepted since all that is found on the market today are lug-handled onion soups. A month later he would note more problems with the onion soup that would require revising the lugs.

The final two items modeled for Coronet were in March: the coupe soup and the open sugar. Originally, Coronet had a covered sugar, but an open sugar was modeled in March 1935 and released into production in July in the same year. Should you find a Coronet sugar which doesn't have the inner flange to hold a lid, then it is an open sugar.

Some of Coronet's first treatments were hand-painted embossing work. Polychrome was the first of these and Rhead notes in January 1935 testing various colors and finally on the 24th: *At* [plant] *6 started line of girls working on Coronet Polychrome.* Other colors of embossing would follow in the same manner as those on Marigold and OvenServe. Coronet is found mainly with decals, but there are silver and gold stamp treatments which mimic the floral verge embossing and there are even some silk screen designs.

Coronet in solid colors is not easy to come by. Melon yellow, sea green and ivory are the only ones found thus far. These are marked with either the standard Coronet backstamp or a Wells Art Glazes marking. At one point, Rhead notes making an inexpensive line of Coronet in Fiesta glazes. Rhead never writes of producing Coronet samples in Fiesta glazes stating such a line would, "cost as much as Fiesta."

Coronet was produced well into the 1940s. Unfortunately, it's backstamp doesn't have a date code so approximating when it was discontinued is difficult. The 1951 edition of *The China and Glass Red Book,* a trade journal listing all shapes made by potteries, lists Coronet as still being available by Homer Laughlin. In the 1952 edition, Coronet is no longer in the listing. Coronet did not receive the enormous amount of treatments that were used on other shapes of the same time such as Virginia Rose and the eggshell lines.

Unfortunately, Coronet backstamps don't have any date codes.

The Coronet dinner plate has a common treatment: red trim with "silver stamps" on the embossing. The stamp design which mimics the Coronet embossing was also used as a decoration on the Marigold shape. The onion soup's embossing is done in green. This hand-painted green decoration is much more common on OvenServe, Virginia Rose and Marigold. Both treatments shown bring out the floral embossing which is sometimes overlooked when Coronet pieces receive just a decal treatment.

This rim soup has the very popular petit-point rose decal which has appeared on almost every HLC shape from the 1930s through the 1950s. It was also used extensively by Harker.

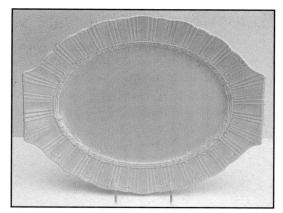

The melon yellow glaze on this Coronet platter is the same used in Wells Art Glazes and embossed OvenServe. Coronet platters come in several sizes and are easily identified by their "fish tail" tab handles.

Coronet plates in Sea Green.

Covered casserole in ivory.

The silver stamp decoration (CO-109) which highlights the embossing is one of the most common treatments on Coronet. Shown are the covered sugar and creamer.

Coronet with hand-painted work, and a decaled teacup.

Coronet Assortment and Values:

10" Plate	$12-14	Gravy Boat	$10-12
9" Plate	$8-10	Gravy Liner	$10-12
7" Plate	$5-7	lug soup	$12-15
6" Plate	$4-5	8" rim soup	$8-10
Teacup	$7-9	8" coupe soup	$10-12
Saucer	$2-3	Casserole	$45-50
Covered Sugar	$18-20	11" Platter	$8-10
Open Sugar	$15-18	13" Platter	$12-15
Creamer	$7-9	15" Platter	$18-20
Fruit Cup	$4-5	Nappy	$10-12
Oatmeal	$6-8	Baker	$8-10
36s bowl	$10-12		

Duratone

Duratone was first produced in October of 1960. The backstamp supports this date since it boats the ware as, "DISHWASHER-PROOF." In general there aren't very many lines prior to 1960 which make reference to dinnerware being dishwasher safe.

The name Duratone has two meanings. First the "Dura" part refers to its durability. Not only was this ware advertised as a dishwasher-proof, but many vintage ads claim Duratone is, "guaranteed oven-proof, detergent proof and stain-resistant. It will not fade, craze or crackle." The "tone" is obvious from the treatments; each has a decal and trim that work together to produce a dominate color or tone. In the past two years I've been able to find only five treatments or tones. Two are in blue, one pink, and yellow and a gray called, "Charm Pattern" and sold through Montgomery Wards. No doubt others will be found. The Spring Garden treatment is the only Duratone treatment I've found where its name is included in the backstamp. All others will have the same backstamp but without a treatment name.

Flatware is the generic coupe shapes that have been used for so many lines of the 1950s, but the hollowware is unique. Sugars, creamers, sauceboats and casseroles were modeled especially for this line and according to the log these shapes were called, "Vogue." The shakers were borrowed from Jubilee and the generic shape jumbo salad bowl was also offered (see the section on Specialty Items for more on the jumbo salad bowl).

Expect large flatware to be marked (platters, dinner plates) while smaller flatware may or may not be marked. Hollowware is never found with a backstamp.

The treatment on this Duratone cup and saucer is called, "Spring Garden." This is by far the most common pattern found Duratone. Also shown is the original box which advertises a 3-piece place setting (cup, saucer, 10" plate) for only 99 cents. The

original prices for Duratone were extremely low: a 7" plate sold for 29 cents, fruit cup for 19 cents, covered sugar *and* creamer for $1.99.

Shown with a Spring Garden 9" plate is a "Buttercup" dinner plate. Its safe to say that Buttercup is the second most common treatment on Duratone.

The name for this treatment is presently unknown, but the decals and trim are combined to produce a pink "tone."

Assortment and values: The pieces listed below the line have not been confirmed as being found with the Spring Garden treatment. In at least three ads, Spring Garden is offered with the most basic of pieces – those above the line. However, the casserole, sauceboat, shakers and jumbo salad have been found with the Buttercup and other Duratone treatments.

10" Plate	$4-5	Oval Platter	$5-7
9" Plate	$4-5	Round Serving Bowl	$4-5
7" Plate	$2-3	Soup Bowl	$2-3
6" Plate	$2-3	Fruit Cup	$1
Cup	$4-5	Covered Sugar	$6-8
Saucer	$1	Creamer	$5-7
Casserole	$10-12	Sauceboat	$6-8
Shakers	$5-7	Jumbo Salad	$10-12

Empress & Kwaker

The earliest ads I could find for Empress and Kwaker come from 1910, but its possible the line was offered earlier. Its doubtful it was too much earlier though, since most catalogs dated circa 1900 often feature The Angelus and Hudson rather than the plain shapes of Empress and Kwaker. While the initial release dates may not be known, it can be said with certainty that both lines became very popular in the 1920s. Each featured dozens of "border treatments" – decals which decorate a narrow space along the rim. The rest of the piece is left undecorated except for gold or colored accents on handles and finials.

Collectors know these two shapes share the same flatware but have different hollowware. Empress hollowware is unusual in that it is widest at its midsection. Handles and finials for Empress were rather simple and curved. Kwaker, on the other hand, has distinctive flat-top handles and finials. There should be no difficulty in telling the hollowware of one line from the other.

The flatware is a different matter. Kwaker and Empress were either marked with a general HLC backstamp or with special markings which contained the shape name. These special marks usually date from the early 1920s. Unfortunately, the majority of pieces will have the generic backstamp which doesn't specify the shape. To complicate matters, treatments were often shared between the two shapes. If a collector finds a piece of Kwaker or Empress with a general mark and without a piece of hollowware, then the item in question could be either Kwaker or Empress.

Kwaker was discontinued sometime in the mid 1940s, but pieces of Empress have been found (namely sugars and creamers) dated as late as 1950. The Kwaker/Empress flatware was picked up to be used with the Willow, Americana, Early American Homes, and Blue Fantasy lines. The Empress teapot was dipped in blue vellum and melon yellow and marked Wells Art Glazes. This was done as a special order, but the retailer's identity remains a mystery. The Empress butter pat was also made in art glazes and the casserole was used with Willow.

Empress Examples:

1912 Magazine advertisement featuring the Empress shape.

Empress dinner plate with a common band treatment: E-1715. This decoration was also used on Kwaker.

Empress Oatmeal, Bouillon and liner. These pieces have a "dull gold coin" treatment called, "Barbara" E-1602. The bouillon cups are smaller than the cream soup cups: bowl diameter: 3⁷/₁₆", liner diameter: 5³/₄". All three pieces are stamped: WARRANTED 18 CARAT GOLD.

Empress cream soup and liner.

Empress cup and saucer.

This "round" covered vegetable has a stylized treatment in conjunction with gold stamp decoration.

The treatment on this "oval" covered dish has a formal "band" design which was a popular type of decoration in the 1920s.

Empress platters with iridized trims are not hard to find. As you can see by the picture, they tend to wear very easily.

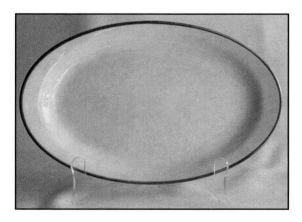

An Empress platter with gold trim.

All Empress shapes, from left to right: A.D. sugar, regular sugar and creamer with very popular blue bird decals and a 48s jug.

Empress 42s and 48s jug – just two of the six sizes of jugs offered with Empress. See section on Trade Sizes in the Appendix for an explanation on "42s" and "48s."

Kwaker Examples:

Shown is Kwaker covered sugar and 6" plate. This treatment, called Ivora, can be found on other HLC shapes, but is most common on Kwaker. The unique combination of red, yellow, green and black keeps it from being confused with other floral decal treatments.

Like other lines produced during the early 20th Century, Kwaker had two types of covered dishes; one oval; the other round. Here is an oval version with one of the many "band" decorations.

Kwaker oval casserole.

K-4115 Kwaker creamer, sauceboat and liner/pickle.

All three pieces shown were made by Homer Laughlin and received a very heavy gold decoration. The sugar and creamer are part of the Kwaker line. The tray became a generic pick up piece as it has also been found in sets of Yellowstone and Wells.

Exotic birds are always a favorite on dinnerware. Here is a common treatment used on Kwaker.

Assortment and Values:

Empress and Kwaker were very extensive lines with multiple sizes of platters, bakers and bowls. There are two sizes of Empress sugars, but only one for Kwaker. The open and covered salad bowls as well as the handled relish were made with Kwaker only.

10" Plate	$6-8	Platter, any size	$12-15
9" Plate	$5-6	Nappy, any size	$8-10
8" Plate	$6-8	Baker, any size	$8-10
7" Plate	$3-4	Coupe Soup	$5-6
6" Plate	$2-3	Rim Soup	$5-6
Fruit Cup	$3-4	Cream Soup	$10-12
Oatmeal	$4-5	Cream Soup liner	$6-7
Teacup	$6-8	Covered Butter	$20-25
Saucer	$1-2	Casserole, oval	$15-18
A.D. Cup	$12-15	Casserole, round	$12-15
A.D. Saucer	$4-5	Teapot	$45-50
Covered Sugar	$8-10	Jug, any size	$15-20
Creamer	$5-7	Covered Sauce Dish	$20-25
Sauceboat	$7-9	Ladle	$25+
Gravy Fast stand	$10-12	Oyster Tureen	$25-30
Bouillon	$8-10	Open Salad Bowl	$18-20
Bouillon liner	$4-5	Covered Salad	$20-25
Handled relish	$12-15		

Epicure & Kenilworth

Epicure

In the very late 1940s and into the 1950s, there were two major groups of new shapes introduced by American pottery companies. The first group consisted of very simple plain round coupe shapes – in Homer Laughlin's case, Rhythm and Jubilee (and its spin-offs Debutante, Skytone and Suntone). The second group is made up of "biomorphic shapes." Such shapes have a fluid or stretched look. Iroquois' Casual China, Impromptu, Stubenville's Contempora, Hall's Tomorrow's Classic and Roseville's Raymor are just a few of these free form lines. Homer Laughlin never produced unconventional lines like those mentioned, but they did come close in 1954 with the dinnerware shape, Epicure.

Designed by Don Shrekengost, Epicure pieces were first modeled in 1954. Because of the way records were kept during this time, its hard to tell the exact date. Items in the modeling log from the late 40s and 1950s were commonly listed simply as "cup" or "plate" without any specific shape reference. Also, sketches were not commonly kept in the log so piecing together a dinnerware line from this time period can be difficult. In 1952 most of the Cavalier shapes were modeled and put into production. With production concentrated on Rhythm, Charm House, Skytone, Debutante and the new Cavalier line, there was no need to design a new shape for 1953. In fact, only 18 pieces were modeled for '53 – one third the amount of shapes created the year before.

Several items in the modeling log at the end of 1953 are more than likely Epicure shapes. They are listed as being modeled from October to December as: Saucer, dropped edge, 8" plate (actual 10"), Cup, Handle, Sugar, Sugar Cover, and Bowl. There is a small sketch in the log beside the October '53 cup which looks like the standard Epicure cup and there is a note stating the shape was, "released for production Nov. 17, 1954." This would coincide with the release dates for other Epicure items. In 1954, more items are modeled but, like all other pieces, there is no mention of the Epicure name – just general item labels. Based on the same type of deduction used for the items listed at the end of 1953, it can be assumed the next pieces were made in August '54. For the rest of the year and into March 1955 all the standard Epicure items were modeled.

One interesting thing to note is the name Epicure is never listed with any of the regular Epicure items modeled from 1954 to mid 1955. The first time the name is mentioned is in reference to Harlequin:

> May 23, 1955   HARLEQUIN HANDLE FOR EPICURE CUP
> June 3, 1955   LARGER HARLEQUIN HANDLE FOR EPICURE CUP

Collectors know these specially made cups as Harlequin large cups. Saucers were picked up from jumbo cups that had been in production for several years. For more on these cups, see the section on Harlequin.

It should be noted the standard cup used for Epicure is a *coffee* cup. There were no teacups designed in the original assortment, but on October 14, 1955, there is an entry in the log for: CUP, EPICURE DINNERWARE SIZE. This is probably a teacup since dinnerware lines usually carried teacups and not the large size coffee cups. While none have been accounted for, the designer, Don Shrekengost, maintained the tea cups were put into production in an article titled, *Epicure* by collector Matthew Whalen (*The Dish,* Vol. 1, No. 2 1998).

There are two specially made items that are not found in vintage ads; the tid bit tray and the nut dish. Tid Bits are made of two plates separated by a white plastic column. To date, only white trays have been found. The nut dishes were promotional pieces for buyers at trade shows. Most are in turquoise and sometimes can be found in their original bag with price list.

Epicure was made in four colored glazes: Snow White, Turquoise Blue, Dawn Pink, and Charcoal Gray. The blue, gray and pink glazes have the appearance of small filings which makes the glaze look textured. The white glaze lacks this special textured look. The body is heavier than normal and, according to backstamps, is oven proof. There are two Epicure backstamps; one with a date code and the other without. Based on the date codes, many assume Epicure was discontinued around 1960.

Shown is one of three different Epicure dinnerware ads that can be found in many 1955 magazines. It offers Epicure in the four colors in a 16-piece starter set for $7.95.

Epicure plates in turquoise, charcoal and pink. Notice the light area at the top of the dropped edge. This is not a manufacturers flaw and is to be expected on all pieces of Epicure.

Epicure Coffeepot

This little Epicure nut dish was a salesman's sample. Included with the dish was a brochure of all the available items.

Covered Vegetable in turquoise.

Another covered vegetable, this time in pink and with an individual casserole for comparison. The individual casserole is the only round piece of lidded hollowware – all others are oval.

Coffee Cup and Saucer in charcoal.

Gravy, lade and shakers in the
four Epicure colors.

Sugar, creamer and rare tid bit tray.

Epicure saucer with a gold shield treatment – a decoration that has only been found on white Epicure coffee cups and saucers. Decorated examples of Epicure are hard to find. There is at least one white Epicure platter known with a green/black swirl treatment.

Epicure Assortment and Values:

10" Plate	$18-20	11" Platter	$18-20
8" Plate	$15-18	9" Platter	$30-35
6" Plate	$4-5	Covered Casserole	$70-80
Fruit Cup	$8-10	Individual Casserole	$50-60
Cereal bowl	$18-20	Gravy bowl	$25-30
Nappy	$18-20	Ladle	$60-70
Cup	$12-15	Coffeepot	$200+
Saucer	$5-6	Tid bit Tray	$200+
Shakers (pr.)	$20-25	Nut Dish	$30-35
Covered Sugar	$18-20		
Creamer	$10-12		

In the fall of 1955 a special line of buffet ware was crafted. Kenilworth, as it would come to be known, was made in the same body and colors as Epicure, however the shapes for these two lines were very different. Most of the Kenilworth items were made to receive special metal fittings. In almost every case the fittings were decorative serving as accents to the bases and lids of hollowware. Several styles of carafes, bowls and casseroles were made in very simple round shapes. In 1957, more items were added to Kenilworth: Coffee pot, sugar, creamer and ice bucket. The '57 coffeepot, sugar and creamer differ from the round Kenilworth pieces with sharp angular handles.

Kenilworth is somewhat easy to find. Since the backstamp makes no mention of Homer Laughlin, most pieces go unnoticed by collectors and dealers. Pieces have been found in all four Epicure colors and some white examples are decorated with decals.

The Kenilworth backstamp.

The ball shape carafes have been found in all four Epicure colors. They come with plastic caps and corks seal and various styles of metal handles.

This is the coffee set modeled in 1957. All four pieces have decorative metal frames. While white is the most common color for all the Kenilworth pieces, examples of the coffee set have been found in turquoise.

Here is a group shot of the two styles of Kenilworth coffee carafes. The example on the far left is in white with casino decals – a common decoration on white Kenilworth. Notice the two styles of handles on the turquoise and white ball shape carafes.

The jumbo salad is in the turquoise Epicure glaze. These may be found unmarked or with a Kenilworth backstamp. The casserole, in pink, has Fiesta-like scroll handles and is complete with metal lid and stand. Most of the time, only the ceramic bases are found. The low bowl has a decal with 50s designs and colors that complements the Kenilworth line.

Kenilworth Assortment and Values: Use low end for white, higher end for other colors and white with decals. Values are for items complete with metal lids and/or attachments.

Coffee carafe - round version	$25-30	Rectangular Platter	$8-10
Coffee carafe - 1957 version	$12-15	Casserole, scroll handles	$15-20
Covered Sugar	$8-10	Jumbo Bowl	$20-25
Creamer	$5-8	Low Bowl	$20-25
Round Tray	$8-10	Ice Bucket (w/glass insert)	$35-40

Fiesta

It would be very difficult to find a line that is more collected and more recognized than Fiesta. It has become so familiar to the general public that when any line of solid colored dinnerware is encountered by a non collector, he or she almost always calls it "Fiesta" when it may not have even been made by HLC. Both vintage (pieces produced from 1936-1973) and contemporary (pieces produced from 1986 to the present) Fiesta have become part of American popular culture.

The first piece to be modeled was a 9-inch "Ring Plate for Colored Glazes" in February 1935. The name "Fiesta" would not be applied to the new line for several months. Interestingly this shape was accepted as the basic design for the flatware. With the development of other shapes, multiple designs of plates were often sketched, modeled and after being reviewed, were subject to being rejected or put into production. In Fiesta's case, there was very little debate as to its design. The second piece was the "Modern Ribbed Teacup and Handles." The body was the standard Fiesta teacup and four versions of handles were considered. All four were rejected in favor of an open ring handle that collectors know of today. Immediately following the teacup and handle was the 10" plate.

On March 2, 1935, Rhead notes making sketches of possible additions to the new shape including steins, a French casserole, and some familiar pieces such as a sugar, creamer and a covered onion soup. For the rest of 1935, pieces were modeled for Fiesta. Some interesting shapes listed in the log that didn't make it into production include the "ringed shape casserole one handle," cracked ice bowl, and a square teapot.

There were several names considered for the new ring shape. On April 1, 1935, Rhead notes working on various colored glazes and wrote in the margin, *Notes on Rhumba Ware.* Four days later on April 5, 1935, Rhead listed the possibilities in his journal: Park Lane, Rhapsody, Plaza, Faience, Tazza, Tazza Faience, and Chalet Faience. Initially, "Fiesta" wasn't even under consideration. On April 9, Rhead wrote in his journal about discussing merchandising for "Faience line." He then makes another entry on the 12th, stating: ... *name for colored glazes DASHE Faience.* Rhead kept referring to the line as, "colored glaze line" rather than committing to the Faience name even though it was an apparent favorite by others who worked at HLC. On April 15, 1935, he notes the name, "Flamingo." The next time he calls the line Flamingo is on April 26: *J.M. Wells went over shape program for Flamingo line.* Finally, on May 14, 1935, the name "Fiesta" is applied to the new shape and on the 17th, Rhead notes making, "...drawings of "Fiesta" stamp for molds and clay stamp."

Over the years the color assortment for Fiesta changed and certain pieces have become more valuable in certain colors. Below is a table of the standard eleven colors with their dates of operation. Those colors made from 1951 until 1959 are commonly called the "50s colors."

Red	1936-1943, 1959-1972	Rose	1951-1959
Yellow	1936-1969	Chartreuse	1951-1959
Cobalt	1936-1951	Gray	1951-1959
Light Green	1936-1951	Dark Green	1951-1959
Ivory	1936-1951	Medium Green	1959-1969
Turquoise	1937-1969		

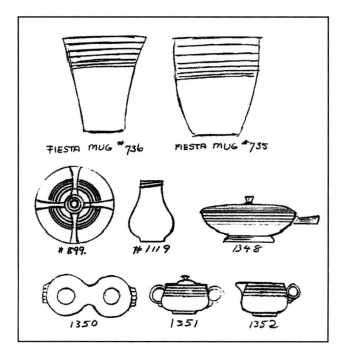

FIESTA MUG #736   FIESTA MUG #735

#899.   #1119   1348

1350   1351   1352

Unfortunately, the sketches in the modeling log start after Fiesta was almost totally developed. Shown here is a sample of Fiesta sketches that appear in the log. On the top row are two water tumblers which Rhead calls, "mugs." He calls model 736 the concave mug and 735, convex. The "concave" version is the one which went into production. The next row shows model 899, a one-piece relish tray that underwent several revisions. The Drip cut syrup base is next followed by an early version of the French casserole, model number 1348 listed as having a capacity of 37.5 oz. and modeled on December 1939. The actual French casserole, a promotional item made in yellow, that went into production doesn't have the pedestal foot as shown with this trial.

In the last row are sketches for the individual cream, sugar and figure-8 tray, another Fiesta promotional set from late December 1939/early January 1940.

Fiesta impressed or "mold" markings and a backstamp

Plates in light green, cobalt, yellow and turquoise.

Shown are the backs of two Fiesta 9" plates. Notice one has a backstamp and the other doesn't. Just because a piece is unmarked doesn't mean it isn't a piece of HLC's Fiesta. While there are many other lines of solid color dinnerware made by different potteries, there should be very little confusion with the distinctive shapes of Fiesta.

8" Deep Plate in cobalt.

Values:

	Red	Cobalt-Ivory	Turq.-Lt. Green - Yellow	50s Colors	Medium Green
15" Plate	$55-60	$50-55	$40-45	$75-85	NA
13" Plate	$35-40	$30-35	$20-25	$45-55	$100+
10" Plate	$50-60	$40-50	$35-45	$70-80	$125+
9" Plate	$35-45	$20-25	$20-25	$35-45	$100+
8" Deep Plate	$40-45	$35-40	$25-30	$45-50	$85-90
7" Plate	$15-20	$10-15	$8-10	$15-20	$50-75
6" Plate	$10-12	$8-10	$8-10	$10-12	$40+

Some of the most sought after pieces of Fiesta: tripod candled holders in yellow, 12" vase in turquoise, 8" vase in yellow, bud vase in turquoise and bulb style candleholders in ivory and cobalt.

Values:

	Red	Cobalt-Ivory-Turq.	Lt.Green-Yellow
12" Vase	$1750-1850	$1550-1600	$1200-1300
10" Vase	$1000-950	$850-900	$750-800
8" Vase	$650-700	$600-650	$450-500
Bud Vase	$95-115	$85-95	$50-75
Bulb Candles, pr.	$100-115	$90-95	$75-85
Tripod Candles, pr.	$700+	$500-600	$450-500

From left to right: water tumbler in red, juice tumbler in cobalt, ice pitcher in yellow, plate in green, 2-pt. jug in turquoise and syrup with Drip cut lid in ivory.

Values:

	Red	Cobalt-Ivory-Turq.	Lt. Green - Yellow	50s Colors	Medium Green
Water Tumbler	$70-75	$60-65	$40-45	NA	NA
Juice Tumbler	_see section later on Juice Sets_				
Ice Pitcher	$175-195	$140-150	$120-130	NA	NA
2-pt. Jug	$80-100	$60-70	$40-50	$130+	NA
Syrup Pitcher	$350+	$350+	$300-325	NA	NA

One of the most desirable pieces of Fiesta, the demitasse coffeepot, was made until circa 1945 and comes in the first six colors only. The regular coffeepot was made longer until the mid 1950s and is found in all the standard colors except medium green. In the foreground is the A.D. cup and saucer in red and the teacup and saucer in cobalt.

Values:

	Red	Cobalt-Ivory-Turq.	Lt. Green-Yellow	50s Colors	Med. Green
Demitasse Coffeepot	$600+	$400-450	$300-350	NA	NA
Regular Coffeepot	$250+	$200-230	$180-200	$350+	NA
A.D. Cup	$45-50	$35-40	$30-35	$400+	NA
A.D. Saucer	$20+	$15-20	$12-15	$100+	NA
Tea Cup	$40-45	$25-30	$20-25	$50-55	$100+
Tea Saucer	$5-8	$4-5	$2-3	$8-10	$20+

The covered sugar in cobalt, shakers in red and stick-handled creamer in turquoise. The creamer was replaced in mid 1937 with a ring handled version.

Values:

	Red	Cobalt-Ivory	Turq.-Lt. Green - Yellow	50s Colors	Medium Green
Covered Sugar	$70-75	$60-65	$40-50	$70-80	$200+
Stick Creamer	$55-60	$45-50	$45-50 (turq. $80)	NA	NA
Shakers, pair	$35-40	$25-35	$20-25	$35-40	$85-100

This style of creamer, known as the ring handled creamer or regular creamer, replaced the stick-handle version in mid 1937. It would continue to be produced until 1969 when it was restyled with a "c" handle. The "c" handle or Ironstone creamer is the style in production today with the reissue line.

Values:

	Red	Cobalt-Ivory	Turq.-Lt. Green - Yellow	50s Colors	Medium Green
Ring Handled Creamer	$45-55	$40-45	$20-25	$50-60	$85-95

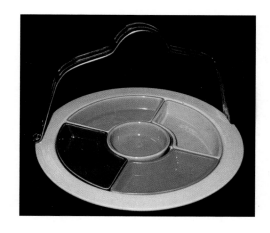

Shown in the six "original colors" is the six piece Fiesta relish with metal attachment.

Values: Complete relish tray - $300-350

On the right is the standard Fiesta casserole in red. To the left is a tricolator bowl. This is the same as the Fiesta casserole minus the foot. These bowls are marked "Tricolator" in the mold and are always found without a lid.

Tricolator bowls in turquoise, yellow and red.

Values:

	Red	Cobalt-Ivory	Turq.-Lt. Green - Yellow	50s Colors	Medium Green
Casserole	$200-225	$185-200	$150-175	$300-350	$900+

Tricolator Bowl, any of the six original colors – $150+

Fiesta fruit bowls: 4³/4" in red and 5¹/2" in ivory. 8¹/2" and 9¹/2" nappies have the same straight side style as the fruit bowls.

Values:

	Red	Cobalt-Ivory	Turq.-Lt. Green - Yellow	50s Colors	Medium Green
4³/4" Fruit	$25-30	$25-35	$20-25	$35-45	$650+
5¹/2" Fruit	$25-30	$20-25	$18-20	$45-50	$85-90
8¹/2" Nappy	$45-55	$40-45	$25-35	$60-70	$150+
9¹/2" Nappy	$55-60	$45-55	$45-55	NA	NA

The ivory carafe is the old version. It has a lid complete with cork and a pedestal foot. The sapphire example is from the new line. It doesn't take a lid and has a tapered base.

Values:

Red	Cobalt-Ivory-Turq.	Lt. Green-yellow
$200-250	175-225	$125-175

The vintage Fiesta teapots: left, in red, large 8-cup size; right, in turquoise, medium 6-cup size. The large version is being used in the new Fiesta line. The major difference between the old and new teapots lies in the lid: old teapots have a "flat" lid whereas new teapots have a "domed" lid (which is actually a modified version of the old coffeepot lid).

The medium teapot isn't used in the new Fiesta line, but you may find them in brown and gold with knob-like finials and unmarked. These come from Fiesta Amberstone (brown) and Fiesta Casualstone/Ironstone (gold).

This is from the modeling log which shows a proposed "Square Fiesta" teapot that didn't make it into production.

Values:

	Red	Cobalt-Ivory	Turq.-Lt. Green - Yellow	50s Colors	Medium Green
Lg. Teapot	$250-260	$225-250	$185-200	NA	NA
Med. Teapot	$250-300	$200-225	$150-160	#350+	$1500+

The 10" compartment plate is the smaller of two sizes. The larger, 12" version, was discontinued early in Fiesta's production. The larger shaker in red is from Fiesta Kitchen Kraft. It is shown with a standard shape shaker for size comparison. The yellow egg cup can be found in the first 10 Fiesta colors – no medium green.

Values:

	Red	Cobalt-Ivory	Turq.-Lt. Green - Yellow	50s Colors	Medium Green
12" Comp. plate	$55-60	$50-55	$45-50 (no turq.)	NA	NA
10" Comp. plate	$45-50	$35-45	$30-40	$70-75	NA
KK Shakers	$85-90	$85-90 (no ivory)	$85-90 (no turq.)		
Shakers, pair	$35-40	$25-35	$20-25	$35-40	$85-100
Egg Cup	$75-85	$50-60	$35-45	$100-125	NA

Shown in medium green is the last standard item made for Fiesta: The 7⅝" individual salad bowl. Besides medium green, it was made in red, turquoise and yellow. They are marked either with a Fiesta backstamp or are marked in the mold.

Individual Salad, any color: $85-95

In 1939, several new shapes were made for Fiesta promotions. The first was a special juice set made up of four tumblers and a juice pitcher. The tumblers were actually made from models that were developed for Kraft Cheese to use as jars. Dozens of jars were made but the size and capacities were constantly under revision. Though the jars never fulfilled their original purpose, they were put to good use with the special promotions.

On March 15, 1939, Rhead wrote of the set: *Cheese Jars for water sets with disk jug . . . Should have 5 oz. capacity, probably cut down 1/4" to lower costs.* Eventually, on July 6, 1939, one of the jars originally designed for Kraft Cheese in May of 1938 was released into production to be used with the new juice set.

It can be assumed the juice pitcher was released at this time as well. It was originally modeled at the same time as the larger disc pitcher in the spring of 1938. The set consisted of a pitcher in yellow and a tumbler in the original colors. Production of the set continued into the late 1940s. When red was discontinued in 1943, rose was picked up from the Harlequin line to serve as a replacement.

There were special sets made in the early 40s that had red juice pitchers. These are much harder to find than yellow ones.

Shown in light green, ivory and red are "Kraft Cheese" jars that were dipped in Fiesta glazes and used with special juice sets.

The promotion was applied two more times. The Jubilee colors, gray, green, beige and pink were used in the very late 1940s and the 50s colors; pitcher in gray and tumblers in dark green and chartreuse along with Harlequin yellow made up juice sets in the 1950s. Many collectors call these Rhythm juice sets because of the color assortment. There may be some problem with this line of thinking as they could be called Harlequin juice sets for the exact same reason. Whether the 50s juice sets belong to either line or are just a special order is currently unknown.

Fiesta shape juice set in Jubilee colors.

Comparison of the Fiesta tumblers. Left: vintage juice tumbler in a Jubilee glaze, Middle: Fiesta 10 oz. water tumbler, Right: tumbler currently in use with the reissue Fiesta line.

Juice Pitcher

Fiesta Yellow	$40-50
Harlequin Yellow	$60-70
Fiesta Red	$250+
Celadon Green	$100+
Gray	$2000+

Juice Tumblers

red-cobalt-ivory	$35-45
turquoise-lt. green-yellow	$20-25
rose	$50-55
Jubilee colors	$90-110
50s colors	$500+

On January 4, 1936, Rhead notes making vellum (ivory) Fiesta with stripes. Unfortunately, the journals don't preserve the details surrounding this line such as were there colors used other than blue and red? Who was the buyer?

The line isn't limited to basic place settings. Many of the more exotic pieces such as tripods, covered

onion soups, mustards and others have been found with the distinctive triple ring pattern. The mustard wasn't released into production until June 1936 so it follows the line must have been made for at least six months and perhaps longer. Shown in the photo are the chop plate with blue bands, and a 7" plate and cream soup cup with red bands.

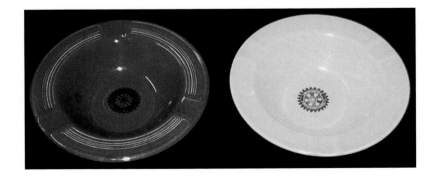

Ashtrays: Fiesta in cobalt on the left and Harlequin in yellow on the right. Both are decorated with a Rotary Club logo.

Values:

	Red	Cobalt-Ivory	Turq.-Lt. Green - Yellow	50s Colors	Medium Green
Fiesta Ashtray	$50-60	$45-50	$35-40	$75-90	$150+

The Fiesta mustard started out as a special item made for Royal Metal. A metal frame was made so the mustard and shakers could be marketed as a "condiment set." Although it was originally intended as a specialty piece, it eventually became a standard Fiesta item.

Values: any color $250-300

Fiesta brochures are very collectible and the earlier the year, the higher the price. Shown is the outside and inside of a four page fold out of a May 1944 version.

Values: 1930s – $75+
1940s – $40-50
1950s – $30-40
1960s – $20-30

Values:

	Red	Cobalt-Ivory-Turq.	Lt. Green - Yellow	50s Colors	Medium Green
ftd salad bowl	$250-275	$225-250	$185-200	NA	NA
11¾" fruit bowl	$250-275	$200-225	$185-200	NA	NA
Utility Tray	$40-50	$40-50	$35-40	NA	NA
Cvrd Onion Soup	$500-600	$500-600 (turq $2500+)	$500-600	NA	NA
12" Comport	$200+	$145-175	$100-125	NA	NA
Sweets compote	$100-125	$85-95	$75-85	NA	NA
Nested bowls					
#1	$250-270	$220-240	$185-200	NA	NA
#2	$95-100	$85-95	$75-85	NA	NA
#3	$110-125	$100-115	$95-105	NA	NA
#4	$130-145	$120-135	$100-125	NA	NA
#5	$150-165	$130-140	$120-130	NA	NA
#6	$175-200	$140-160	$135-155	NA	NA
#7	$250+	$200-225	$185-205	NA	NA

Nested bowl lid, any color, size 1 through 4: $800-1200 each

	Red	Cobalt-Ivory	Turq.-Lt. Green - Yellow	50s Colors	Medium Green
Tom & Jerry Mug	$75-80	$60-65	$45-50	$65-75	$90-110
Cream soup cup	$70-90	$45-55	$30-35	$100+	$3000+
Sauceboat	$55-56	$45-55	$25-30	$75-85	$175+
12" Platter	$40-50	$35-40	$25-35	$55-60	$150+
Desert bowl	$50-60	$45-50	$25-35	$80+	$500+
Disc Pitcher (64oz.)	$145-150	$100-125	$85-95	$225-250	$1500+

	Yellow	Cobalt	Turquoise	Red
Figure-8 Tray	NA	$65-70	$200+	NA
Ind. Sugar	$85-100	NA	NA	NA
Ind. Creamer	$55-65	NA	NA	$200+
French Casserole	$250+	NA	NA	NA
Promotional Salad	$100-120	NA	NA	NA

Fiesta Casuals

Mixing solid color hollowware with decorated flatware was first done in the early 1950s with Dura-Print, but by the 1960s, more and more lines were being offered with the solid color hollowware and decorated flatware (i.e. Ironstone, Orbit and Regency). In the mid 1960s, Fiesta shapes were used in at least two forms. Both lines were marked with the special name, "Fiesta Casuals" and were limited with platters, 10" plates, 7" plates and saucers as the decorated flatware and 8" nappies, 5½" fruit, teacup and sugar and creamer as solid color hollowware.

These Fiesta 7" plates have the two Fiesta Casuals treatments. On the left is "Yellow Carnation" which makes use of yellow Fiesta hollowware. On the right is a plate from a line which uses turquoise hollowware. Most collectors know this as, "Hawaiian 12-Point Daisy" but in at least two ads from 1965, the line was offered as "Turquoise Cornflower" along with "Yellow Carnation."

Values for Fiesta Casuals, either decoration:

10" Plate	$15-20
7" Plate	$20-25
Platter	$20-25
Saucer	$3-5

Sheffield Amberstone and Coventry Casualstone

In 1967, HLC made a special line for J&H International (for more on this company, see section on Markings). This would be the first of several specially made lines that was sold under the name "Sheffield." In this case, the standard Fiesta line was modified into "Sheffield Amberstone." Many of the standard items were restyled, some left alone, and a few items not before offered with Fiesta made an appearance. They were all brought together with a new brown glaze and the flatware received a special black decoration. A breakdown of the assortment is given below with values.

Fiesta Casualstone is basically the same as Amberstone except the base color is a rich gold glaze and flatware is decorated with a different design. This was one of two lines made for Coventry Ware, Inc. – the other being Coventry Castillian on the Granada shape. The assortment for "Coventry Casualstone" is identical for Amberstone. Both lines are very easy to find.

The Sheffield Amberstone handled tray is a chop plate with metal holder.

The restyled mug, shown in the brown glaze from Amberstone was also used in Casualstone, Ironstone and Sheffield Dresden.

Coventry Casualstone cup and saucer.

Casualstone pie plate.

Amberstone and Casualstone butter dishes make use of the Orbit shape.

Casualstone covered marmalade and sauceboat. The marmalade with a modified finial was used only with Casualstone and Amberstone. The sauceboat on the other hand is in antique gold and could come from Casualstone or Ironstone which both used the same gold glaze.

Assortment and Values:

Note: The markings from the hollowware was removed but once in a while a piece of Amberstone or Casualstone is found with the impressed Fiesta logo.

Pieces taken directly from Fiesta:

13" Chop Plate	$18-20
Oval Platter	$15-18
10" Plate	$5-7
7" Plate	$4-5
6" Plate	$2-3
Saucer	$1-2
Sauceboat	$15-18
Disc Pitcher	$50-60
Shakers	$10-12
Deep Plate	$8-10
Ashtray	$30-35

Restyled Pieces of Fiesta:

Sugar	$8-10
Creamer	$4-5
Coffeepot	$65-75
Teapot	$45-50
Casserole	$55-65
Marmalade	$65-70
Fruit Cup	$4-5
Nappy	$12-18
Teacup	$4-5
Mug	$30-35

Pieces Created for Amberstone and also used with Casualstone:

Sauceboat stand	$35-40
Pie Plate	$30-35
Jumbo Salad	$25-30
Oatmeal bowl	$4-5
Handled Tray	$18-20
Butter (Orbit shape)	$25-30

Fiesta Ironstone

The standard Fiesta line was no longer offered in 1969. Instead, a new line called, "Fiesta Ironstone" took its place. The assortment was made up of pieces designed for Amberstone with some deletions. Three colors made up Fiesta Ironstone: antique gold (the same color from Coventry Casualstone), turf green and mango red – the same "radioactive" red from the standard Fiesta line. The five "large" pieces from Fiesta Ironstone; disc pitcher, coffeepot, teapot, casserole and jumbo salad were only made in antique gold so don't expect to find them in the turf green glaze or red. If you find a red disc pitcher, then its from regular Fiesta and not part of Ironstone.

Fiesta Ironstone was discontinued in January of 1973. Almost every piece is unmarked.

The Ironstone (or Casualstone) coffeepot on the left is shown with a standard Fiesta coffeepot for comparison. The only major difference involves the shape of the finials.

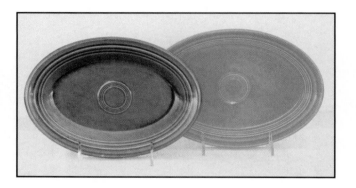

The sauceboat stands measure 9" and are very desirable in red. The example on the left is in Ironstone's turf green. To the right is contemporary Fiesta small platter which is very similar to the Ironstone sauceboat stands. All Ironstone, Casualstone and Amberstone sauceboat stands are unmarked.

The jumbo salad was made in only two colors; brown for Amberstone and gold for both Casualstone and Ironstone. A few unusual jumbo bowls have been found in a gold glaze with a dark green air brush trim.

Nappy in Antique gold (Casualstone or Ironstone), 6½" bowl in turf green (Ironstone) and 5½" bowl in brown (Amberstone).

Assortment and Values:

	Antique Gold/Turf Green	Red
12" Platter	$10-12	$15-20
10" Plate	$8-10	$25-30
7" Plate	$4-5	$8-10
Teacup	$5-6	$8-10
Teacup, Ironstone shape in turquoise, yellow or medium green – $45-50		
Saucer	$1-2	$2-3
6½" Bowl	$4-5	$6-8
5½" Bowl	$3-4	$5-6
Nappy	$12-18	$20-25
Jumbo Salad	$25-30*	NA
Sugar	$8-10	$18-20
Creamer	$4-5	$8-10
Casserole	$55-65*	NA
Coffeepot	$65-75*	NA
Teapot	$45-50*	NA
Disc Pitcher	$50-60*	NA
Sauceboat	$15-18	$40-45
Sauceboat stand	$35-40	$95+
Shakers, pr.	$10-12	$35-40
Mug	$30-35	$40-45

(*) *Indicates Antique Gold only*

Contemporary Fiesta

Homer Laughlin made numerous trials of shapes from the vintage Fiesta and Ironstone shapes in 1985. In early 1986, the Fiesta line was officially reissued in five colors with an assortment of 23 items:

10" Plate	Disc Pitcher	Tripod Candleholders	Creamer for Tray
7" Plate	Juice Pitcher	Bulb Candleholders	Figure-8 Tray
Cereal	Sauceboat	Individual Sugar	Medium Vase
Teacup	Coffeepot	Sugar for Tray	Large Teapot
Saucer	Casserole	Individual Creamer	Bud Vase
Shakers	Chop Plate	8" Nappy	

This comes from an original 1986 brochure that shows the initial offering of accessory items for the new Fiesta line. Notice the coffeepot, casserole, and sugar are from the Ironstone shapes. The casserole, coffeepot and sugar were all restyled. Several coffeepots and sugars in this style have been accounted for in the new glazes, but they are very hard to find. Strangely, the large teapot is shown

with a vintage medium teapot lid! This was later changed to a dome shape lid resembling the vintage coffeepot lid.

Over the years new shapes and colors have been added. There have been some limited edition colors which has fueled a contemporary Fiesta collecting craze in the last six years. It started with the limited run color, lilac. Special pieces have also been made which have become collectible especially the three Millennium vases.

Most pieces made from old molds will have the same cast marking. The backstamp has been different from the original ever since 1986. Old *backstamps* have the letters in the word Fiesta all lower case and in the new versions, the letters are all upper case. There are over a dozen types of Fiesta markings from the old and new lines, but when trying to determine old from new, color is the key.

Since Fiesta was reissued in 1986, HLC has assigned treatment numbers to the colors. A breakdown with production dates is given here:

F-100	White	1986-present
F-101	Black	1986-1998
F-103	Rose	1986-Present
F-104	Apricot	1986-1998
F-105	Cobalt	1986-present
F-106	Yellow	1987-present
F-107	Turquoise	1988-present
F-108	Periwinkle	1989-present
F-109	Seamist	1991-present
F-113	Lilac	1993-1995
F-114	Persimmon	1995-present
F-116	Sapphire	1996-1997
F-117	Chartreuse	1997-1999
F-118	Pearl Gray	1999-present
F-119	Juniper	1999-12/31/2001
F-102	Cinnabar	2000-
F-302	Sunflower	2000-
F-323	Plum	2002-

Notice F-102, Cinnabar, is out of order. The number was originally used in 1986 to designate a light gray that was under consideration but didn't make it into the original color assortment. Also, numbers are used for other treatments on Fiesta such as F-123 for "Cranberry" which is white Fiesta with a red stripe and F-122 for "Aegean" – white Fiesta with a blue stripe. There is also a raspberry color, but this was used for the limited to 500 special presentation bowls to commemorate the 500 millionth piece of Fiesta made in 1997.

The 10" (medium) vase in rose, disc pitcher in lilac, and shaker in new chartreuse are shapes from the old line. The tumbler, shown in sapphire, is wider than the old version and the teacups have a "c" handle; not the ring handle found on vintage cups.

A comparison of old and new Fiesta teacups. The periwinkle and cobalt examples on the left are from the new line – note the "c" handle. The teacups on the right, in yellow and gray, are from the old line – note the ring handle.

These rang shakers were modeled by John Stoakes. The holes for the shakers are arranged in the letters "S" and "P". The colors shown are persimmon, white and turquoise.

The snack plate, and mini disc pitcher are pieces unique to new Fiesta. The mug has a fluted opening and a set of rings – old mugs are straight sided with no rings at the opening. The tripod candleholder is the same shape used in both the old and new lines.

Pedestal mug, tripod bowl and sauceboat.

Millennium Candlesticks can be identified by their special Y2K raised mold markings.

A specially decaled white Fiesta mug with the old style eagle over lion backstamp.

Hostess tray and 5" bowl in turquoise.

The 9" plate is from a special line called, "Water Colors." Behind it is a chartreuse 10" dinner plate with "Mystique" – one of three treatments made for Mega China.

Coffeepot in the desirable lilac color.

Side view of a presentation bowl.

One of the newest items added; the trivet.

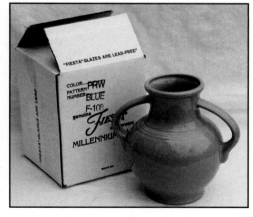

Millennium I vase in periwinkle.

Juniper glaze on a generic shape plate and a cinnabar bud vase.

Lilac was limited to a two year (1993-1995) run and sapphire was made for only six months in 1996. Both have become very collectible and prices have risen for both over the past few years. HLC has released limited colors since these two namely Chartreuse and Juniper, but its too soon to place values on these. Since Apricot has been discontinued in 1997, prices for once common pieces have started to elevate. Apricot vases and coffee servers have recently sold for over $50.00 each.

Values for Lilac Fiesta:

Bouillon 6¾ oz.	$30-35	Plate, dinner 10½"	$35-40
Bowl, cereal 14 oz.	$20-25	Plate, luncheon 9"	$50+
Bowl, rim pasta 12"	$40-45	Plate, salad 7¼"	$20-25
Bowl, rim soup 9"	$40-45	Plate, bread & butter 6⅛"	$10-15
Bowl, serving 39¼ oz.	$50-55	Plate, chop 11¾"	$60+
Bowl, soup 19 oz.	$30-35	Platter, oval 9⅝"	$35-45
Bowl, cereal 6½"	$20-30	Platter, oval 11⅝"	$35-45
Bowl, fruit 5⅜"	$15-20	Platter, oval 15⅝"	$45-50
Butter dish	$50-55	Sauceboat	$50+
Candleholder, pyramid	$500+	Saucer, A.D.	$10-12
Candleholder, round	$75-85	Saucer, tea	$4-5
Casserole	$150	Shakers, pair	$50-60
Coffee server	$85-105	Sugar bowl	$70-80
Creamer	$25-30	Sugar/Creamer/fig.-8 tray set	$75-85
Cup, A.D.	$45-50	Teapot	$85-95
Cup, Tea	$15-20	Tray, relish/utility	$30-35
Mug, Fiesta	$25-30	Tumbler	$15-20
Napkin ring	$25-30	Vase, bud 6"	$85+
Pie baker	$85-95	Vase, medium 9½"	$250+
Mini disc pitcher	$45-50		
Juice disc pitcher	$65-85		
Large disc pitcher	$45-50		

Values for Sapphire:

Bowl, serving 39¼ oz.	$25-35	Plate, dinner 10½"	$30-35
Bowl, soup 19 oz.	$20-25	Plate, salad 7¼"	$10-15
Carafe	$45-55	Platter, oval 13⅝"	$20-25
Clock	$35-40	Tray, tab handles 12"	$55-65
Teacup	$10-15	Tumbler	$10-15
Saucer	$4-5	Vase, medium 9½"	$175-200
Disc Pitcher	$25-35		

Fiestaware 2000

Designed by the late Jonathan Parry, Fiestaware 2000 is unlike any dinnerware line produced by HLC. It was made as a limited assortment with basic sizes of plates, bowls and a mug with saucer. The frame has bold abstract designs and the top of the verge is decorated with a small set of rings. Samples were made in early 1999 in several new Fiesta glazes until it was decided the official color assortment would be Pearl Gray, Persimmon, Cobalt and the limited edition color, Juniper.

A large pitcher was modeled but wasn't put into a standard run. The line is currently not being produced, but there's no reason why it couldn't be brought back in the future and possibly expanded. Expect the flatware to have a Fiestaware 2000 backstamp with rising sun and the mug to have a mold mark version.

Fiestaware 2000 in cobalt and persimmon.

Fiestaware 2000 cobalt plate.

Fiestaware 2000 mugs in the official colors; Juniper, Persimmon, Pearl Gray, and Cobalt.

Georgian and Georgian Eggshell

There are two lines made up of Georgian shapes. They differ in that the first version, Craftsman or "Georgian Ivory" is of an ivory body and the later line, Georgian Eggshell, is made up of the light weight body originally designed for Nautilus Eggshell. Craftsman was the first to be developed in the summer of 1933.

In August, five sizes of plates and two saucers were made, but these were plain rim shapes. It wasn't until September that the dash-dot rim embossings were added. After a design was accepted, the hollowware pieces were crafted in October. A new "neutral" or ivory colored glaze was developed for the new shape and various names were under consideration. At first, Rhead drew up a "Georgian" backstamp. This marking contained a guarantee that the ware was "crazeproof." Rhead notes on October 18, 1933: . . . *on "Crazeproof." Raises question as to what will be asked with regard to other wares if this new glaze is guaranteed:* It was decided then that the word "crazeproof" wasn't necessary in the marking. On the next day Rhead makes an entry about two marks for the "Craftsman" shape. Even though this would become the "official" name for the line, Rhead and others at HLC would continue to use the term "Georgian" with regard to the shapes and treatments.

Rhead wrote in his journals about the first fourteen treatments for Craftsman on October 21, 1933. He listed these as:

G-1	Rosolane	G-8	Sienna
G-2	Mauvette	G-9	Chartreuse
G-3	Octavia	G-10	Carnelain
G-4	Primoline	G-11	Glaire

G-5	Gugenia		G-12	Aspasia
G-6	Gobalin		G-13	Aurelia
G-7	Adelaiad		G-14	Priscilla

More pieces were modeled in November such as the AD cup and saucer, various small bowls, two nappies and a baker. On December 2, 1933, Rhead notes: *Made line drawings for patent office "Craftsman" trademark.* With the shapes, treatments and markings in place, production on the new line was ready to begin.

On January 3, 1934 the first Craftsman pieces came out of the kilns. Rhead commented on the wares saying: *Colors a little strong but ware is favorable. Gilding rather skimpy . . . Not enough effort among those getting this out to make a finished product.* For the next few weeks, there was more trouble with the color and detail of the stronger decals such as Mauvette, but apparently the "effort" must have improved since Craftsman treatments were soon picked up by several retailers.

The expensive treatments, such as those already listed, each had a special Craftsman decal-like backstamp with the treatment name. An entry from Rhead's journals dated January 8, 1934 explains why other treatments are given more generic Craftsman backstamp: *Cheaper Craftsman sets to be marked also "Craftsman"* [in] *gold stamp.* There are some pieces which are marked with a general HLC backstamp. Since these usually come from the late 1930s, it may be the case that all the specially created Craftsman markings were abandoned.

Craftsman Examples:

This is one of several types of Craftsman backstamps used on Georgian during the 30s when sold through Sears. Shown is the marking used on "Elaine." Other than the Wells peacock marking, the Craftsman backstamps are the only multicolored marks used by HLC. "Cheaper" Georgian treatments are marked with a silver Craftsman marking or with a "Georgian Dinnerware" backstamp.

Craftsman dinner plate.

Mauvette treatment, G-2, on a sauceboat.

While this piece is marked, "Georgian Dinnerware by Homer Laughlin," it lacks the typical dash-dot embossing usually found on the rim. The stars are little silver stamps.

Georgian Eggshell:

In 1940, it was decided that the Georgian shapes would be made in the light weight "eggshell" clay. It had been considered several times over the years after the introduction of the first eggshell line, Nautilus Eggshell, but Georgian was always put aside while other eggshell lines such as Nautilus and Theme were favored. In Georgian's case, development was quite easy as the shapes had been in production for several years in the form of Craftsman. The only work involved remodeling the existing pieces so they could be made with the different body. A special Georgian eggshell mark was made in May 1940.

There were several items added that were never part of the older Craftsman line, but were specially made for Georgian: lug soup, teapot, salt and pepper shakers, a chop plate, salad bowl and an 8" square plate. In December 1940 two items are listed in the log as being modeled for Georgian Eggshell, but none have been found: the A.D. coffeepot and an A.D. sugar.

Georgian Eggshell was almost immediately put into production. While its predecessor, Craftsman, never achieved major success, Georgian Eggshell would be produced well into the 1950s. Almost every retailer in the 40s and 50s carried at least one pattern on Georgian Eggshell. In Montgomery Ward's case, multiple treatments were offered including: Cashmere, Rambler Rose, Chateau, and Berkshire. Its interesting that the Georgian shape was the last to be made in the eggshell weight in the late 30s and early 40s era yet it became one of HLC's best selling lines.

Most pieces were given the Georgian Eggshell backstamp with a date code. Official treatment numbers were prefixed just like Craftsman with a "G" but the actual numbers started much higher in the 3000s. This was done so there was no confusion with the two shapes.

Georgian Eggshell Examples:

Backstamp for Georgian Eggshell.

Ad from 1953 featuring "Bouquet" on Georgian Eggshell. This large rose decal is often found on the Liberty and Virginia Rose shapes. When on Georgian Eggshell, its official number is G-3528.

Here is a good contrast between "realistic" and "stylized" floral treatments which is representative between two different eras. The dinner plate is from the mid 1940s and is called, "Chatham." Notice how the floral arrangement has a realistic look in comparison to the sauceboat.

The sauceboat, dated 1953, has a "stylized" treatment. The decal looks like something hand drawn and is in sync with 1950s design. This treatment is called, "Star Flower."

Another interesting thing to note is how the plate from the 40s has more decorative elements than the 50s sauceboat. The plate has not one, but two sets of gold trim; on the rim and a laurel ring on the verge. In between is a pastel blue/green band. All three work together to frame the floral decal treatment. The sauceboat, on the other hand, has a very simple and more direct design: decal and blue trim.

The Chatham treatment
on a creamer.

"Rambler Rose" (VM-2) is the name of the treatment on the Georgian Eggshell rim soup. This is one of the few times the treatment name is given along with the standard backstamp.

The creamer has a very common and popular treatment: Nassau.

81

This Georgian Eggshell teapot has been decorated with floral decals. The most dominant flower in the treatment is a red poppy.

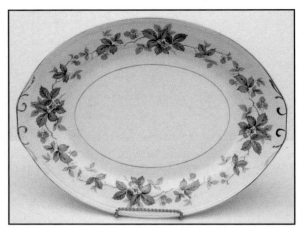

"Greenbriar" on a Georgian Eggshell platter.

Georgian Eggshell cup and saucer with a blue and green floral decal. The official treatment number is: G-3381.

Georgian Eggshell demitasse cup and saucer. The demitasse cups with any treatment will be unmarked, but accompanying saucers should carry the Georgian Eggshell backstamp.

Shakers with gold trim.

Tea set with the "Norway Rose" decal made for Cunningham and Pickett.

This Georgian Casserole is from a set that uses Liberty's Queen Ester rose decal. The large pink rose is revealed on the inside bottom of the base. The official treatment number is: G-3388.

"Cashmere" was sold through Montgomery Wards and is one of the most common of the Georgian Eggshell treatments.

The tulips seen on these pieces of Georgian Eggshell are much more common on Kitchen Kraft.

Assortment and Values: Items with (*) are found in eggshell weight only:

10" Plate	$8-10	Sauceboat stand	$6-7
9" Plate	$5-6	Shakers*	$10-12
8" Round Plate	$8-10	Cream Soup Cup	$7-9
8" Square Plate*	$8-10	Lug Soup	$8-10
7" Plate	$4-5	15" Platter	$15-18
6" Plate	$2-3	13" Platter	$12-15
Teacup	$4-6	11" Platter	$10-12
Saucer	$1-2	9" Platter	$10-12
A.D. Cup	$8-10	Chop Plate	$18-20
A.D. Saucer	$7-8	Casserole	$20-25
Covered Sugar	$10-12	9" Baker	$7-9
Creamer	$6-8	10" Baker	$7-9
Sauceboat	$7-9	10" Nappy	$10-12
Gravy Fast stand	$12-15	9" Nappy	$7-9
Fruit Cup	$4-5	Teapot*	$30-35
6" Oatmeal Bowl	$4-5		

Granada

First produced in the mid 1960s, the Granada shape was used mainly as a promotion for L & H International's Sheffield lines. According to the HLC mold notes, by early 1967, Granada consisted of plates, bowls, shakers, butter dish, teapot, jug, utility bowl, ashtray, sauceboat and coffeepot.

Some of the shapes would undergo minor revisions, but there is basically one style: round shape with an embossed scalloped. On flatware, the scallop is towards the rim; on hollowware it is almost mid-body. The hollow forms are cylindrical with a stretched appearance. This stretch feature is repeated on the handles.

Gold and green are the most common colors used on the Granada shape. Granada in gold was sold as "Coventry Castilian." Flat pieces from this line had a black decoration. Green Granada was sold as "Sheffield Granada." This shape would continue to be produced into the 1970s.

"Coventry Castilian" shakers in their original packaging. The dinner plate has the black stamp design found on flatware from Coventry Castilian.

The ashtray can be found with the Coventry Castilian design and in the speckled green glaze used in Sheffield Granada. Don't expect to find these in other glazes or treatments. The utility bowl in the rich gold glaze comes from a Coventry Castilian set.

The gold glaze on the sugar and creamer is heavily speckled. These could belong to several different lines since hollowware was never decorated. Once in a while, lids on sugars, casseroles, coffeepots, etc. will be in a contrasting color – usually black.

"Sheffield Granada" handled tray. These trays, like those from Fiesta Amberstone and Casualstone, are chop plates with holes which were drilled while the plates were in a "greenware" state (semi-soft clay before first firing). They were assembled at HLC.

The design on the gold speckled plate is a combination black-brown design. In the foreground is a soup/cereal bowl in an olive green glaze – a glaze similar to that is used with Sheffield Granada, but without specks.

"Golden Harvest" is the name of this common treatment on Granada. The gold glaze is speckled unlike the gold color used on Coventry Castilian.

Here we see a blue version of the Golden Harvest treatment. The base color is a lightly speckled ivory glaze and the decoration is a combination of dark and light blues. As with most other lines of the 1970s and 80s, only the flatware receives a decoration.

This plate is marked, "Golden Harvest II."

This yellow floral decaled Granada shape dinner plate dates from 1978.

Granada ad showing Sorrento and Sonesta. Notice the Sorrento line uses the Golden Harvest II plate.

These pieces are on display at HLC: Granada teapot in the familiar speckled glaze developed for the Sheffield line, a coffeepot in a light gray glaze and a covered sugar in a transparent olive green color.

Values for Granada:

Plates, any size	$2-3	Shakers, pr.	$5-6
Soup/Cereal	$1	Casserole	$12-15
Rim soup	$1-2	Coffeepot	$15-18
Teacup	$1-2	Teapot	$12-15
Saucer	$1	Butter	$5-6
Mug	$1-2	Ashtray	$8-10
Sugar	$5-6	Handled Tray	$3-4
Creamer	$4-5	Gravy Fast Stand	$5-6
Utility Bowl	$2-3	Gravy liner	$2-3
Pitcher	$8-10	Soup Tureen	$12-15

Harlequin

Throughout the years, the Homer Laughlin China Company produced wares for F.W. Woolworth's: OvenServe with green hand-painted embossings, Marigold with simple platinum trim, Yellowstone Vellum with the pastel rose decal, specialty salad bowls and more. Up until the mid 1930s, Woolworth's would use specific treatments, but the shapes themselves were not exclusive as many other retailers carried OvenServe, Marigold, Yellowstone, etc. with different decorations. However, in March 1936, Rhead worked on a shape that was intended as a Woolworth exclusive and made use of silk screen decorations on the rim.

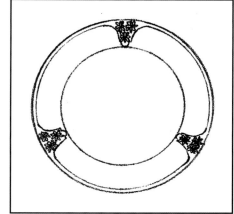

The shapes modeled were basically the then new Brittany shape but with periodic embossing of daisies. The rough sketch (not from the modeling log) is of a plate which mold notes describe as, "3 panel for silk screen." In March of 1936 the 9" plate, cup and saucer were the only pieces modeled.

The line was never extended beyond these three pieces and it wasn't officially released into production. There is at least one known example of a saucer with the embossed daisies. Its complete with a red silk screen design and backstamped with a date code: "C 36 N 6" or March 1936 Plant 6.

While Woolworth's didn't get their three-panel silk screen shape, several months later in May, a new line was considered which would go on to become Harlequin. Rhead wrote of the new shape on May 15, 1936: *Going over material for new colored glaze shapes and model outline.* The next day he writes: *J.M. Wells – new shape for Syndicate stores. Colored glazes similar to Fiesta practice.* In June, several different designs of 9" plates were made as well as solid color glazes. It should be noted that in the modeling log there were a total of nine "new" styles of plates, but it isn't clear if all were under consideration for Harlequin.

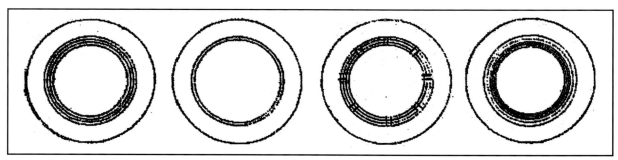

Here are four of the nine plates modeled in June of 1936. The first should be familiar to Harlequin collectors. This shape was listed in the log as: 7" Plate, embossed lines on ball. (Remember that it was common for potters to use trade sizes so the 7" plate was actually around 9". The "Ball" is another name for the verge – the area from which the well changes into the rim.)

The second plate is identical to the first model, except the inner two rings are missing. The third example has the familiar Harlequin type rings, but they are divided by segments resulting in "8 panels" as listed in the modeling log. The fourth plate modeled (not shown) is listed as having an "egg and dart edge" it also had six petals and two verge rings. The fifth version modeled has a style summed up by its log description: " 7" plate similar decoration as fiesta, but on ball, not on edge."

There were four other plates modeled, but it's not clear if these were intended as alternates or for another line. Three had rings on the verge, but also varying small embossed floral designs. The last plate is listed as: " 7" plate raised edge, line on ball." Whether or not these last four were under consideration isn't certain, but with the first five, there were certainly enough options.

While the various plates were being crafted, tests of colors were being made. One of the first colors was the bright Harlequin yellow which Rhead commented on as, "The finest yellow I have ever seen on tableware." On June 18, 1936, he writes on color development: . . . *Assembled possible colors. Find that green is weak . . . to arrive at middle green on the same scale as stain on W.S. George greens rather than greens of the "Victoria" – a yellow green type. J.M. Wells states that the final selection will range from 3 to 4 colors, but that we should plan a comprehensive series. Shape is to be dipped in each glaze.* After several glazes were developed, samples were made in the various styles of plates. On July 10, 1936, Rhead wrote a letter to Beleinger that the first model with "the turned lines inside the verge" was accepted by Woolworth's and was released into production. Further, drawings were made for the teacup and this would, as Rhead wrote, "determine character of hollowware and other items." More color samples were also being made at this time.

In mid July '36, two styles of teacups were modeled based on Rhead's sketches. The first had a curved body and the other was a conical shape. Both had curved handles, but alternates were made with angular handles for the cone cup. From here two styles of hollowware started to be crafted: a "convex" shape – the curved rounded body and the "straight sided" shape or the cone shape. While a particular style for the hollowware had not yet been decided upon, several flatware shapes were being made: a "rolled top" nappy and fruit were modeled in late July '36 as well as the 10" plate and the 8" deep plate in the first week of August.

On August 1, 1936 Rhead wrote in his journal: *Woolworth colored glaze* [teacups] *out. Also extra plates. Bad dipping and green too transparent. The conical cup is much better than the convex cup and the glaze behaves much better . . .* The next shape made was the casserole. At this point a style of hollowware was not yet determined. First came the convex casserole with ball shaped handles and finials followed by the "straight sided" or conical casserole. Immediately after the straight sided casserole was modeled, the convex sugar was made. On August 13, Rhead commented on the progression of the hollowware: *Trouble with new casserole* [convex shape] *Knobs are not finished properly. Working on new type of lug and on the straight sided shape. Hollowware is proceeding slowly.* He did in fact make new "lugs" for the convex casserole and at least one example is known to exist in the mauve blue glaze. Another change was made to both casseroles with the elimination of the foot.

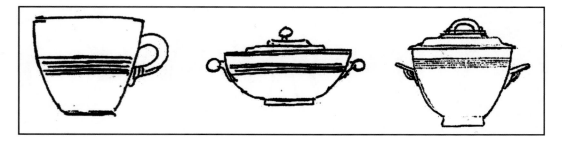

Above are modeling log sketches of "concave" pieces of Harlequin under consideration: teacup, casserole and covered sugar.

On the last week of August, the glaze trials were much better and a style of hollowware was finally accepted as Rhead notes on the 28th: *J.M. Wells approved new conical casserole. Not to change manufacturing . . . convex shape is out. The latest green is O.K. Type not to be changed.* With conical shape as the basis, the rest of the hollowware was made. The last piece modeled in August was the "straight sided" creamer. Though no other records or sketches exist of this shape, it's safe to assume this is the high lip version since it was later released into production. The first item modeled at the beginning of September was the straight sided covered sugar.

From the beginning, several models of handles for the teacup were considered. On September 17, 1936, a teacup handle design was chosen as was the color assortment: *J.M. Wells O.K.'d straight cup handle. Released to Pittenger. Final colors: blue, green, pink, yellow.* (It should be stressed that whenever Rhead refers to a maroon or burgundy color, he almost always calls it "pink." He also did this with the maroon colored treatment that was used on the Quaker Oats Harvest line and with the dark red Americana and Early American Homes decorations.) On the 21st, the line was finally named Harlequin and more pieces were released into production.

By the end of September 1936, Harlequin, which started out rather chaotic, was now in production with four colors. The original assortment included:

10" Plate	9" Plate	7" Plate	6" Plate	Teacup	Saucer
Oval Baker	Sugar	Creamer	Fruit Cup	Nappy	Shakers
Double Egg Cup	Deep Plate	Casserole			

The line remained largely unchanged for the next several months with one major exception; the creamer. On October 27, 1936, Rhead notes: *Released Harlequin jug, new model #700 No. 3 Harlequin cream. New model to replace old shape.* In the modeling log, #700 is listed simply as: Jug 48s. (For an explanation on the numbers used in trade sizes, see the appendix.) This was the second high lip creamer with the longer spout. In an entry dated February 9, 1937 yet another creamer was requested: *Letters from Woolworth . . . The Harlequin creamer – The new spout pours all right but they want it more graceful. To work out new adjustment.* Towards the end of February, Rhead had a new creamer made. It was listed in the log as model number 773: 48s Jug Harlequin and was released into production on March 3rd. With these entries, the following dates can be established for the various Harlequin creamers:

High lip, short spout: September 1936 – October 27, 1936.

High lip, long spout: October 27, 1936 – March 3, 1937.

Regular Creamer: March 3, 1937 until line was discontinued in 1964.

For several years after its introduction, pieces were often added to Harlequin. Dates given in the list below are the original modeling dates.

1937	
March	11" Platter, 5 11/16" Fruit Cup
September	Demitasse Cup and Saucer
1938	
January	Regular Ashtray, 13" Platter, Tumbler, Single Egg Cup
February	Nut Dish, Marmalade, Teapot, Cream Soup
April	22-oz. Jug, Sauce Boat
November	Novelty Creamer

1939
January   Individual Creamer
August   Basketweave Ashtray
September   Salad Bowl, Ashtray Saucer, "Harlequin Animals"

1940
January   Syrup
March   Fruit bowl 4¾"*
April   Candleholder**, Relish Dish, Oatmeal 6⅜"
November   36s Bowl ***

　　　 *　 Not released into production
　　 **　 Three versions made, only one released
　 ***　 Two versions made, only one released

　　Several pieces were remodeled in the 1940s for the automatic jigger (as were pieces from many other lines) but there were no new additions until 1955 with the "large" cup and saucer. In late 1942, production of dinnerware was cut back. Many patterns and more "exotic" accessory shapes were discontinued. In some cases, entire lines (namely Modern Farmer) were discontinued all together. With other shapes, assortments can be easy to figure out by using vintage ads, but since Harlequin was carried by only one retailer, Woolworth's, and since they didn't issue the same kind of brochures or catalogs found with other lines, the exact dates when Harlequin pieces were discontinued aren't known. Over the years collectors have been able to figure out which pieces were dropped in the 1940s based on if they are found in the 50s colors or not.

　　Harlequin started out with four colors: a red, green, blue and yellow. Collectors call yellow "Harlequin Yellow" to avoid confusion with the slightly darker yellow used with Fiesta. The blue has been called, "Mauve Blue" for many years, due to the Harlequin coverage in Huxford's Fiesta books. When this shade is used by other companies such as Knowles, W.S. George, etc. it is almost always called, "Medium Blue." The red for Harlequin is maroon or burgundy and green is called "Spruce."

　　The next two colors added to Harlequin were tangerine (Fiesta red) and turquoise. Though the exact date when the colors were added can't be pin pointed, it was probably done between March 1937 and January 1940. This is because the second high lip creamer was replaced in March '37 and none have been found in red or turquoise. The relish was added in January 1940 and bases are always turquoise and at least one of the inserts seems to always be red.

　　Three colors were discontinued in the early forties: maroon, spruce green and red. On May 29, 1941, Rhead notes how the Harlequin and Fiesta glazes were selling:

Colored glazes selling as follows:

Harlequin	*Fiesta*
1. *Yellow*	1. *Tangerine*
2. *Tangerine*	2. *Yellow*
3. *Blue*	3. *Turquoise*
4. *Turquoise*	4. *Blue*
5. *Crimson*	5. *Ivory*
6. *Green*	6. *Green*

　　Soon after, he starts to work on other glazes for Harlequin. On July 2, 1941, he wrote: *Two salmons and a gray on Harlequin . . .* Evidentially, the "Crimson" or maroon was replaced by one of the salmons and today's collectors call this color, rose. Maroon was also being used in Tango and the color was discontinued from that line as well and Fiesta red served as a replacement.

The next color dropped was spruce green. Unlike maroon, a new color wasn't developed. Instead, the green used in Fiesta at the time, "light green", was picked up as a replacement. This must have happened at the same time many pieces were being discontinued since it has been well documented that certain pieces are very difficult to find in light green. These include the candle holders, single egg cup, nut dish and several others and when found in light green, their prices are higher than those in other colors.

Red was no longer offered in 1943. It contained uranium and the U.S. government seized control of the element due to W.W.II. It was therefore discontinued from the Fiesta and Harlequin lines. It should be pointed out its entirely possible red and spruce green were discontinued at the same time. This would mean that Tango was no longer offered since red was dropped.

By 1943 the Harlequin color assortment was changed to: Harlequin yellow, mauve blue, turquoise, rose and light green. In 1951, three colors developed for another Woolworth line, Rhythm, were added to Harlequin (as well as Fiesta): forest green, gray, and chartreuse. Mauve blue and light green were discontinued, but yellow, turquoise and rose continued. In 1959, Harlequin's color assortment changed for the last time. Red was reintroduced, a new green was added. The "Rhythm colors" and rose were discontinued. The result was Harlequin in four colors: Harlequin yellow, turquoise, red and green – a.k.a. "medium green." More pieces were discontinued when this color change occurred and are hard to find in medium green: service water jug, 22-oz. jug, novelty creamer.

Harlequin was finally discontinued in 1964 after almost 30 years as a Woolworth's exclusive.

In May 1978, HLC began working on a modeling program to reissue the Harlequin line at Woolworth's request. The limited line included the 10" and 7" plates, cup and saucer, cereal and serving bowls, creamer and a covered sugar. Only the sugar was modified from its original, the others were based on vintage models except for the chop plate which didn't exist in the older Harlequin line. The only piece considered that didn't make it in the reissue assortment was the 9" plate.

The colors included yellow, turquoise, coral and green. The line was sold until 1983 and serving bowls, 10" plates and chop plates usually have a general HLC backstamp along with the year.

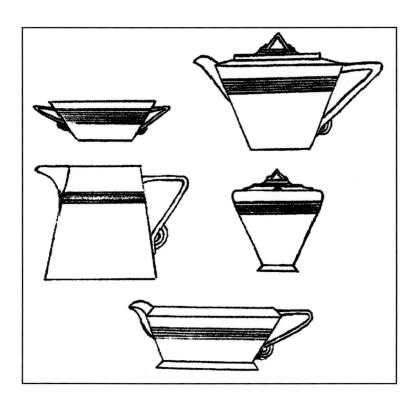

Modeling log sketches of standard pieces of Harlequin: top – cream soup cup, teapot; middle – 22 oz. jug, covered marmalade; bottom – sauceboat.

Teapot in blue and covered casserole in maroon.

These "toy creamers" were made in the first eight Harlequin colors and are very hard to find in light green. Shown (left to right) are: red, spruce green, unusual white glaze, maroon, and mauve/medium blue.

Harlequin sugar in red and creamer in turquoise.

The red creamer is called a, "novelty creamer." Note the rings on the center of the body. If you find a solid colored ball shape creamer without rings on the body, then it was probably a Sevilla Pottery product and not made by HLC. The large cup on the right is made up of an Epicure body with a specially made Harlequin handle. See the specialty items section for more on this cup and its corresponding saucer.

10" Plate in the bright Harlequin yellow glaze.

Double eggcup in light green.

The shaker in turquoise is standard. The other was decorated by an outside company. The all over gold design was used by several decorators and can be found on HLC, Taylor Smith & Taylor, Knowles and others potteries wares. The original spruce green color is visible from the inside.

Oval baker in rose and the regular cup and saucer in blue.

Candleholder in spruce green.

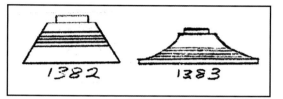

Sketches of alternate Harlequin candleholders that didn't go into production.

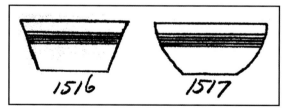

Model 1516 is the straight sided 36s bowl that was shelved in favor of 1517 which became the standard 36s bowl for Harlequin.

Standard Harlequin 36s bowl in rose.

22 oz. Jug in the coveted medium green glaze.

Harlequin Assortment and Values:

	maroon spruce green red	mauve blue yellow rose turquoise light green	chartreuse gray dark green	medium green
10" Plate	$20-25	$18-20	$30-35	$50-55
9" Plate	$15-18	$10-12	$18-20	$40-45
7" Plate	$8-10	$7-9	$12-15	$15-20
6" Plate	$6-8	$4-5	$10-12	$15-20
13" Platter	$20-25	$15-18	$25-30	$180+
11" Platter	$18-20	$12-15	$25-30	$180+
Sugar	$30-35	$20-25	$35-40	$125+
Reg. Creamer	$10-12	$7-9	$15-18	$60-70
Teacup	$10-12	$8-10	$12-15	$20-25
Saucer	$3-5	$1-2	$6-8	$12-15
Nov. Creamer	$20-25	$12-15	$30-35	$1200+
Sauceboat	$18-20	$12-15	$25-30	$175+
Shakers, pr.	$15-20	$15-20	$30-32	$200+
Fruit Cup	$10-12	$8-10	$15-18	$40-45
Oatmeal	$18-20	$12-15	$25-30	$55-65
36s bowl	$30-35	$20-25	$40-45	$125+
Nappy	$18-20	$15-18	$30-35	$100+
Ind. Salad 7³/₈"	$20-25	$15-18	$30-35	$85+
A.D. Cup	$45-50	$35-40	$100+	$325+
A.D. Saucer	$12-15	$8-10	$25-30	$60-75
Cream Soup Cup	$20-25	$15-20	$50-65	$850+
Rim Soup	$18-20	$12-15	$40-45	$95-110
22 oz. Jug	$60-75	$40-50	$60-75	$500+
Ball Jug	$70-80	$35-45	$125+	$1800+
Teapot	$150-175	$125-135	$200+	$500+
Casserole	$95-110	$85-95	$150+	$500+
Basketweave Ashtray	$30-35	$20-25	$100+	$250+
Eggcup, double	$18-20	$12-15	$30-35	$200+

	maroon spruce green red	mauve blue yellow turquoise rose	light green
Reg. Ashtray	$50-60	$40-45	$65+
Ashtray Saucer	$60-75	$50-55	$75+
High Lip Creamer	$125-150 (either version in mauve, yellow, maroon and spruce only)		
"Toy" Creamer	$20-25	$18-20	$75+
Baker	$20-25	$12-15	$30-35
Eggcup, single	$25-30	$18-20	$100+
Marmalade	$200-225	$180-200	$350+
Syrup	$375+ (any color)		
Relish Tray	$250-275 (turquoise base, any color inserts)		

	maroon spruce green red	mauve blue yellow turquoise rose	light green
Nut Dish	$20-25	$18-20	$55+
Candleholders, pr.	$300+	$350+	UND
Butter (Jade)	$125-150	$95-110	$95-110
Tumbler	$35-40	$25-30	$25-30
Jumbo Cup	$300+ (any color)		
Jumbo Saucer	$150+ (any color)		

Harlequin Animals

The animals were made for Woolworth's and dipped in the four original Harlequin colors: maroon, spruce, mauve blue and yellow. Seven were modeled but only six went into production on October 25, 1939. The six standard animals in the order in which they were modeled are: lamb, penguin, cat, fish, duck, and donkey. A turtle was created after the donkey, but it didn't go into production. (There are two unusual entries at the same time of the animals; "Indian Model" and "Indian Woman Model." Like the turtle, these are not noted as being officially made.)

The duck seems to be a copy of a set of ducks made by another pottery. The lamb looks very much like a scaled down version of a McCoy vase. In fact, all six animals may very well be copies or modified versions made by other potteries. One thing is very clear, other companies had access to the same molds and produced animals that are almost identical in weight and size. The donkey and duck shown are two such animals. They are identical in every way to HLC's version except they are done in white. Most of the time they are found with gold accents. Huxford's have coined these as "Mavericks."

HLC probably produced these figures for only a two or three years at the most. They were makers of dinnerware and kitchenware and novelty items such as Harlequin animals were not the focus of their production.

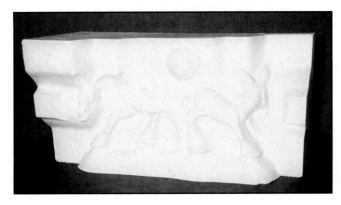

This is one of the original Harlequin animal donkey molds in storage at HLC.

Fish in mauve blue and cat in maroon.

Duck and Donkey. Except for the white glaze, these are identical to the standard HLC animals. These "mavericks" are worth much less than HLC's.

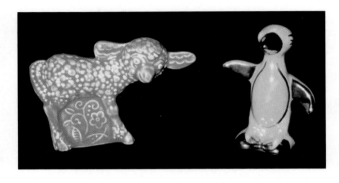

The lamb is unusual since its glazed in Fiesta's light green. The penguin is glazed in Harlequin yellow, but someone decided to give him a gold paint job!

Animals in standard colors, each: $200+
Mavericks: $20-45 (depending on workmanship)

There are a number of Harlequin Animal fakes circulating in the collector market. They are generally smaller than HLC's animals and are in non-standard colors such as turquoise, cobalt and Fiesta red. HLC did produce several sets of animals in Fiesta colors, but most of these remained at the plant.

Look at the underside of the animal. If it has the same color glaze on the inside as it does on the outside, then chances are very good that its a Homer Laughlin product. If, on the other hand, the inside doesn't have a solid color glaze, then it was definitely *not* made at HLC.

Table Fair

Originally called, "Concept," Table Fair was produced in 1980. It uses flatware which was brought out with the reissue Harlequin line a few years earlier: 10" plate, round chop plate, 7" plate and soup/cereal bowl. Hollowware was specially modeled for this line and unlike Harlequin's conical hollowware, Table Fair's was cylindrical. All pieces of Table Fair hollowware were made to include the Harlequin-like rings. The Harlequin saucer was not used. Instead an oversized version was made to accommodate the mug-like cup.

There were three major types of decorations on speckled glazes: plain, strawberries, and wheat. Only flatware such as the 10" plate, 7" plate and chop plate received decals. All hollowware will be in the speckled glaze.

Apparently, HLC toyed with the idea of making Table Fair in pastel glazes as several trials have been showing up in recent years. These pastel glazes are much harder to find than the plentiful speckled glazes. Table Fair will have a general HLC backstamp.

The treatment on this 7" plate is called, "Bennington." It appears on reissue Harlequin flatware, but the hollowware used is from International. The two sets of shapes are brought together with the Desert Stone speckled glaze and cobalt blue trim. Expect the basket decal only to appear on flatware.

This Harlequin shape saucer comes from a line made in the early 1980s which is a combination of Harlequin flatware and Ironstone hollowware. There is also a green version of the heart decoration.

Assortment and Values for Table Fair and related lines:

10" Plate	$2-3	Cereal	$1-2
7" Plate	$1-2	Utility Bowl	$4-5
Chop Plate	$3-4	Sugar	$2-3
Cup	$1-2	Creamer	$1-2
Saucer	$1	Handled Shakers	$3-4
Nappy	$2-3	Butter Dish	$2-3
Casserole	$6-8	Teapot	$5-7

Hearthside

First made in 1971, Hearthside is a ringed shape. On flatware, the rings are confined to the rim and, on hollowware, they can be found towards the base. This is a typical 70s line of dinnerware with golds, greens and browns as the primary colors. In one advertisement, color seemed to be the pitch for Hearthside:

The popularity of color was never greater than it is today, as shown by the desire of a large majority of the tableware buying public. Seven original contemporary [treatments] in green and gold glazes that are certain to attract customers. All patterns sealed under the glaze for lasting beauty.

Many treatments will involve some sort of black stamp decoration in the same spirit as White Dover and Granada. Once in a while, a line will offer the lids of hollowware in contrasting colors. Since, in general, flat pieces were the only items to receive decorations, hollowware can be interchanged between lines of the same color.

There are some pieces of Hearthside flatware are showing up in the secondary market in the reissue Harlequin colors: coral, green, yellow and turquoise. The Hearthside shape did not last beyond the late 1970s.

The treatment on the small Hearthside plate is called, "Concept" (HS-208) and is rather easy to find. The chop plate has an uncommon green/brown decoration.

1970s ad showing "Concept" and "Sungold" (HS-203). Note how two different types of decorated flatware uses the same hollowware.

Hearthside ad for "Jubilee" (HS-209) and "Sun Gold."

"Pimlico" (HS-207) and "Surfside" (HS-202).

The brown glaze is so thick on this Hearthside 6" plate that it almost entirely masks the black stamp decoration.

These Hearthside 6" plates show a common problem with the speckled glazes used in the 1970s. They are from the same line, but the example on the right has a glaze that is so heavy it looks like it could be from a different line.

Hearthside cereal bowl and cup. The best thing about Hearthside, and other 70s lines, is that since hollowware didn't receive a decoration, it can belong to several different lines.

Hearthside shakers.

This Hearthside dinner plate from 1977 has a speckled glaze and colorful decal. Most of the gold, green and brown glazes that were popular in the early 1970s were replaced by white and ivory speckled glazes by the late 70s.

Values for Hearthside:

Plates, any size	$2-3	Shakers, pr.	$5-6
Soup/Cereal	$1	Casserole	$8-10
Rim Soup	$2-3	Nappy	$4-5
Teacup	$1-2	Coffeepot	$8-10
Saucer	$1	Teapot	$8-10
Sugar	$5-6	Butter	$4-5
Creamer	$4-5	Gravy	$5-6
Utility Bowl	$2-3	Gravy Stand	$2-3

Hudson

In the early days of Homer Laughlin, attempts were being made for HLC wares to gain the same acceptance of British imports. Many English patterns and shapes were copied by HLC in the very late 1800s and they even adopted the now famous "eagle over lion" backstamp to signify American's presence in the dinnerware industry. By 1900, focus changed from competing with British wares to French. Many of the older plain shapes such as Shakespeare, Victor and Golden Gate were being replaced by ornately shaped copies of French Haviland lines. (Remember it wasn't until the late 1920s that most potteries designed their own wares opting instead to purchase shapes from an outside company and most of these were copies of successful European lines.)

Various examples of HLC ware from circa 1900:

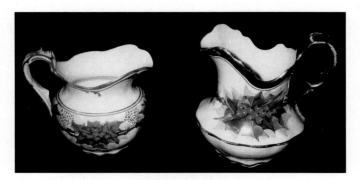

Colonial Creamers with holly decals.

Genesse cup and saucer.

Genesse plate with gold decoration.

The Angelus dinner plate.

The Angelus platter with holly decoration.

One of the first Haviland look-alikes offered by HLC was Hudson. This shape, introduced circa 1900, continued to be produced until the 1920s. In almost every ad from the early 1900s, mention is made to French wares or decorations which were popular during the time. The following are extracted from two Sears ads from the early 1900s which featured treatments on HLC's Hudson shape. The first is with regard to a rose decal decoration on Hudson and the second deals with the shape itself.

". . . Not a cheap ordinary decoration, but an exquisite colored decalcomania imported from France. . . "

"American dinnerware made of pure white semi-porcelain in a new Haviland shape by the famous Homer Laughlin China Co."

It seemed to be a good idea to sneak in a mention of France in any manner! This shape was an instant hit and was carried by several other potteries at the same time. This wouldn't be the last time American companies would carry a French copy. At least nine U.S. potters offered Haviland's Ransom shape. HLC's name for this line; Republic.

Hudson is often found in a white body with floral decals. One of the most common Hudson treatment is, "Majestic." Occasionally, Hudson pieces were made in colorful treatments for the Art China line. Since HLC was still in its infancy and hadn't perfected glazes, dinnerware pieces are often found crazed. The shapes are scalloped and embossed, though one has to look carefully for the light embossing found on the rim, particularly on the flatware. Markings include a general HLC mark with the Hudson name in script or a generic HLC backstamp with date code.

Vintage ad featuring the Hudson shape – circa 1915.

Hudson Plate.

A shape not often found in lines after the 1920s: a spooner.

Hudson covered sugar and creamer.

Hudson covered butter with blue floral decals.

Hudson covered casserole.

Assortment and Values for Hudson:

10" Plate	$6-8		Celery Tray	$15-18
9" Plate	$5-6		Platter, any size	$12-15
8" Plate	$6-8		Nappy, any size	$8-10
7" Plate	$3-4		Baker, any size	$8-10
6" Plate	$2-3		Coup Soup	$5-6
Fruit Cup	$3-4		Rim Soup	$5-6
Oatmeal	$4-5		Cream Soup	$10-12
Teacup	$6-8		Cream Soup liner	$6-7
Saucer	$1-2		Covered Butter	$20-25
A.D. Cup	$12-15		Casserole, oval	$15-18
A.D. Saucer	$4-5		Casserole, round	$12-15
Coffee Cup	$12-15		Teapot	$50+
Coffee Saucer	$6-8		Jug, any size	$15-20
Covered Sugar	$8-10		Covered Sauce dish	$20
Creamer	$5-7		Spooner	$15-18
Sauceboat	$7-9		Bone dish	$10-12
Gravy Fast stand	$10-12		Cake Plate	$15-18
Butter Pat	$8-10		Coffeepot (pick-up)	$25-30

Ironstone

Before presenting HLC's Ironstone lines of the 1960s and 1970s, a discussion of the term "Ironstone" is necessary. It was used 100 years ago to describe the durability of wares since the body contained stone. Such shapes from this era are rather heavy and sometimes even "clunky." Homer Laughlin, and other potteries still in existence in the 60s and 70s, used the term Ironstone to promote the strength of their ware, but it is anything like the bulky wares of the early 1900s.

If all of Homer Laughlin's lines were to be ranked in terms of collectibility, then the ironstone shapes of the 60s and 70s would be at the bottom of the list. Most of these shapes were given different names over the years such as Palette Ware, Serenade and Century Service. For the most part, there was consistency with the various lines. For example, if a particular treatment had a Bristol sugar, then there was also a Bristol creamer, Bristol coffeepot, etc. However, in some cases, any shape could be used making classification difficult. There are some ads showing treatments using coupe shape flatware, a Bristol sugar, an Orbit Coffeepot and a Regency creamer! This would be like having a line in the 1940s using Brittany flatware, a Serenade sugar, a Fiesta coffeepot and a Harlequin creamer! This was never done with "vintage" lines, but in the 60s and 70s, anything was fair game.

The following examples are just a few of the many shapes used with Ironstone lines including the different names applied at various stages.

Palette Ware

Palette Ware is a backstamp found on plain round coupe shapes. What's unusual about this marking is that it has a copyright date of 1961. Several Palette Ware pieces have been found: various sizes of plates, platters and bowls. Each has the same type of thick solid color ring towards the edge, but the center decoration may be different.

This is the most common Palette Ware decoration: the single solid green ring with no further decoration.

Marked, "Palette Ware" is this 1963 calendar plate with a pink band.

Serenade Hand-Decorated

After the use of the name Palette Ware, HLC marked pieces as "Serenade Hand-Decorated" and "Color Harmony." Interestingly, the marking used for Serenade Hand-Decorated is a revised version of the old Serenade marking used with the pastel line from the late 30s to early 40s. The similarity between the two lines ends with the backstamp.

There were several Serenade H-D lines from the early 1960s which combined decorated Rhythm flatware, cups from Charm House and a sugar and creamer from Triumph. The example shown is one of the lines called, "Blue Aster." The Charm House cup has an exterior glaze to match the blue from the flatware. The Triumph sugar and creamer (made in a semi-porcelain body for this line) will have the same type of exterior glaze. A similar line, "Orchard" was also made. The treatment consists of dark red crab apples with olive green hollowware.

Though it looks like a Palette Ware example, this piece is actually marked with the Serenade Hand-Decorated mark.

Ironstone ad from the late 1960s/early 1970s of "Crazy Quilt" and "Nordic."

This is a common treatment called, "Blue Duchess" C-305, with the "C" standing for Century Service – a name used to describe Ironstone shapes around 1971 as a result of HLC's 100 years of operation. Examples of Blue Duchess may be found with a Serenade HD or the Color Harmony marks. Hollowware for this line is the same generic type shown in the Crazy Quilt and Nordic ad, but examples of Charm House with blue exteriors are sometimes found.

Bristol

The hollowware for Bristol is very distinctive with its bell-bottom shape. Teacups, sugars, creamers and coffeepots have all been found and mainly with exterior glazes. The Jubilee shakers were picked up with sets using Bristol hollowware.

Two ads for Ironstone shapes using Bristol shape hollowware.

Bristol shape coffeepot in a green glaze.

Bristol sugar with yellow exterior glaze.

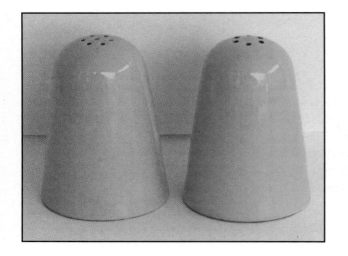

Jubilee shape shakers with exterior yellow glaze. The undersides are white indicating these were used with the Ironstone lines. One such pair was erroneously listed on eBay as rare Jubilee shakers in Harlequin yellow. They were actually meant to be used with one of the Ironstone lines.

The blue creamer and gold shakers are from HLC's Provincial – a shape very similar to Bristol though not as curved. Provincial was first made in 1968 and Bristol followed in 1970.

Mikasa

Shown are three treatments from a line that was made for Mikasa. Backstamps for all three have the general HLC marking along with a special backstamp that reads: "Mikasa Collection 70" along with the treatment name. Hollowware for this line is called, "Continental" and has a cylindrical shape with "pinched" necks. Each piece of hollowware was glazed with a solid color exterior to match the thick band towards the rim on the flatware. The green banded plate is called, "Fire Flower", the black version is "Scottsdale" and finally, the yellow is "Paisley."

Jade

In early spring of 1931, work began on producing a triangular shaped line. By March, a triangle plate and cup and saucer were modeled and samples were made, however, development on the new shape stopped soon after. After the success of Century and similar square shapes by other potteries, it was decided to instead create a second square shape.

The Jade shape was first produced in late 1931. It was developed along with the "Clair de lune" glaze – special vellum glaze with a green cast. In August of 1931, after vacationing in Toronto, Rhead notes on checking up on the "square shape." A definite design and name hadn't been decided upon, but by mid August it was determined that the shape should be simply a convex square shape with a narrow rim. Before modeling actually began on any of the shapes, trials were being made of the Clair de lune glaze. Pieces from other lines were given the special color, but none of the samples were acceptable. It would take two more months and several more tests until Clair de lune was perfected.

After the initial of tests for Clair de lune, Rhead made sketches of the various "square" shapes. Development of the new line was put on hold for almost two weeks while the Art Department temporarily shifted its attention to another new shape, Ravenna.

By early September '31, the name, "Jade" was being used to refer to the line and Rhead had finished several sketches. These were then turned over to Al Kraft for modeling. The first pieces made were 9" plate, teacups and sugars. Samples of these three pieces were made in the Clair de lune glaze and were approved by J.M. Wells in early November. With the general shapes and special glaze finally in place, production began and more items were added.

Jade was also made in the then one-year old Vellum glaze, however, at the Pittsburgh show in January of 1932, only Jade in Clair de lune was introduced to the public. Clair de lune, French for "moonlight," has a texture similar to vellum and in certain lighting even looks like the ivory glaze. Jade with Clair de lune was often advertised as, "moon light captured in dinnerware." The "moonware" was obviously not well received by the public since very little Jade Clair de lune is found today. Records indicate that in 1932, it did have moderate success in terms of sales falling behind the best sellers of the year: Yellowstone Ivory, Yellowstone Vellum, Century Vellum, Ravenna and Orleans. The company must have realized early that Clair de lune was not going to have the success that they had anticipated. With the exception of embossed OvenServe, the Clair de lune glaze was not officially used on any other shape. During 1933, Jade Clair de lune was still being made, but more attention was given to patterns on Jade Vellum.

The last time Rhead mentions altering any of the Jade shapes is in July of 1932 when he notes remodeling the dinner plate to have a circular center. To date, only square wells have been found so the circular versions may not have been put into production.

The question that remains is: why was Jade not a success? It certainly wasn't because of poor publicity or marketing. The shape along with Clair de lune was offered in several trade publications and was prominently displayed for buyers at trade shows. Several retailers carried Jade, but it just didn't sell as well as other shapes.

Could it have been the decorations? Unlikely since, while there were hosts of decals made especially for Jade, there were many treatments borrowed from other shapes. For example, "Clematis" was an excellent seller on Wells as was "English Garden" on Century, but the combination of the treatments on Jade never gained any real acceptance. It also wasn't necessarily the glazes. While Clair de lune fizzled out quickly, Jade was also made in Vellum which was popular on other shapes from 1932 until the late 1940s.

All that is left is the Jade shape itself. There were several square lines being produced in the 1930s, but these had scalloped corners or other variations. W.S. George's "Lido" and HLC's "Century" were successful square shapes, but had a "folksy" appearance and lacked elegance. On the other hand, Jade was much closer to being a true square than the others. Many agree that Jade is one of the most graceful shapes HLC has produced. Could this be why Jade was not popular? It is apparent that the public's tastes leaned towards more "busy" shapes and strayed away from the clean, elegant look of Jade. By 1934, it was overshadowed by embossed lines such as Orleans, Virginia Rose, OvenServe and Marigold, and was eventually discontinued.

Collectors today can appreciate the sleek lines of the flatware and the formal style of the hollowware with their pronounced pedestal feet and regal finials and handles. Though Jade was unpopular in its original run, it has become one of the most sought after decaled HLC lines. The Spanish theme treatments, "La Hacienda" (on Vellum) and "Spanish Wall" (on Clair de lune) are both highly collectible. Expect most Jade to have a general HLC backstamp, although some early pieces of Jade Vellum may have the Wells peacock multi-colored mark.

The decal on the Jade dinner plate is called, "Black Tulip" J-224. It is much more common on the Century shape, but can also be found on Wells. The ivory tray in the back measures 11½" by 10½".

Here is a Jade soup bowl in the green cast Clair-de-lune glaze. In the background is a Yellowstone plate in vellum to show the differences between the two glazes. The decal on the soup bowl is "Minuet" and comes from a family of decals depicting a colonial couple in different scenes. They were also used on Marigold with red trim in the mid 1930s.

Hard to find Jade cream soup and liner in the Clair de lune glaze with gold trim.

Jade covered sugars. The blue medallion treatment is J-56 and can also be found on Century, Republic and Virginia Rose. It was originally used by Knowles Taylor & Knowles of East Liverpool, Ohio. Between the two sugars is a 7" plate and fruit cup with the J-9 decoration.

Jade sugar and creamer with pastel rose decals.

The red glaze on this Jade teapot is very unusual. It is only on the exterior of the base and lid.

Old southwestern theme decals such as "La Hacienda" are very popular on Jade. This pattern is also called, "Monastery".

This Spanish wall platter is trimmed in both green and platinum. Many beginners make the mistake of identifying this as a piece of Century because of the tab extensions. Remember that Jade's platters have square corners and Century's are scalloped. The official treatment number is J-7.

This is the Jade shape butter dish. After the Jade line was discontinued in the 1930s, the butter dish continued to be produced into the early 60s as a pick up piece. It was used with various treatments in Century (in favor of the Century shape round covered butter), Nautilus, Marigold, Virginia Rose, and in solid colors with Riviera and Harlequin.

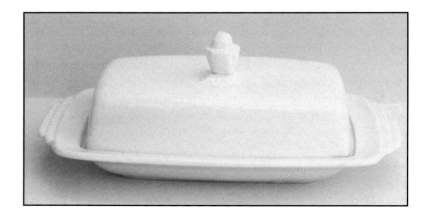

Jade Nappy

Assortment and Values for Jade:

10" Plate	$12-15	Fruit Cup	$6-8
9" Plate	$8-10	6" Oatmeal Bowl	$6-8
8" Plate	$12-15	9" Baker	$8-10
7" Plate	$5-6	10" Baker	$8-10
6" Plate	$5-6	Nappy	$12-15
Teacup	$12-15	15" Platter	$20-25
Saucer	$5-6	13" Platter	$18-20
A.D. Cup	$25-30	11" Platter	$12-15
A.D. Saucer	$10-12	Cream Soup Cup	$20-25
Covered sugar	$12-15	Cream Soup Liner	$12-15
Creamer	$8-10	Deep Plate	$8-10
Sauceboat	$12-15	36s Bowl	$12-15
Sauceboat Stand	$8-10	Covered Jug	$75-80
Gravy Fast Stand	$15-18	Covered Syrup	$50-60
Covered Butter Dish*	$30-35	Teapot	$75-80
Handled "Cake" Plate	$15-18	Covered Casserole	$45-50

* Since the Jade shape butter was used with so many lines, it may be worth more depending on the line. Virginia Rose, Harlequin and Riviera butters are worth more than one with a Jade treatment.

Jubilee & Debutante

Jubilee

In 1948, after almost six years without introducing a new line, HLC produced the Jubilee shape. The simple streamlined form satisfied the growing demand for more casual shapes of the late 1940s. Jubilee, so named to celebrate HLC's 75th anniversary, was initially used in two forms: solid colors and decals. It was also used for two other lines, Skytone and Suntone, but those are discussed in a separate section.

The solid colors for Jubilee consisted of four pastel shades: Celadon Green, Mist Gray, Cream Beige and Shell Pink. Except for special promotional items such as the Fiesta shape juice set and Kitchen Kraft mixing bowls, the Jubilee pastel colors were not used on any other HLC shape. Those with large collections of Jubilee, Fiesta and Rhythm believe the Jubilee gray is not the same that was used in the other two lines.

In comparison to HLC's other solid color lines, Jubilee was not a very good seller. As with Serenade and Nautilus in the early 40s, Jubilee just could not compete with TS & T's Lu-Ray Pastels which continued to be produced well into the 1950s. The Jubilee backstamp never carried a date code so its not clear when the line was discontinued.

There are a few interesting notes about this shape. There was no oval baker – a standard item in most HLC lines. The absence of oval bakers would continue with shapes made after Jubilee. The shakers would be used with several other lines. Obviously they were used with the Jubilee spin-offs: Debutante, Skytone and Suntone, but they were also picked up by Cavalier, Duratone and several Ironstone shapes of the late 1960s and early 1970s. HLC is still producing the Jubilee shaker to this day with "Diplomat" sets – a combination of Cavalier and Brittany shapes.

Jubilee coffeepot in gray.

6" plate in pink and creamer in beige. Because of its design, the creamer looks as if it should have a lid, however, one was never made.

Covered sugar in gray with cup and saucer in green.

Demitasse cup and saucer in pink and fruit cup in beige.

The Fiesta juice set with pitcher in green and tumblers in gray, beige, and pink.

Debutante

At the same time Jubilee was released, the Debutante line was being made. The Debutante shape is identical to Jubilee except it was made in white with decal treatments. There are two items made for Debutante and not for Jubilee: the lug soup and the 15" platter. These two shapes were also used with Skytone and Suntone. Many consider Debutante a separate shape since it has its own backstamp (this time with a date code) and its own set of treatments. Most of these decorations are colorful floral decals. To maintain the casual look, most of the treatments didn't have gold or silver trim. Official treatment numbers have a "D" prefix and, since there are no oval bakers, are often found on the underside of the nappies.

As with Jubilee, Debutante was not produced for more than five or six years.

Debutante mark.

Debutante 10" Plate.

Montgomery Wards ads from the early 1950s featuring the Debutante shape.

Assortment and Values for Jubilee and Debutante: *Use the higher end for Jubilee prices.*

10" Plate	$8-10	Egg Cup	$12-15
9" Plate	$7-8	Gravy Fast Stand	$10-12
7" Plate	$5-6	Cov'd Casserole	$20-25
6" Plate	$5-6	Cov'd Sugar	$8-10
Teacup	$7-8	Creamer	$6-8
Tea Saucer	$1-2	15" Chop Plate	$10-12
Coupe Soup	$6-8	Shakers, pair	$8-10
Cereal Soup	$5-6	Coffeepot	$30-35
5½" Fruit	$5-6	Teapot	$20-25
11" Platter	$8-10	A.D. Cup	$15-18
13" Platter	$7-8	A.D. Saucer	$4-5
7½" Nappy	$8-10		

Debutante only:

15" Platter	$12-15	Lug Soup	$5-6

KK Bowls in Jubilee colors: **Fiesta Juice Set in Jubilee colors:**

6" in Shell Pink	$90-110	Juice Pitcher in Celadon green	$125+
8" in Celadon Green	$90-110	Tumbler: any color	$90-110
10" in Mist Gray	$100-125		

Kraft Blue / Kraft Pink

In the 1930s several potteries were producing wares with solid color clays. These pieces would then receive a clear glaze and the colored body would show through. The Crooksville China Co. and the Taylor Smith and Taylor China Co. both used pink bodied ware for a number of years before Homer Laughlin attempted such a line. HLC would initially take a different direction producing blue body ware instead of pink.

In the first few months of 1937, HLC considered producing already existing shapes in "blue bodies." By July, it was decided a new line would be created with an embossed thick rope border and first few pieces of this line were modeled: sugar with cover, teapot with cover and the creamer. The new line would be unlike colored bodies produced by other potteries in that the applied handles and finials were made in a white clay producing contrasting colors with hollowware. The first design for the teapot and creamer has the familiar "tips" on the top of the handles. These handles also had small extensions on the top part. Alternate versions with the top part completely smooth and without the extensions were modeled, but the original designs were accepted.

Once the sugar, creamer and teapot were approved, the rest of the Kraft Blue shapes were modeled. From August to September 1937, the plates, platters and bowls were created. Two other shapes were made at this time: a handle to be applied to Willow body teacups and a double egg cup. A special "Kraft Blue" backstamp was made on September 30th and on October 25, 1937, the new line was released into production. There are some pieces of Kraft Blue that can be found with a general HLC backstamp, but most will have the special Kraft Blue mark.

Two more items were added to Kraft Blue in April 1938: 10¼" dinner plate and a cream soup cup. Like other hollowware, the cream soup cup has a blue body and while handles. On January 27, 1939, Rhead notes working on a "small ball jug, blue jug with white handle." This piece was based on the Harlequin novelty creamer. The Harlequin rings were removed and a new rope handle was made. This handle had to be made separate from the body so it could be made in white. This early rope handle version was not released into production and on May 29, 1939, a new style was being considered. The handle was to be plain and the rope design would be moved to the neck of the body. This too was not accepted and finally, at the end of June '39, the creamer with a plain blue body and plain handle was modeled. This is the style collectors will find on the market today.

Original sketches for Kraft Blue. The last row is of an egg cup and cream soup – both of which are standard Kraft Blue and Kraft Pink items. The novelty creamer, shown as model 1201, is the original design which called for a rope shape applied handle.

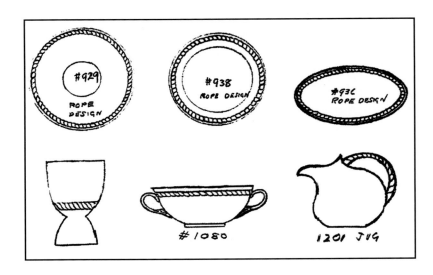

An oatmeal was made in 1941 and released into production in April of that year. It was the last piece added to Kraft Blue. Why this line wasn't expanded with casseroles, sauceboats and other hollowware forms isn't clear. It does seem certain that it started out being made for Woolworth's, but other retailers would carry the line – plain and later with decals. On April 5, 1941, Rhead writes, "Pink Kraft plates and teas for Woolworth's." Kraft Pink was approved and put into production shortly thereafter. Now Homer Laughlin was producing a pink bodied ware that others had been making for years. The assortment for Kraft Pink is identical to Kraft Blue, though don't expect pink to be as easy to find. Kraft Pink novelty creamers are quite rare followed by teapots and cream soup cups.

Kraft Pink was not produced beyond the late 1940s, but Kraft Blue lasted until the early 1950s. A second line, Skytone, also used the blue body clay. This line, based on the Jubilee shape, began production in the summer of 1950. There are many instances where sets of Skytone are found with pieces of Kraft Blue mixed in and vice versa. Both lines share the highly stylized floral decals popular in the 1950s. Skytone's shapes are very distinct from Kraft Blue so there should be no confusing the two. Both lines were almost always marked, however, there are some pieces showing up that have the "wrong" markings. Recently, a Kraft Blue novelty creamer was found with a Skytone backstamp. Also, a Skytone demitasse cup and saucer was found with a Kraft Blue marking. This raised the question: are these mistakes or were shapes borrowed and then given a different marking? In the case of the novelty creamer, none were ever offered in the known vintage Skytone brochures and ads so Kraft Blue novelty creamers marked Skytone are probably mistakes. Kraft Blue never had demitasse cups and saucers so it could very well be the case that Skytone versions were picked up and then marked appropriately.

There are several treatments that can be found on Kraft Blue. The stylized decal shown on these 7" plates is the most common and was an exclusive for G.C. Murphy's. Its official number is: GCM-101.

Kraft Blue Creamer with the "Marcia" decal.

Kraft Pink Sugar. Don't expect to find treatments on Kraft Pink.

On the left is a Harlequin novelty creamer in gray. The Kraft Blue and Kraft Pink novelty creamers to the right were made based on the Harlequin model. The handle was separated and made in white while the base was made in the colored clay.

The Kraft Pink bowl in the background measures 6" in diameter. The Kraft Blue creamer is the standard shape. You will also find a novelty creamer based on the Harlequin shape (without rings) in both Kraft Pink and Kraft Blue.

Kraft Blue Teapot.

Assortment and Values: Use lower end for Kraft Blue and higher end for Kraft Pink.

Teapot	$20-35	Platter, any size	$12-18
Creamer	$4-9	10" Plate	$15-20
Sugar	$8-12	9" Plate	$10-12
Ball Cream	$25-40	7" Plate	$5-7
Cream Soup	$10-15	6" Plate	$4-5
Double Egg Cup	$12-20	Teacup	$6-9
Nappy	$8-15	Saucer	$2-4
Oatmeal, 6"	$5-7	Oval Baker	$8-10
Fruit Cup, 5"	$4-5	Deep Plate	$6-8

Hand Painted Ware (Peasant Ware)

The Peasant Ware line consists of Kraft Blue shapes in a tan body with hand-painted treatments. One of the first times Rhead mentions the line in his journals is with regard to the body. Several colored bodies were considered until a tan colored clay was decided upon at the end of November 1939. After samples of Peasant Ware were reviewed, a special backstamp which read *Peasant Ware, Hand Painted, Homer Laughlin, U.S.A.* was made on January 14, 1940. There were numerous hand-painted designs being tested at this time such as a rooster, house, ship, different figures and several others with trim varying in widths.

Rhead mentions the line again on March 23, 1940: *JMW spoke about Handpainted Peasant line for Woolworth's. Trying it without* [trim]. *House to be more solid. Also chimney to be perpendicular. Color to be stronger . . .* It was determined in April 1940 the line would consist of a 9" plate, cup and saucer, 6" bowl, teapot, creamer and sugar, but on May 23, 1940, Rhead notes the line making use of all the Kraft Blue shapes except the 10" plate, baker, novelty creamer, and cream soup cup. The final designs are also listed at this time as House, Flower Pot, Windmill and Ship. One of the last times Rhead writes on working on Peasant Ware is in June of 1940.

This is one of the most difficult HLC lines to locate. Pieces that are found often are marked with the same backstamp Rhead wrote about in January 1940, but without the Peasant Ware name. Not every piece has the same decoration and so far, only three of the four treatments mentioned in the May 23, 1940 entry have been found; Ship on the teapot and 7" plate, House on the sugar and 9" plate, Windmill on the teacup.

Peasant Ware teapot with the "Ship" treatment.

Value: UND

Fruit Skin Glazes

In early 1941, Sears and Roebuck approached Homer Laughlin about producing a line of solid colored dinnerware. Sears had offered several lines of colorware in the past including Granada by French-Saxon and Valencia by Shawnee. In March 1941, work began on modeling a new shape and producing new colored glazes.

The glazes developed for this new line with heavily textured specks would become known as "Fruit Skin Glazes." The shapes created for this line had an embossed rope decoration at the rim in the same manner as Kraft Blue. The first pieces modeled for this line were a plate and a casserole. Unfortunately, there are no sketches for any of the shapes created for this line in the modeling log. On March 6, 1941, Rhead notes: *First molted glazes out on rope. Casseroles and plate – very promising.* More shapes were created and on March 12th, Rhead makes the following entry:

> *McDonald [buyer for Sears] and J.M. Wells in. Both approved. Favorable toward Fruit Skin Glazes. Also discussed new shape. They both like the rope pattern and covered cream soup. Saw new skeletons of soup tureens . . . It seems definite we will have a new shape. I want to get away from the rope border and am working on leaf and other motif [s]. J.M. Wells stated if we could not spray these glazes, they could be dipped.*

Work proceeded with developing new shapes and more glazes. Rhead notes a blue and salmon as the next two colors, but that the specks had to be reduced so that when applied to smaller items, they will be proportional. Sketches of hollowware without the rope border were drawn up on March 19th. Rhead describes these as: "globe" shape casserole, sugar and creamer. The next entry, dated March 22, 1941, foreshadows the fate of Fruit Skin Glazes:

> *. . . letter from Sears (McDonald) to the effect that we should work on a cheaper glaze effect than Fiesta. McDonald likes new glazes . . . wants the best thing we ever did at Syndicate prices. Hope this does not spoil line as planned for the general trade. Have been wondering what to do to meet this lower cost range.*

Development continued on the special glazes and the doubt from the previous entry seems to be put aside when Rhead notes on March 28th: *J.M. Wells likes new glazes. Will make for Sears & Roebuck.*

On May 21, 1941, Rhead writes of more optimism with the new line:

J.M. Wells up. Said we would make full line of colored glazes. Mr. Mash said the glazes were exceptional and should be successful. Also that the shapes "Tree Platter", Divided baker, etc. would help to sell the ware. Not to be concerned about price of the new items.

From May to July, nineteen items were modeled for Fruit Skin glazes. Other lines were being considered for Sears such as Modern Farmer in Serenade glazes. In June, more trials of Fruit Skin glazes were being made on Modern Farmer and Swing and samples were sent to Sears for approval. Ten more items were modeled, the last being a nappy at the end of October. One of the last times Rhead mentions Fruit Skin Glazes was on October 21, 1941: . . . *on "Fruit Skin Glaze" Relish and Snack Plates . . . concerned about production. Explained that these are planned as special items to meet California development, etc.*

Sears never did carry the Fruit Skin Glazes line. In the 1941/1942 season, their catalog offered a line of solid colored dinnerware made by a California pottery. Never had Homer Laughlin devoted so much time and resources into developing a line that didn't go into production. This line is being presented here for two reasons. First, collectors get a chance to see what could have been. The final assortment probably would have undergone some changes since there were several different styles from which to choose. Then there's the name itself which could have been changed by Sears and a special backstamp would have been created.

The "what if" side to Fruit Skin Glazes is appealing enough to present it here, but what's even more exciting is samples of this line have been found outside the factory. At least one "tree platter" (a rope shape oval platter with a "tree" cut into the well to catch grease) and cream soups have been discovered thus far. Who knows what other shapes and colors might surface?

This purplish dish is one of the few pieces fruit skin glazes to be found outside Homer Laughlin. It is marked on the underside with the glaze number, 4904.

These two photos, taken at HLC, show the coupe shape rope flatware with specially made pieces of hollowware.

Items for Fruit Skin Glazes as listed in the modeling log in 1941:

March CASSEROLE ROUND [covered cream soup]
       COV. DISH OVAL
       PLATE 8"
       SALAD BOWL
       CUP TEA & HANDLE
       SAUCER TEA
       PLATE 7"
       HANDLE CUP (an extra for the previous cup)
       FRUIT BOWL

May   DESSERT 6³/₄"
       PLATE 8" ROPE CHANGED
       PLATE 6"
       BOWL SALAD
       DESERT, IND.
       SAUCER TEA
       CUP, TEA

June   TRAY CRACKER
       SALAD BOWL
       BOWL BERRY W/ TURNED FOOT
       CUP TEA
       BOWL BERRY W/ STUCK ON FOOT
       SAUCER, A.D.
       CUP A.D.

July   BAKER DIVIDED
       BAKER NOT DIVIDED
       TEAPOT
       SUGAR
       CREAM

August DISH 16½" X 10½" CREAM,
       HLD CHANGED

September COVER DISH
           SUGAR
October   SQUARE RELISH TRAY
           DISH TRAY
           BOWL
           BAKER – STRAIGHT SIDED
           NAPPIE

While Fruit Skin Glazes never went into production, at least one of the shapes was put to good use. On December 23, 1941, records indicate the 10" rope plate being ordered for a special souvenir plate:

Mr. J.M. Wells asks for a plate with 6 famous American Scenes from Washington similar to the Vernon Kilns pattern. It is to be the Rope plate without the rim and in Ivory body. The subjects to be incorporated into one all-over design are: 1. Mount Vernon, 2. Capitol, 3. White House, 4. Washington Monument, 5. National Gallery of Art, 6. Supreme Court Building. Also U.S. Seal. To be printed first in Willow Blue.

The special plate was made in 1942 and in the same blue color used for Blue Willow. Shown in the photo is an example with all the elements from the original order. Washington DC plates will have a special blue Homer Laughlin marking.

Blue DC plate: $10.00-12.00

Liberty

In late 1941, HLC made plans to produce a line which would feature early American scenes reproduced from Joseph Boggs Beale paintings as a Woolworth's exclusive. Beale (1841-1926) was an American artist well known for historical and religious illustrations. The new shape was named, "Liberty." It was probably given this name to reflect the theme of the Beale treatments. One of the first mentions in Rhead's journals regarding the new line occurred on December 23, 1941: *Mr. J.M. Wells also asked about the subjects for the Beale series. I understand that the series is to be done by the photo-engraved method.*

The first Liberty piece modeled was the 9" plate on January 1942. After being accepted, the following items were created from mid January to early March; 10", 8", 7", 6" plates, saucer, teacup, sugar, oatmeal, creamer, 8" deep plate, 9" nappy, 8" nappy, 8" baker and 12" oval platter. Only two items were revised: the sugar and creamer. Its noted they were remodeled with "flared tops."

From late March to June, work commenced on creating the various patterns for the Liberty shapes (known at the time as "Beale patterns" in company records). On Monday, June 22, 1942, two entries in Rhead's Journals discuss the new treatments: *Beale samples out this afternoon. Could be a lot better printing. Most items lack detail and fine tonal variations.* Work commenced on improving the quality of the prints, but on July 24, 1942, another change was made, this time with regard to the shape which resulted in a heavier and sharper gadroon edge. In August and September all the existing Liberty shapes were remodeled and a new item was added; the sauceboat.

Before continuing with Liberty's development, it should be noted that Rhead was in failing health in mid 1942. From his journals, its apparent he eventually died of mouth cancer, but he suffered from the condition for a long time. On April 29, 1941, Rhead notes: *To Wheeling to see Phillips. Worried about mouth. Ordered me to go to Cleveland* [Clinic] *at once. Radium or surgery . . .* For the rest of 1941 and into 1942, Rhead would make numerous entries about making trips to the Cleveland Clinic. In late 1941, Rhead spent fewer and fewer days at HLC. Work continued as usual and the journals were maintained by another. It's not clear who this was, but it was someone who worked in the Art Department. In mid 1942, Rhead would often come to work at noon or later to oversee the progression of shapes and patterns – including Liberty.

It's noted several times in the 1942 journal that Rhead would often leave the area and return. An entry from March 17, 1942 states: *Mr. J.D. Thompson brought up the good news that Mr. Rhead is feeling much better and will probably be home around the twenty-ninth or thirtieth of this month.* He did return but eventually went to New York and in October was hospitalized. An entry dated November 2, 1942 hints at his planning to return to HLC: *Letter from Mr. Rhead asking about report to USPA. Also about book cases for his library which is to be moved here.* On the next day, November 3, 1942, there is the single entry: *Mr. Rhead died last night.* Frederick Hurten Rhead was buried in New York on the morning of November 5, 1942. He was 62 years old.

Towards the end of '42, the revised Liberty shape and the perfected "Beale Patterns" now called, "Historical America" was put into production. Two more items would be added in 1943: the covered casserole in February and the teapot in late March.

Historical America was produced for many years after 1942 and is very easy to find in today's market. Red is by far the most common color, but once in a while, blue examples can be found. Exactly when HLC started using the Liberty shape with floral decals and other decorations isn't clear but based on backstamps, it must have been very soon after its introduction. It became one of HLC best selling shapes for decals with production lasting into the late 1950s. Historical America will have its own special backstamp but decaled Liberty will have a generic HLC mark.

Contrary to popular belief, the flatware from Liberty and Newell are not the same. The gadroon embossed rims may be similar but each line has distinct rim size and scallop design. Their holloware is anything but similar. While Newell's gadroon is placed on the rim (like most other potteries gadroon shapes), Liberty's is placed low on the body. There's a bit of irony with these two similar shapes in that Newell was the first line Rhead designed for HLC and Liberty was the last.

Historical America Examples:

"The Pony Express" nappy.

"Franklin's Experiment" cup and "Arrival of the Mayflower" saucer.

Liberty Examples:

Vintage ad showing Currier & Ives decals on the Liberty shape with two different borders. The gold filigree border was called, "Sun Gold" and the light blue border was, "Blue Heaven." 61 piece service for 8 sold for $29.95 and 103 piece service for 12 sold for $49.95.

It could be argued that "Dogwood" or L-613 is the most popular decal for the Liberty shape. It can also be found on Rhythm (RY-106) and Virginia Rose, (VR-445) but it is much more common on Liberty.

Here's a treatment whose name is commonly listed on the reverse of dinner plates: Queen Esther. The large floral decal can also be found on Georgian Eggshell and Theme, but without the gold regal-like medallions. Instead, Georgian Eggshell will have a thin floral ring around the large decal.

This Queen Ester sauceboat shows how a treatment translates from a piece of flatware to hollowware: a smaller "sprig" of the large flower used on the flatware now graces the sides of the sauceboat. The number of leaves and small blue background flowers has been reduced, and a singular gold medallion is located at the very front of the boat.

The 36s bowl shown here demonstrates a common feature on Liberty: the gadroon "border" found on the rims of flatware is placed towards the base and not at the opening. In general, other gadroon shapes, by HLC and other companies, have the rope-like border at the openings. This may be helpful to remember when "out in the field" and encountering gadroon shapes. Liberty's low gadroon placement occurs on the oatmeal bowl, sugar, creamer, sauceboat, teacup, teapot and covered casserole.

The 9" plate on the left is commonly known as "Spring Wreath." It appears on Virginia Rose and Kitchen Kraft OvenServe as well as other HLC shapes. To the right is another floral treatment with a hand-painted look that is rather common on the Liberty shape. In the front is a poppy decoration – one of several treatments on Liberty sold through Woolworth's. Its official treatment number is W-146.

This treatment originated on the Coronet shape as CO-100 and can also be found on Virginia Rose and Georgian Eggshell.

Here's another Woolworth line, this time, "Apple Blossom" or W-246.

Liberty Creamers with the Ivy and Dogwood decals.

The pink and gray floral decals on this round serving bowl are common on Liberty, but can also be found on Georgian Eggshell, Virginia Rose and Marigold.

10" plate with Autumn Leaves treatment.

Assortment and values for Liberty: Use higher end for popular decals such as Dogwood and Historical America.

10" Plate	$8-10	Baker	$7-9
9" Plate	$6-8	Nappy	$7-9
8" Plate	$8-10	Fruit Cup	$2-3
7" Plate	$4-5	36s Bowl	$5-6
6" Plate	$2-3	6" Bowl	$5-6
Teacup	$5-6	Deep Plate	$5-6
Saucer	$1-2	15" Platter	$12-15
Sugar	$12-15	13" Platter	$10-12
Creamer	$6-7	11" Platter	$10-12
Sauceboat	$8-10	Casserole	$25-30
Sauceboat Stand	$6-7	Teapot	$25-30

Marigold

Marigold is listed in Rhead's journals for the first time on the 16th of November, 1933. The entry is rather vague: "Commenced modeling new shape for Woolworth." By December this new line was being called the "Daisy Shape" for lack of a better name. Plates were made with silver stamp decorations (for some reason these early pieces were fired at Edwin M. Knowles' electric kiln) and after being approved, the teacup was ordered. Its capacity was to be identical to the OvenServe teacup which is why both cups have very similar bodies – save the embossings.

On January 1, 1934, Rhead was sketching other pieces of Marigold, however, there were no major developments with Marigold for almost a month since attention was given to expanding the very successful OvenServe kitchenware. In February, work resumed on the "Daisy Shape" and would continue for the next five months. The first items to be added are listed in the following entry:

> 02.05.34 – *JMW daisy shape for Woolworth's or Newberry. Teas, 6", 7" bakers, 7", 8" dishes,* [snip] *sugar, creamer, 6" deep plate, 4<sup>1/2" fruit and oatmeal, 5" fruit extra large, 36s bowl, oatmeal, 7" coupe to commence modeling as early as possible.*

The modeling of the shapes listed in the entry above began immediately. According to the modeling log, several types of "fan" embossings were considered in the original design from December: 5 scallops, 5 pointed scallops, 6 scallops, tulip and tulip-deep flute. The accompanying drawing for the first style, "5 scallops" shows the familiar fan embossing. The only major difference from the original concept and the pieces modeled in February involved the addition of the "inside line."

While the "Daisy Shape" assortment was being crafted, treatments were being considered. The earliest of which involve hand-painting the "fan" embossings. Green, blue and pink underglaze fan treatments were the first, but other colors such as maroon and yellow would follow. A special backstamp was made and the idea was passed onto the already existing Virginia Rose shape in May of '34.

On April 14, 1934, Rhead notes in his journal that "Marigold" is the new name of the daisy shape. Samples were made of Marigold with the hand-painted fans and were shown to retailers. By the end of May, Rhead states: *the green* [hand-painted] *Marigold is selling . . . must get out other colors.* In June, a new item was added; the sauceboat. More pieces were ordered in October: square plate, casserole, 15" platter and the pickle. The assortment remained unchanged until 1935 when, in January, the 8" nappy and 8" baker were modeled. In February, the last piece was made: the 42s jug, commonly called a "milk pitcher."

Modeling of Marigold went rather smoothly. There were only three "problem" items; the casserole, platter, and square plate. The first casserole had handles which "curled" upwards. Production of this style casserole lasted from November of '34 until July of '35 when it was decided that Virginia Rose casserole handles would be more appropriate on the Marigold body. Whether this was done for production reasons or aesthetics is unknown, but collectors are left with two different Marigold casseroles.

The square plate underwent at least one revision because of its shape and rim. Marigold has a very large rim which makes many non-circular flatware's rim and well out of proportion. In fact, Rhead commented on this with regard to the platters in June of 1934: "*. . . Do not like the proportion of the dish. Believe that rim is too wide in proportion to the well of the dish. May remodel.*" He never did remodel any of the platters.

Production of the many hand-painted fans was limited, but the green underglaze and red/black overglaze treatments were made for several years. Silver and gold stamps were rather common place on Marigold (as well as Virginia Rose) and dozens of examples are found today. But when collectors encounter Marigold, it is usually with decals. Several of these treatments will have a special verge gold decoration – a type of decoration that was used more on Marigold than any other HLC shape.

In 1937 Marigold was given a special green glaze. The green is darker and much more consistent than other HLC greens made at the time. Green Marigold is usually found marked with date codes from 1937 and 1938. Other than green and plain ivory, which is the same ivory glaze developed for embossed OvenServe, and an unusual yellow glaze, Marigold hasn't been found in any other solid color.

Many new collectors confuse the embossings of Marigold with Virginia Rose (see the Virginia Rose section for a comparison of the various embossings). Virginia Rose and Marigold were basically made side by side in plant 8. In fact, there are cases in which complete sets of Virginia Rose are found with some Marigold mixed in, as well as pieces of Marigold with the general Virginia Rose backstamp.

No new items were added to Marigold after the 42s jug in 1935. There were several pickup pieces such as the Jade butter and cable egg cup. These two pieces have been found with various Marigold silver stamp decorations and mixed in Marigold sets.

Marigold was no longer offered by Homer Laughlin after 1952.

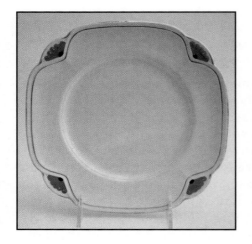

This Marigold square plate features a popular treatment: red/black fans, M-110. In a 1934 article several such treatments were mentioned appearing on the then new Marigold shape. Three were underglaze: pink, blue and green; and two were over the glaze: coral and black & blue and yellow. Of the underglaze colors, green is the easiest to find with blue and pink next. As for the over glaze treatments, the combination of coral [red] and black, M-110, is rather common.

Here is another over glaze fan treatment: light blue and dark blue combination with gold trim.

Sometimes, the under-the-glaze hand-painted treatments will have this marking instead of the generic HLC backstamp. This is the only case in which the shape name, "Marigold" appears in a backstamp. A similar marking was used for hand-painted treatments on Virginia Rose.

A Pound Sterling Price Guide from May of 1937 lists several other "fan" decorated treatments. They are: M-109 green & blue fans with gold edge; M-111 yellow & black fans; M-136 green & blue fans with silver edge; M-140 black solid fans.

The 10" plate in the background has the same type of underglaze green hand-painted work found on OvenServe, Coronet and Virginia Rose. Shown in front of the "green fans" examples is a 6" plate.

Marigold platter with the red pig decal.

The large looking creamer is actually a milk jug. These are hard to find and generally always have the platinum decoration. Woolworth's sold Marigold with the platinum trim for most of the shape's production run which explains why it is in such abundance. In vintage ads, Woolworth's never glorified the line with a name. Instead, it was often offered as simply, "Platinum Dinnerware." The official number for this ware is W-134.

The Marigold fruit cup is wearing a rather common decal: M-212.

The creamer and covered sugar has the small sprigs found in the M-212 treatment.

The rose decal on this Marigold 10" dinner plate is very common on Virginia Rose. The petit point house decal on the little fruit cup was used extensively by Crooksville Pottery and is not easy to find on HLC shapes.

Marigold rim soup – M-201 decoration.

Solid green Marigold. Sets are often found with "open sugars" and both rim and coupe soups are known to exist in this rich green color. Don't confuse this glaze with Fiesta's light green which was also in production in the late 1930s.

This 7" plate is part of an over-decorated combination set by Pacific China. For more, see section on Decorators.

Here is an original style Marigold casserole with the standard handles. Soon after its introduction, the handles were replaced by the smaller Virginia Rose versions.

Marigold dinner Plate with "green fans" and a platter with green wash trim.

Century lug soup with Marigold's "Springtime" treatment.

Marigold Assortment and values:

10" Plate	$8-10	Oval Baker	$8-10
9" Plate	$6-8	Oatmeal	$5-6
8" Square Plate	$8-10	Fruit Cup	$4-5
7" Plate	$4-5	15" Platter	$15-18
6" Plate	$4-5	13" Platter	$12-15
Teacup	$5-6	11" Platter	$10-12
Saucer	$1-2	Sauceboat	$8-10
Covered Sugar	$12-15	Sauceboat Stand	$8-10
Creamer	$8-10	Rim Soup	$6-8
Milk Pitcher (42s)	$18-20	Coupe Soup	$10-12
Casserole with		10" Nappy	$12-15
Marigold handles	$70+	9" Nappy	$10-12
Casserole with Virginia			
Rose handles	$30-35		

Modern Farmer

The Modern Farmer shape is one of the most unusual lines put out by HLC. The flatware can best be described as a coupe shape with pleated ripples. Creamers, sugars and sauceboats have a stretched appearance and exaggerated handles. Modern Farmer was based on a shape made by James River Potteries of Hopewell Virginia and once in a while a James River version will be found with a "JR" backstamp. James River also produced a rippled ringed shape called, "Cascade" which is very similar to Modern Farmer, but the ripples aren't pleated.

The first time Rhead mentions Modern Farmer is on June 19, 1940: *McDonald, Sears Roebuck here. Wants to make James River line.* McDonald was the buyer for Sears who worked closely with HLC and other potteries. During the next month, most of the Modern Farmer items were modeled and by August 3, 1940, they was released into production.

Sears picked up the new shape and sold it for several seasons with various decal treatments. They offered at least two: "Gascon," a blue floral treatment and "Breton" – a multicolored and multi-sprig treatment that would later become known as, "Priscilla." Other commonly found treatments include one with small yellow daisies and another with the ever popular petit point rose. Several other treatments can be found, but don't expect the large library of decals commonly associated with Virginia Rose, Marigold and other shapes. At one point, HLC toyed with the idea of making Modern Farmer in the Serenade glazes for Sears. Samples were made in 1941, but the line never materialized. It was during this time that Rhead was working on Fruit Skin Glazes – a new line of colorware using new shapes and glazes that ended up being shelved. (For more, see section on Kraft Blue.)

The shakers come in two versions: plain Swing and Swing with ripples. Sears Ads from the 1940s will either show one or the other, but never both. There are also ads that show a tall spiral type shaker that may have been made by James River and not Homer Laughlin. There is no evidence that HLC produced any Modern Farmer shakers except the modified Swing version.

Modern Farmer makes use of the general HLC backstamp. If the date codes are accurate, then the line was not produced much longer after 1943. Most shapes and lines were cut back due to W.W.II and it seems that Modern Farmer was discontinued all together. With a short production life, small number of treatments and a minimal assortment, Modern Farmer is a limited line in every sense of the word.

"Gascon" is the name of the treatment on this Modern Farmer 9" plate. It was a Sears exclusive in the early 1940s. Dinner plates were commonly marked with a double back-stamp as shown. Of the few modern Farmer treatments, this seems to be one of the most common. Its official treatment number is MF-3.

Before Sears sold "Gascon," they sold this pattern called, "Breton." A 32-piece set could be purchased in 1940 for $4.39. Its official treatment number is MF-2.

Sauceboat and stand with the little yellow daisies treatment.

The hollowware for Modern Farmer is rather large in comparison to other HLC shapes. Shown is a Modern Farmer sugar with small daisy sprigs. Its capacity is 16 oz.

Decoration MF-14 on a Modern Farmer baker. This pattern was also used on Theme Eggshell as TH-6 and on Liberty as "Greenbriar" for Cunningham and Pickett.

Modern Farmer sugar and creamer with an all over gold decoration.

Assortment and Values:

Cup	$5-6	Casserole	$20-25
Saucer	$2-3	13" Platter	$10-15
9" Plate	$6-8	11" Platter	$8-10
6" Plate	$4-5	Pickle	$8-10
7" Plate	$4-5	Sugar	$10-12
Fruit Cup	$4-5	Creamer	$6-8
Lug Soup	$6-8	Sauce Boat	$10-12
Coupe Soup	$6-8	Nappie	$8-10
Shakers, pr.	$10-12	Baker	$8-10

Nautilus & Nautilus Eggshell

Nautilus

The Nautilus shape started out as a very plain round shape with a single sunken ring around the edge. On the other hand, the hollowware was ornate with shell finials and handles and little scroll feet. Modeling began in July of 1935 with a 9" plate with a "deep ball, sunken bead and a plain edge." Several other versions were modeled, but it was the sunken bead that was accepted. From August to October, several casseroles were modeled: "Pain Sunken Bead", "Sunken Bead on Edge Ring Handled" and "Sunken Bead Plain Cover Oval Handles." The next two pieces were the ring handled creamer and sugar to match the ring handled casserole. Unfortunately, there are no known sketches of these ring handled pieces.

On October 1935, the familiar Nautilus casserole was modeled: "Casserole Shell Handles Four Footed." With the basic shapes for the flatware and hollowware approved, the rest of Nautilus was made. The flatware was modeled with ease, however the same cannot be said for the hollowware. The casserole required several revisions so the shell handles would come out right in the finished product. The feet for the hollowware underwent several changes. On March 20, 1936, and entry in Rhead's journals discusses one of the problems with the hollowware: "... *Nautilus cream. Casting holes in foot too prominent. This piece and the sauceboat to be taken care of – went to Al Kraft* [modeler]." On the same day an entry is made regarding the teapot which confirms what may collectors have always suspected: "*Pittenger phoned about Nautilus teapot. Told him that J.M. Wells had not included it in the line. He suggested the Wells teapot. Suggested that we decorate one and show it to J.M. Wells.*"

While Rhead doesn't mention of the Wells teapot again, it must have been picked up since sets of Nautilus are sometimes found with a Wells teapot. Nautilus was offered in early 1936 and would continue to be produced into the early to mid 1950s. Almost every piece (except teacups and AD cups) will be marked with a special Nautilus backstamp which Rhead notes making on December 26, 1935.

Besides the Wells teapot, there are several other pick up pieces such as the Baltimore mug, Cable egg cup and the Jade butter dish. These pieces will have a general HLC mark. Even though Nautilus pieces will be marked as such, there should be no confusion with other shapes, especially the hollowware. The shell handles and scroll feet were never used by HLC in any other line.

Nautilus casserole with black and red trim.

Magnolia on Nautilus was sold through Cunningham & Picket.

Creamer and sugar with the "Early America" treatment.

Nautilus baker and sauceboat with the N-259 decoration. This line was sold with light green Fiesta to create one of the four "Fiesta Harmony" set in the late 1930s.

Both in the brown glaze used in Sheffield Amberstone are the Nautilus teacup (left) and the modified Fiesta cup (right). Brown Nautilus teacups aren't terribly rare and are sometimes found in Fiesta Amberstone sets.

Pastel Nautilus

Soon after the pastel line Serenade began production in 1939, HLC toyed with the idea of making one of its already existing shapes in pastel glazes for Woolworth's. In September, the following shapes in the Serenade colors were ordered for testing purposes: Wells, Harlequin, Nautilus, Coronet, Republic, Virginia Rose and Swing. Several more trials and samples were made until it was finally decided that the pastel glazes would be used on Nautilus.

The regular Nautilus line was used so don't expect to find the eggshell version hollowware in pastel glazes. There were only two changes to Nautilus to make this line. One involved modifying the teacup by making it larger. The other was the addition of a double egg cup with Rhead notes as the Kraft Blue egg cup without the rope embossing.

Pastel Nautilus was released to be sold through Woolworth's in early 1940 in the standard Serenade glazes: pink, green, yellow and blue. Almost every piece is found with a Homer Laughlin/Nautilus backstamp.

Pastel Nautilus 7" Plate

The eggcups used in Pastel Nautilus are basically Kraft Blue eggcups without the rope embossing.

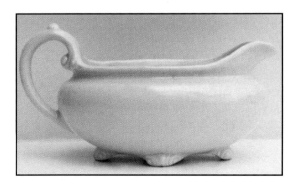

Sauceboat in pink.

Nautilus Eggshell

Almost a year had passed since the regular Nautilus line was put into production when HLC decided to use the shape as a basis for a new type of body called Eggshell. Rhead always called this a "talc body" but it was really a special combination, light weight clay. Some vintage ads identify the primary mineral involved as Tremolite – Calcium Magnesium Silicate Hydroxide $Ca_2Mg_5Si_8O_{22}(OH)_2$. The shapes for Nautilus Eggshell are the same as regular Nautilus except for the hollowware.

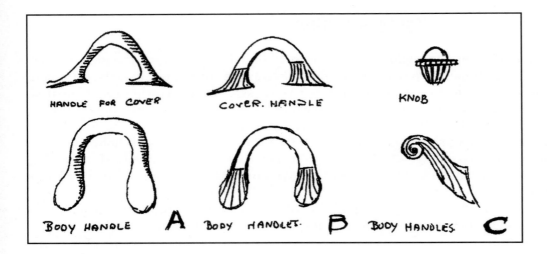

The casserole was basically the same capacity as the regular version but the scroll feet were replaced with a rounded foot. Three different handles and finials were considered and tested. The first two were "open" handles and finials, but it was the closed scroll handles and knob finial that was chosen – shown from the original sketches as style "C". A smaller knob version was also made for the sugar. The creamer and sauceboat were also made with rounded feet and the little "thorn" atop the handles was removed. While the design of the flatware was not changed, appropriate molds needed to be made for the new type of body.

Rhead notes making the Nautilus Eggshell backstamp on December 28, 1936 – two days over of being exactly a year since he made the regular Nautilus marking. The new line was offered in January of 1937.

When it became apparent eggshell was a good seller, HLC decided to make more shapes in the light weight body. Swing came next in late 1937, Theme in 1939 and Georgian in 1940. Interestingly when several new pieces were being made for Georgian, several were also made for Nautilus Eggshell which weren't previously offered. In August 1940, the Nautilus Eggshell salad bowl, teapot and square plate were modeled. When the regular Nautilus pieces were being remodeled for eggshell, Rhead noted on February 2, 1937: *Will not make 8" nappy in Nautilus Eggshell.* It is interesting that a change of heart must have occurred with the introduction of the salad bowl in 1940. Shakers were modeled for Eggshell Georgian during this same time, but Rhead notes that instead of making a new shape for Eggshell Nautilus, the Swing shakers would be used instead.

Hundreds of decals were used on Nautilus Eggshell from its introduction until it was discontinued in the early 1960s. Almost every retailer offered the line since it was simply designed yet elegant. It was a sharp contrast to the Art Deco/Streamline shapes of the 30s and 40s as well as the casual lines of the 1950s. In most catalogs from the 50s, Nautilus Eggshell is often offered side by side with Georgian Eggshell and the last eggshell shape made by Homer Laughlin, Cavalier.

Nautilus Eggshell
marking.

This ad from a 1950s whole-sale catalog features, "Corsage." This same pattern on Nautilus was sold through Montgomery Wards in the mid 1950s as Nassau.

This massive 15" platter has the "Nantucket" treatment. This has become very popular in recent years and, while not impossible to find, may be priced a little high because of demand. Expect shakers to be in the Swing shape which were borrowed for many Nautilus Eggshell lines.

The platinum band treatment is common on Nautilus Eggshell. Its official number is N-1219 and when it appears on Swing, the treatment is called, "Chanson." You may find a similar pattern on Taylor Smith and Taylor's Laurel shape called 601.

N-1219 Sauceboat. Notice the foot and handle difference from the regular Nautilus line.

"Cardinal" Platter.

The "Ferndale" treatment on this plate can also be found on Georgian Eggshell.

"Ferndale" Sugar.

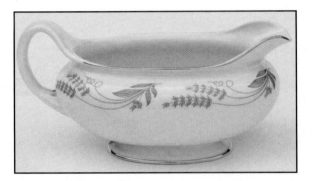

Sauceboat with a stylized blue and gold wheat treatment.

Covered casserole with pink and blue flowers – similar in style to Ferndale.

The "square" plate shown here is Eggshell Nautilus. Its shape was the basis for the Georgian Eggshell and Theme Eggshell square plates. Its official treatment number is N-1583.

Assortment and Values for: Nautilus and Nautilus Eggshell. Items marked with an asterisk (*) are in eggshell only.

10" Plate	$8-10	Casserole	$20-25
9" Plate	$6-8	Cream Soup*	$8-10
8" Plate	$6-8	Cream Soup Liner*	$4-5
Square Plate	$6-8	Lug Soup	$5-7

7" Plate	$4-5		Deep Plate	$5-7
6" Plate	$4-5		Gravy Fast stand*	$8-10
Fruit Cup	$4-5		Sauceboat	$6-8
6" Bowl	$5-6		Sauceboat stand	$4-5
Teacup	$6-8		Sugar	$8-10
Saucer	$2-3		Creamer	$5-7
A.D. Cup	$8-10		10" Baker	$10-12
A.D. Saucer	$5-6		9" Baker	$8-10
15" Platter	$12-15		10" Nappy	$8-10
13" Platter	$8-10		9" Nappy	$8-10
11" Platter	$8-10		Teapot*	$25-30
Chop plate	$12-15		Shakers, pair*	$8-10
Pastels Eggcup**	$15-18		Eggshell Eggcup	$6-8
Pastels Teacup**	$10-12			

** The pastels eggcup and teacup were used in the Nautilus Pastels line only.

Newell

Named after the town in West Virginia where five of the Homer Laughlin plants are located, Newell was the first line of dinnerware Rhead designed. It was first offered to the public in 1928 and would last into the mid 1930s. Gadroon shapes were becoming popular with other potteries in the late 1920s and Newell was HLC's first gadroon line. Two more would soon follow based on Newell: Trellis and Old Roman. Both lines used many of the flat pieces from Newell with the addition of embossed patterns along the rim. Newell is easier to find than these "spin-off" lines. (It should be mentioned that the Newell and Liberty shapes have very little in common. Liberty was another gadroon line first offered by HLC in 1942. These two lines have distinct shapes, rope embossings, treatments and come from different eras.)

Newell isn't that difficult to find so it must have been a very good seller in its day. Flatware such as plates and platters are especially easy to find. The handled tray and pickle may be a little more difficult to locate. Sugars, creamers and sauceboats are much easier to find than larger hollowware such as the casserole, jug and teapot.

Newell is almost always found in either white or the light yellow glaze with decals, but once in a while plain light yellow pieces show up. The majority of decals used on Newell are highly stylized and very colorful floral treatments. Most pieces are marked with a general HLC backstamp. Since the old East Liverpool factories continued operations until 1929, some Newell pieces will have the "L" as the location in the backstamp. (For more, see section on markings.)

Blue bird decals on any dinnerware line command high prices. Here we see a variant of the standard blue bird decals on a Newell dinner plate.

This very colorful treatment (N-2023) is rather common on the Newell shape. Shown are the oval baker, covered sugar, sauceboat, sauceboat stand, cream soup and liner.

Six inch plate with a common red and blue floral treatment.

Newell platter with decals that are also found on Virginia Rose.

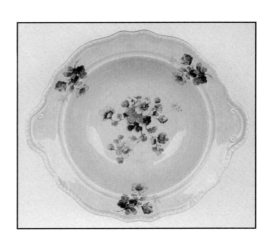

This Newell covered casserole in the light yellow glaze has small floral decals around the lid and rim, but hidden on the inside bottom is a large sprig. Its official treatment number is N-2528.

To the left is the smallest size of several jugs offered with Newell; the 48s jug. Beside it is the regular creamer.

Here the 48s jug is being used as a creamer with the regular covered sugar. Its not unheard of to find sugar and creamer sets from Newell, Century, Trellis and other lines with a 48s jug instead of the regular creamer.

Newell egg cups.

Assortment and Values for Newell

10" Plate	$8-10	Handled Tray	$12-15
9" Plate	$6-8	Platter, any size	$8-10
8" Plate	$8-10	Nappy, any size	$7-9
7" Plate	$5-7	Baker, any size	$7-9
6" Plate	$4-5	Coupe Soup	$6-8
Fruit Cup	$3-4	Cream Soup	$18-20
Oatmeal	$5-6	Cream Soup Liner	$10-12
Teacup	$6-8	Bouillon	$10-12
Saucer	$2-3	Bouillon Liner	$6-8
A.D. Cup	$10-12	Casserole	$20-25
A.D. Saucer	$5-7	Covered Butter	$12-15
Covered Sugar	$8-10	Jug, any size	$12-15
Creamer	$5-7	Teapot	UND
Sauceboat	$10-12	Egg Cup	$15-20
Gravy Fast stand	$12-15		

Old Roman

Old Roman is one of the most intriguing lines Homer Laughlin produced. Very little is known about this shape, however a brief history can be pieced together based on the examples found thus far. First, the shape for Old Roman can best be described as a scalloped shape with gadroon edge and rim embossing. The flatware – plates, saucer and bowls are basically Newell pieces with added embossings. The known hollowware: creamer, sugar, and teacup were specially made for Old Roman.

Old Roman is not at all readily available. The known pieces have been found in light yellow glazes and the solid color, Sea Green. Usually they are marked, "Wells Art Glazes" or "Old Roman." There are some examples that sport decal treatments, but most Old Roman found today will be in a solid color with no other types of decoration.

Unfortunately, Old Roman isn't found with date codes in its backstamp, but its safe to say it was made in late 1930 to early 1931. This estimate is based on several reasons. First, the assortment includes a square plate which is the Wells square plate with the Old Roman embossed design. (Interestingly, the Newell-type gadroon edge found on every other piece of Old Roman wasn't added.) Secondly, the Wells Art Glazes marking found on Old Roman wasn't used until 1930 on pieces made in solid colors, namely the Wells shape itself. Finally, the first journal of Rhead's that HLC has is from 1931. In it he makes the following entry on March 20, 1931: *Old Roman sprayed cup badly peeled. Too heavy yellow glaze and heavy color.* He never mentions the Old Roman shape again in the '31 journal or any year that follows.

The dinner plate, glazed in sea green, is backstamped, "Old Roman" (with no mention of Homer Laughlin). You may find some solid colored Old Roman with the Wells Art Glazes backstamp as well. The green coloring brings the embossing to life which is not easily achieved with the standard yellow glaze the shape usually receives. Like Trellis, the general shape of the flatware including the gadroon border is taken from the Newell shape.

Old Roman rim soup and creamer in the green glaze. While the flatware is a modified version of Newell, the hollowware was specially created.

Old Roman "square" plates. The one in the background has the "Old Roman" backstamp.

Old Roman fruit cup.

Old Roman saucer with the Wells Art Glazes mark.

Assortment and Values for Old Roman:

9" Plate	$12-15	9" Baker	$15-18
6" Plate	$8-10	Teacup	$12-15
Square Plate	$18-20	Saucer	$5-7
Rim Soup	$12-15	Creamer	$15-18
Fruit Cup	$8-10	Open Sugar	$20+

Orbit

The Orbit line consists of flatware from Brittany or Rhythm (depending on the treatment) and specially made hollowware. These hollow pieces, coffeepot, shakers, teacup, sugar, creamer, sauceboat fast stand were modeled in November/December of 1962. The covered butter was modeled in February of '63 and the line was put into production soon after.

The majority of flatware comes from Brittany – a plain round rim shape, but there are a few treatments that make use of Rhythm – a plain round coupe (rimless) shape. All the bowls come from Rhythm. A full breakdown of flatware is given in the values section. Only the flatware (excepting bowls) receives decal decorations along with colored trim. 12" Chop plates were called for in the new Orbit line, but since a chop plate didn't exist in Rhythm and the Brittany example was 13", two 12" chop plates in the Rhythm and Brittany style had to be created.

The decals are stylized and bold using only a few tones. The hollowware's exteriors are done in solid colors to match the trim of flatware done in blue, green, gold and tan. This makes any piece of hollowware usable with several different types of decaled Orbit flatware. If you find a piece of flatware (plates, platters or a saucer) then it is easy to determine the color of the corresponding hollowware. However, since hollowware is found in solid colors only, such pieces can belong to several lines.

Expect most flatware such as the dinner plates, platters, chop plates and large serving bowls to have a general HLC backstamp. The smaller flatware and all of the hollowware are always found unmarked. Since flatware has the general HLC backstamp, there is also a date. The latest date found on Orbit flatware so far is 1970.

Orbit is an interesting line to collect, especially the hollowware. The pronounced cylindrical bodies and oddly shaped handles combine to make a unique design. Even the shakers are atypical with their slender and tall appearance. Most of the Orbit pieces are not too hard to find. The coffeepot and sauceboat stand are the only two standard items which pose any kind of challenge. The teapot and covered casserole were modeled in 1969, but its not certain if they were put into production. Orbit was one of the first lines designed by Vincent Broomhall who became Art Director at HLC in October of 1962.

The Orbit creamer in tan – one of the four exterior glazes.

Orbit plate with the "October Leaves" treatment. Its easy to tell from the colors in the decals and trim that this calls for tan hollowware.

8½" serving bowl with tan colored interior.

Orbit coffeepot, covered
sugar and creamer in green.

Orbit covered sugar and creamer in blue.

Orbit shakers and covered butter in green. Unlike other
pieces of Orbit that take a lid, the covered butter will have
the lid in a solid color and the base in plain white. The butter was picked up by other lines including Sheffield
Amberstone and Coventry Casualstone which primarily
used Fiesta shapes.

1960s ads showing "Fashion" and "Trent" on the Orbit shape.

Assortment and Values for Orbit:

Flatware Brittany or Rhythm (decaled)

12" Chop Plate	$6-8
10" Dinner Plate	$3-4
7" or 6" Plates	$1-2
Saucer	$1
11½" Platter	$3-5
13" Platter	$6-8

Flatware: Rhythm (colored)

Charm House Cereal	$1-2
Coupe Soup	$1-2
Nappy (interior color)	$2-3

Hollowware – Exterior solid colors. Lids should be white and each piece has a white tapered foot.

Covered Sugar	$5-7	Sauceboat Fast stand	$8-10
Creamer	$3-4	Covered Coffeepot	$15-20
Shakers, pair	$5-7	Butter dish	$5-7
Teacup	$1-2		

Ravenna & Orleans

These lines are being presented together since they are very similar in design and were developed at the same time. The general description for the flatware for Ravenna and Orleans is the same: round scalloped shapes with heavy embossed rims and fluted verges. New collectors have a hard time telling the two apart, but after viewing a few pieces, the differences become very noticeable. On the left is an Orleans plate in an art glaze and to the right is a decaled Ravenna plate. There are two major differences: 1. Orleans has small flur-de-lis shapes around the rim. This results in little "bumps" in the outline. 2. Orleans has fewer and wider flutes at the verge; Ravenna verge flutes, or ribs, are very narrow. Their flatware may be similar but their hollowware is very distinct. Ravenna's has a rim — an uncommon feature on HLC dinnerware whereas Orleans' is much more conventional.

Ravenna was the first to be modeled. On August 27, 1931, Rhead notes, *"Worked on Rose 7" plate (Ravenna.)"* He continued to model this plate – which actually measured 9" since Rhead used trade sizes in his notes – along with a 5" (actual size 7") plate until August 31st. At the time, work was proceeding slowly with Jade and for the month of September, sketches for both shapes were being made and reviewed. In October there was little activity with Ravenna. The only piece Rhead even mentions that month was a 9" nappie since work was focused on Jade and the Apple Tree bowls. However, on November 2, 1931, J.M. Wells approved the Ravenna shape and ordered the following to be made (actual sizes): 12" platter, sauceboat, casserole – with and without cover, 10" and 6" plates, and an 8" deep plate with the note: "large as possible." For the rest of November, Ravenna pieces were modeled and decaled samples of flatware were being made to be shown to various buyers.

Ravenna wasn't even four months old when, on November 30, J.W. Wells orders a "modeled plate for Woolworth's." By December 14th, the new modeled plate was produced. J.M. Wells took samples of the new plate, called Orleans at this point, along with sketches of teacups to New York. Two days later on the 16th, Rhead notes: *"JMW phoned from NY that Frantz* [buyer for Woolworth's] *was interested in modeled plate."* By then most of Ravenna had been modeled with the exception of the sauceboat which was finished on December 21st. Many collectors are surprised that HLC would produce two very similar shapes. Keep in mind that Ravenna was made for the general trade while Orleans was originally intended as an exclusive.

On January 18, 1932 new items were ordered to be added to Orleans. Most of these new shapes were pieces of hollowware which were totally dissimilar to their Ravenna counterparts. The new items are listed in Rhead's journals as: teas, 6" baker, 36 bowl, 7" dish [platter], 4" fruit, 6" nappie, oatmeal, 4", 5", 6", 7", 8" plates, 6" deep plates, cream, open sugar, 8" dish, 7" nappie, and a 7" coupe soup.

In February, most of the Orleans pieces were being modeled and Ravenna with decals was being made for buyers such as J.C. Penney. More items were ordered to be added to Orleans in March and April: 36s jug with cover, cream soup, 10" dish, casserole and casserole cover. New pieces were also ordered for Ravenna: 7" baker and a pickle. These would be the last pieces made for the line. There was a jug ordered for Ravenna in August 1933, but it was never modeled. The actual date Ravenna was discontinued isn't clear, but most agree it was by the late 1930s.

While Ravenna was short lived, Orleans continued to endure. Orleans patterns were being made in late 1932 and for 1933 more pieces were made in February: 8" baker, 6" dish, 5" fruit, 8" nappie, 36s jug. It was made with decals and various platinum trims for Woolworth's and continued with very little change until March 1936 when the sugar was remodeled to accept a lid and the covered casserole was made. On June 8, 1936, samples of Orleans were ordered in the Art Glazes. This is the only date Rhead gives for Orleans in Art Glazes, and they must have been accepted since Orleans has been found in at least two Art Glaze colors: peach and rust. Orleans Art Glazes was given a special name, "Antique Orleans" and even had its own backstamps.

Along with decals and art glazes, Orleans was made with several transfer designs. Orleans was phased out by HLC in the late 1940s. Some pieces have been found with backstamps dating as late as 1946. While it was produced for almost 15 years, examples are not easily found today. Plates and platters may be common, but the hollowware – sugars, creamers, casseroles, etc. are rather difficult to find. This is also the case with Ravenna.

Because of the similarity in flatware, Orleans and Ravenna are often confused for one another. As already stated, their hollowware is very different. This may be why Orleans was more successful than Ravenna. There weren't too many companies producing hollow forms with rims. Taylor Smith and Taylor produced such a line called, "Marvel" released in 1932 – the same year as Ravenna. Marvel was produced for several years and is easy to find today. Perhaps this competitive line is another reason why Ravenna failed. Ironically, in early 1933, HLC would adopt five pieces from Marvel's line to produce "breakfast sets" for Quaker Oats and called this new shape, "Chelsea."

Expect to find Orleans with a general HLC backstamp except for those pieces in art glazes which will be marked either "Antique Orleans" or simply, "Antique." There were two marks used with Ravenna. The first was the name "Ravenna" in caps and the other is the general HLC mark.

Ravenna Examples:

This marking makes no reference to HLC or any date. If a piece of Ravenna is found marked, it will either have the type shown, or a generic HLC backstamp with date code.

Shown is a dinner plate with a luster trim and colorful birds decal. The exact same treatment decal and luster trim was also used by Harker, Knowles and several other potteries of the Ohio River Valley area.

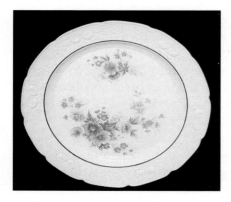

Ravenna dinner plate with floral decal.

Wild poppy decal on a Ravenna Platter.

Ravenna open sugar and creamer.

Ravenna sauceboat.

Orleans Examples:

"Antique Orleans" is a line which uses the Orleans shape in solid colored glazes. At least two such glazes have been accounted for: peach and rust from Wells Art Glazes. The marking used on these pieces simply says, "Antique Orleans" with no mention of Homer Laughlin. Since Orleans blanks would ordinarily receive a generic HLC backstamp, the Antique Orleans must have been special order since pieces were specially marked. Of Homer Laughlin's colorware lines, this is most difficult to find.

Markings found on rust glazed Orleans saucer and platter.

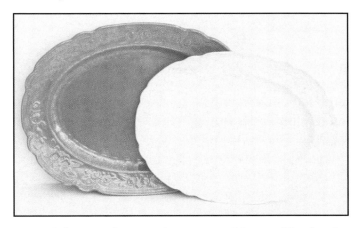

Orleans platters in rust and ivory. The back-stamp on the ivory platter is from 1946.

The Orleans fruit cups and saucer have a triple platinum ring set.

The creamer has a floral decal treatment common to the Orleans shape: O-79. The oval baker has a red transfer design of a castle. This was decorated in the same manner as other transfer lines; Willow, Americana, etc.

Very hard to find Orleans jug.

The Orleans sugar is the second style that was first made in March 1936. The original version from 1932 was an *open* sugar and the tops of the handles were placed high on the base and ended at the opening. Though an open example isn't shown, the placement of its handles is very much like that shown with the creamer which underwent no changes during its production run. When it was decided to add a cover to the sugar, the older open version had to be remodeled since the handles were in the way of the lid. The *covered* sugar has the tops of its handles placed lower on the body.

Orleans dinner plate with tulips. This treatment was also used on Virginia Rose.

Assortment and Values for Ravenna:

10" Plate	$12-15
9" Plate	$8-10
8" Plate	$10-12
7" Plate	$6-8
6" Plate	$4-5
Teacup	$6-8
Saucer	$2-3
Sugar	$12-15
Creamer	$8-10
Sauceboat	$12-15
Rim Soup	$6-8
15" Platter	$15-20
13" Platter	$12-15
11" Platter	$10-12
Pickle	$10-12
Fruit Bowl	$4-5
36s Bowl	$10-12
Nappy	$8-10
Baker	$8-10
Casserole	UND

Assortment and Values for Orleans:

10" Plate	$8-10
9" Plate	$7-9
8" Plate	$10-12
7" Plate	$5-6
6" Plate	$4-5
Teacup	$8-10
Saucer	$2-3
Sugar, open	$10-15
Sugar, covered	$25+
Creamer	$6-8
Sauceboat	$12-15
Rim Soup	$8-10
15" Platter	$12-15
13" Platter	$10-12
11" Platter	$10-12
Pickle	$8-10
Fruit Bowl	$5-6
36s Bowl	$10-12
10" Nappy	$10-12
9" Nappy	$8-10
8" Baker	$8-10
9" Baker	$8-10
Casserole	$50+
Jug	$30-35

Regency

The Regency shape was first developed from the end of December 1965 to June 1966. The first few items were test pieces such as the teacup and creamer. These new items had "ribs on bottom" as noted in the modeling log. Three 10" plates – with and without ribs were then produced. Work on developing Regency stopped in mid January 1966 while one of the newest shapes, White Dover, was expanded. On February 26, attention was again given to Regency and a "straight" cup with ribs was made. Most of the standard Regency items would soon follow.

From March 1 to July 1, the following pieces were modeled for Regency: Saucer, two styles of cups, coffee pot, sugar, creamer, sauceboat, sauceboat stand, lug soup, 7" plate, casserole, fruit, 10" and 9" nappies, 11" and 13" platter, butter cover, coupe soup, chop plate, two teapots, jumbo cup, salad bowl, snack plate and shakers. While a total of three cups had been designed, only one was put into production. There were also various finial or "knobs" under consideration for lids. Unfortunately, sketches for these alternates are not in the modeling log. The butter was made up of the base from Orbit and a lid made with the Regency ribs.

In September 1966 some changes were made. The Regency sauceboat was remodeled and three new items were added: 5" dish, coffee saucer (to go with the jumbo cup,) and a 6" plate. After the modeling of these three pieces, there were no more items added, nor were any of the existing shapes revised.

Compared to other shapes which were introduced in late sixties such as Orbit, White Dover and Granada, Regency is rather hard to find. Flatware is rather easy to come by, but the hollowware can be scarce. Expect only large pieces of flatware to have a general HLC backstamp along with a year. Though most of the pieces from this line are unmarked, there should be no confusion with other shapes. The ribs can be found on every piece including small items like fruit cups and saucers. Expect hollowware to have exterior colors with white lids and flatware to have stylized treatments. Regency was only made for a few years so the number of decorations available is limited. Official Regency treatment numbers have the prefix, "Reg."

Regency shape coffee server and teapot.

Malibu (Reg-801) is the name of the decoration on the 10" plate. Also shown is the Regency sauceboat.

This is one of the Sheffield lines discussed in the section on Markings. Its called, "Sheffield Serenade" and comes complete with a handled tray.

Regency shape teacup and shakers.

Values for Regency:

Plates, any size	$2-3	Shakers, pair	$5-6
Fruit Cup	$1	Casserole	$12-15
Lug Soup	$1-2	Coffeepot	$12-15
Teacup	$1-2	Teapot	$8-10
Saucer	$1	Butter	$4-5
Sugar	$5-6	Handled Tray	$3-4
Creamer	$4-5	Platters	$3-4
Sauceboat	$4-5		

Republic

Republic was introduced in 1915. In one ad, it was offered as a shape that, "*. . . has been produced in obedience to popular demand. Excepting the hollowware, we do not claim it for any degree of originality.*" The ad does state that when it comes to decoration, they, "do claim originality." At least eight American pottery companies produced a shape similar to Republic. Prior to the late 1920s, it was common for potteries to purchase molds from a single supplier. Harvey Duke writes in his book on Pottery and Porcelain (see bibliography) that all of these shapes were based on Havilland's Ranson shape. The flatware for all of these lines are the same but the hollowware will have subtle differences. The finials on HLC's are rope-like but with W.S. George's they are more bow-like.

Republic had an assortment of approximately 70 items. As the years went on, most of these items became discontinued. Lines from the early 20th Century often had five to seven sizes of platters, bakers and nappies. This "overkill" of shapes was further extended with a round casserole as well as an oval version. It was typical for lines from circa 1900 such as The Angelus, Hudson, Kwaker, Empress, Genesee, Niagara and Republic to have very extensive assortments.

Sometimes the rim embossings are confused with Marigold and Virginia Rose. (See the Virginia Rose section for a comparison of the various embossings.) At least one treatment was offered on Republic in the late 1960s so its production run extends almost fifty-five years. For the entire run, Republic was marked with a general HLC backstamp and date code.

Almost every piece of Republic found will have floral decals. The demitasse cups and saucers were picked up by Tango rather late in its run and was offered in Fiesta red, Harlequin yellow, blue and Spruce green. If any other shape is found in solid color glazes that is also unmarked, then it is almost certainly a W.S. George piece. They made their Raddison shape (the name for their version of Republic) in various solid colors primarily in the 1930s. Scio's version, called Ransom, is sometimes marked with a USA impressed mark. All other companies making shapes similar to Republic will have appropriate backstamps with the companies name so there should be very little confusion.

An early Republic covered sugar with gold stamp decoration.

"Priscilla" on a Republic sugar. This decal is easy to find on Nautilus and Kitchen Kraft. It's rather difficult on Modern Farmer. The treatment was also used by Universal Potteries of Cambridge, Ohio on Camwood Ivory – a plain round rim shape.

Not only does the Republic shape get confused with Virginia Rose, but so do some of its treatments. This one in particular always seems to be misidentified as VR-128, Fluffy Rose and sometimes as JJ-59, Moss Rose. While the colors and shapes of the flowers may be similar (especially with VR-128) the arrangements are distinct. Its official number is: R-3543.

"Pastel Rose" Republic Baker.

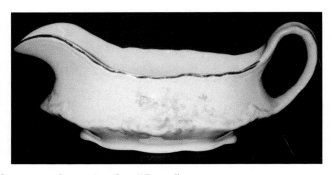

These two photos show a cup and saucer and a sauceboat in the "Jean" treatment – a common decoration on the Republic shape.

This dinner plate has a grouping of colorful pastel flowers which can also be found on Virginia Rose.

This Republic plate has a gold garland/chain treatment that is more common on the Liberty shape.

From a distance, this plate looks like Marigold since it has a "silver stamp" treatment which is in the style of Marigold embossing. When viewed up close, its revealed that its in fact the Republic shape and, according to the backstamp, it was produced in the early 1950s.

"Susan" is the name of the treatment on the Republic shape in this late 1940s ad from Montgomery Wards. The yellow and orange floral decal was also used on Kitchen Kraft. To the left of Susan is "Gold Circle" on the Virginia Rose shape.

Assortment and Values for Republic:

10" Plate	$8-10	Covered Butter	$20-25
9" Plate	$6-8	Platter, any size	$10-15
8" Plate	$10-12	Nappy, any size	$7-9
7" Plate	$5-6	Baker, any size	$7-9
6" Plage	$3-4	Coupe Soup	$6-7
Fruit Cup	$3-4	Casserole, round	$12-15
Oatmeal	$4-5	Casserole, oval	$15-18
Teacup	$4-5	Jug, any size	$15-18
Saucer	$2-3	Teapot	$25-30
A.D. Cup	$8-10	Oyster Tureen	$20-25
A.D. Saucer	$5-7	Covered Sauce Dish	$18-20
Covered Sugar	$10-12	Ladle	$25+
Sauceboat	$6-8		
Gravy Fast stand	$10-12		

Rhythm

In 1948, HLC started work on a new shape for Woolworth's. Several different designs were considered for ringed hollowware, but it was evident that from the start the flatware should be coupe shaped. On November 12, 1948, a 10" plate was listed as: *8" Plate M – Coup*[e] *Woolworth.* A second Woolworth plate was modeled on January 17, 1949 this time with a "ringed center." Two other items were made that year: April 17, Cup, Lined for Woolworth and July 1, Woolworth Cup with Rings. No other pieces were modeled the entire year while the Art Department worked on developing the Charm House shape.

When Charm House was basically complete, attention was given to the "Woolworth" line. The 10", 9", 8", 7", 6" plates, a remodeled teacup, fruit cup, sugar and cover, creamer, 9" nappie (casserole base), casserole cover and coupe soup, were all modeled from March 3 to June 22, 1950 – all without rings. Work on the new line was suspended from June 24 to July 17 while the necessary changes were being made to the Jubilee shapes for Skytone.

Two new pieces were added at the end of the summer of '50: the sauce boat on August 22nd, and a teapot on September 14th. These pieces were still being referred to as "Woolworth" shapes or as "WW Coupe." The modeling log listing for the sauceboat indicates it was released into production on September 25th. This is the only release date listed for the Woolworth coupe line which was named, "Rhythm."

Several shapes were remodeled over the years and there were only a few new pieces added. The water jug was modeled on July 3, 1951 and the 15" platter on February 13, 1952. The snack plate – which is only found in solid colors – is also not explicitly listed in the log. There are, however, multiple listings for various "T.V. Plates" and one of these may be the standard Rhythm snack plate.

Rhythm had two pick up pieces. The shakers came from Swing and the soup/cereal bowl is from Charm House. It can be identified by the distinctive mushroom shape and was commonly marked with the Rhythm backstamp. Examples with the Rhythm backstamp can be found in sets of Dura-Print and another 50s shape that picked up the bowl; Cavalier. In turn, the Charm House shape picked up the Rhythm sauce boat to replace the gravy fast stand.

Rhythm was sold through Woolworth's but it was also picked up by virtually every other retailer of the 1950s. Coupe shapes were very popular and almost every company was making them. Universal's Ballerina, Knowles' Accent, Taylor Smith & Taylor's Versatile all had the same general "look" of HLC's Rhythm and and were released around the same time. Rhythm was made in solid colors and with a wide range of decals – both stylized and realistic. No matter what the decoration, pieces are marked with the same "Rhythm" backstamp with a date code. Official numbers for Rhythm decals start with an "RY."

There are several highly collected treatments on Rhythm. The "American Provincial" treatment consists of a set of decals which vary from one piece to the next. For example, dinner plates will have a farmer and his wife, water jugs will have a bird and the sauceboat will have a simple flower. The solid colors, chartreuse, gray, maroon, dark green and Harlequin yellow, were very popular in the 1950s. Since many companies made shapes similar to Rhythm and in similar colors, its easy to confuse one maker with another. In almost every case, Rhythm will be marked as such.

Based on backstamps and vintage ads, it's reasonable to say Rhythm was not made beyond 1963. While the hollowware may have been discontinued then, the flatware was used with several other shapes from the late 1960s into the early 1980s.

Backstamp for Rhythm.

Oval platter in maroon. Sometimes Rhythm and other 50s dinnerware shapes, like Universal's Ballerina or Salem's Ranchstyle can be confused with one another. These other shapes have *round* serving trays and platters, Rhythm's are *oval*.

Glazed in Harlequin yellow, these Rhythm salt and pepper shakers were borrowed from the Swing shape.

Rhythm sugar and creamer in gray. The creamer shown is the taller of two sizes. Both sizes seem to be equally as common whether they are in solid colored glazes or with decals.

The "small" Rhythm creamer is back-stamped 1951 and is glazed in rose. While this color was used in the Harlequin and Fiesta lines at the time, it wasn't standard for Rhythm. It is shown with a Charm House sugar in maroon for color comparison.

The divided snack plate was made in solid colors only.

Desert Flower is the name of the treatment on this platter. All the flatware from the Desert Flower line comes from Rhythm, but the hollowware is solid color Charm House in chartreuse.

"White Flower", shown on a small Rhythm platter, was sold exclusively through J.J. Newberry Co. and its official number is JJ-152.

The white Rhythm jug is more than likely an untreated blank. This piece, along with the 15" platter, was never meant to be dipped in the solid colors and usually have decal treatments.

Here we have a comparison of two 50s lines which often overlap. The yellow creamer is a piece of Charm House hollowware. This is part of a set where the flatware is Dura-Print. (See Charm House for more on Dura-Print.)

The creamer in gray is the "tall" Rhythm creamer. The handles are very similar on the two pieces, but every piece of Charm House will

have a mushroom shape. Rhythm's is more straight sided with a tapered base.

This shape sauceboat was used with both Rhythm and Charm House (Dura-Print and Applique) hollowware. Expect to find it in solid colors not standard in Rhythm, but ones that are standard with Dura-Print such as turquoise, brown and black. The treatment on the Rhythm sauceboat shown is from the American Provincial (RY-104) line.

Cherry Blossom treatment with gold trim.

Oriole decal (FP-67) on Rhythm.

Tall creamer in chartreuse, 10" plate and sauceboat with stylized treatments.

Wheat Pattern on Rhythm.

"Gold Crown," with the Lifetime China backstamp, was made with Rhythm flatware and Cavalier hollowware.

This "Wells High School" decorated Rhythm plate was given to graduating seniors in 1962. The W. E. Wells High School was located across the street from the Newell plants. The building still stands, but it is no longer used as a school.

While spoon rests may have been designed for Rhythm in solid colors and decals, they have been found in Harlequin colors and with Dura-Print treatments.

Rhythm cup and saucer with Duratone creamer.

Assortment and Values for Rhythm:

10" Plate	$8-10	15" Platter**	$15-18
9" Plate	$6-8	13" Platter	$12-15
8" Plate	$15-18	11" Platter	$12-15
7" Plate	$4-5	9" Platter	$8-10
6" Plate	$2-3	Fruit Cup	$2-3
Teacup	$5-7	Cereal (Charm House)	$5-6
Saucer	$1-2	Coupe Soup	$6-8
Snack Plate*	$30-35	Nappy	$6-8
Tall Creamer	$4-6	Casserole	$20-25
Short Creamer	$6-8	Teapot	$18-20
Sugar	$6-8	Water Jug**	$18-20
Sauceboat	$5-7	Spoon Rest, Solid Color	$150-175
Shakers (Swing)	$6-8	Spoon Rest, Decaled	$45-50

* Solid Color Rhythm only
** Decaled Rhythm only

KK Bowls in Rhythm colors:		Fiesta Juice Set in Rhythm – 50s – colors:	
6" in dark green	$125+	Juice Pitcher in gray	$2000+
8" in Harlequin yellow	$100+	Tumbler	$500+
10" in chartreuse	$175+		

Serenade

The development of Serenade can be summed up in one word: rushed. On December 8, 1938, Rhead notes: *JMW ordered new spiral shape modeled for January.* The first pieces of Theme were being designed and modeled at the time, but both Rhead and modeler Al Kraft immediately worked on a 10" "Spiral" plate. More than likely Kraft modeled the body of the plate and Rhead worked on the rim embossing. On the 10th, Rhead sketched two "Spiral" casseroles and notes that J.M. Wells picked one with a "convex top cover." By the 14th four pastel glazes were chosen.

During the last week of December, the shape had been approved and was named, "Serenade." It was decided to make a new backstamp and to model more pieces. From the 1st of January, 1939 to the first week of February, all the standard Serenade pieces were modeled. There were only minor alterations such as a modification to the teapot cover and to the tea saucer. The first teacup handles were also replaced since, as Rhead notes, the handle was, "too heavy."

While the Serenade shapes were developed with ease, the same cannot be said for the glazes. There was no trouble noted with green and yellow, but blue and pink presented some problems. Rhead notes that some of those working on Serenade's development didn't like the blue being used. There are several notes that Serenade blue was, "too gray." Also, there was problems with the pink glaze.

On January 18, 1939 after several trials of pink, Rhead notes: *Serenade pink glaze not right.* He also mentions several blue samples, but considering the gray cast found on blue Serenade found today, they must have been rejected. By mid February, there were still problems with pink. On the 13th Rhead records a possible solution: *Suggested to A.V.* [Albert Victor Bleininger who worked mainly on clay and glaze development at HLC until 1945] *that we make a light salmon terra cotta to replace the present Serenade pink which is not yet right. A.V. states that he is trying #7 kilns where there are no chrome fumes.* Rhead never again writes of the salmon terra cotta. A pink glaze was finally accepted late February and samples of Serenade and other shapes such as Virginia Rose,

Nautilus and Century 6" plates were being made in four "Serenade glazes."

By April 1939, Serenade, with its shapes, glazes, pamphlets and backstamps, was complete. Rhead notes some dissatisfaction with this line on May 10, 1939: *Serenade being shipped. Fair results in color. Would have like to have had more to try with regard to glazes. Texture and colors not good enough.* The line was offered for the first time in trade publications on July 1939.

Why was HLC in a hurry to market Serenade? The answer lies with Taylor Smith & Taylor's Lu-Ray Pastels which had been released a year earlier. Its pastel glazes were a sharp contrast from the bold Fiesta-like colors and became an instant best seller. Several pottery companies released similar lines soon after Lu-Ray Pastels became popular. Other such lines were "Deanna" by Knowles and "Elmhurts Pastels" made by W.S. George. They were first offered to the public at the same time as Serenade, and while Deanna had some success, Elmhurst Pastels was a poor seller. Despite being produced into the 1940s, Serenade never gained the wide spread popularity of Lu-Ray Pastels.

Serenade was HLC's first pastel colored line. The matte textured pastel glazes were used with another HLC shape, Nautilus, and a special Serenade Kitchen Kraft casserole was made as a promotion for Royal Metal and M. Seller's (for more, see sections on Nautilus and OvenServe). In 1948, HLC would make another attempt with pastel glazes in the form of Jubilee. Keep in mind that Serenade, Nautilus and Jubilee were the only shapes HLC made in pastel glazes. "Shenandoah Pastels" was made by Paden City Pottery of Paden City, West Virginia, though some make the mistake in labeling it as HLC.

Reverse of a promotional pocket calendar from the early 1940s.

Serenade dinner plate in the standard blue pastel glaze.

This Serenade 9" plate in a rich turquoise glaze is on display at HLC. It may have been a color under consideration to replace the standard blue which Rhead called "too gray".

Teapot in pink and shaker in yellow.

Pickle dish in green.

Creamer and sugar in pink.

Serenade Assortment and Values:

10" Plate	$15-18	Chop Plate	$18-20
9" Plate	$8-10	12" Platter	$15-18
7" Plate	$6-8	Pickle Dish	$10-12
6" Plate	$5-7	Sauceboat	$8-10
Teacup	$8-10	Shakers, pair	$10-12
Saucer	$2-3	Nappy	$18-20
Fruit Cup	$4-5	Casserole	$20-25
Lug Soup	$6-8	Teapot	$75+
Deep Plate	$6-8	KK Casserole (see Royal OvenServe)	
Sugar	$10-12	base only	$40-45
Creamer	$6-8	lid only	$100+

Skytone & Suntone

Skytone

The concept for Skytone was the same as Kraft Blue; blue body (Jubilee) shapes with white handles and finials. Before the line could be produced, three changes would have to be made in order to get the desired blue/white contrasting effect. The handles and finials on Jubilee were applied except in three cases; the teapot, coffeepot and creamer. With these three pieces, the handles are actually part of the body resulting in one piece.

In the summer of 1949, special molds were made separating the handles from the bases of the teapot, coffeepot and creamer. With this change, the handles could be made in a white body and then applied to the blue bases. With the addition of a lug soup (which came from Debutante), Skytone was ready to go into production.

Skytone was offered by various retailers and was a good seller all through the 1950s. Pieces can be found plain or with decals. Almost all of the Skytone decals are highly stylized floral treatments that resemble one another. It's not unusual to find a set with two or more different decals. Though produced for over ten years, there are not very many different Skytone decals when compared to the vast number used by other decalware.

It's also not surprising to find Kraft Blue shapes mixed in with Skytone sets. The Kraft Blue shape was made into the mid 1950s. Due to this overlap, Kraft Blue and Skytone often share shapes and decals – in some cases, they even share backstamps. (For more, see section on Kraft Blue.)

Because it was such a good seller in the 1950s, Skytone is very easy to find today. Collectors can afford to discriminate against pieces with scratched decals and worn platinum trim. Flatware and larger hollowware commonly have the Skytone backstamp. More often than not, there is also a date code.

Marking.

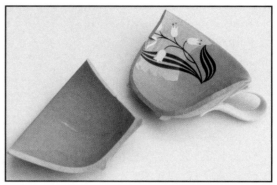

This broken teacup reveals the blue clay used in all Skytone pieces.

Outside and inside covers of a Skytone brochure.

The "Stardust" treatment (HLS-180) is by far the most common decal found on Skytone. Shown are the creamer, 6" plate and covered sugar. This decal can be found on Cavalier as "Grey Dawn."

Salt and pepper shakers with the HLS-205 decoration. This is one of the few Skytone treatments which uses pink in the flowers.

This Skytone plate has two unusual features: a stylized decal of three birds (usually Skytone decals are floral in nature) and thick platinum trim.

The decal on the teacup is called, "Blue Mist" and its official treatment number is HLS-230. It was sold through Montgomery Wards in the mid 1950s. Shown with the teacup is a plain and harder-to-find demitasse cup.

To the right is the gravy fast stand with the "Marcia" treatment. This was sold through Sears in the mid 1950s. When Skytone was first offered, the fast stand bowls, decaled or plain, were done in blue and the attached saucer in white. Sometime around 1955, both components were made in blue only. There are a few fast stands that have been found with the *bowl* in white and the *base* in blue however these are much harder to find than the other two versions. To the left is a Marcia serving bowl with the official treatment number, SR-180. Generally, Skytone treatment numbers begin with HLS, but in this case, the SR stands for Sears and Roebuck.

Sometimes when the Marcia treatment is found on Skytone dinner plates and platters, there is a double marking in gold. It is Sears' special "Harmony House" mark they commonly placed on their dinnerware lines no matter which pottery made them. Keep in mind that "Harmony House" is a Sears marking, and not HLC's.

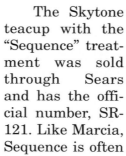

The Skytone teacup with the "Sequence" treatment was sold through Sears and has the official number, SR-121. Like Marcia, Sequence is often found with the special Harmony House backstamp. Sometimes collectors call this "Atomic" because of the intertwined swirls.

The Skytone fast stand with a blue base and white top are the most difficult to find of the three versions. In the background is a 10" plate with the HLS-247 treatment.

Skytone serving bowl with the gold stamp decoration: PG-113.

Skytone demitasse cup and saucers are hard to find, but this example is unusual in that the saucer is marked, "Kraft Blue." Is this a mistake or did Kraft Blue, which was in production at the same time as Skytone and used the same blue color clay, pickup the demi cup and saucer?

This OvenServe custard was made in the same blue clay used with Kraft Blue and Skytone. It is the only one known at this time.

Suntone

Suntone is the same as Skytone but with a brown or dark terra cotta clay used for the bodies. The handles and finials are the same white bodied versions used in Skytone. However, there are several differences between these two lines. First, Skytone was sold either plain or with decals. Suntone is found plain. While there are decorated Suntone examples at HLC, none have been found on the open market. One such decoration was a dark green treatment similar to Quaker Oats' Pastoral.

Suntone is marked much in the same manner as Jubilee. It carries the line's name and the fact that it was made at Homer Laughlin, but there is no date code. In contrast, Skytone almost always has a date code.

It should also be noted there are miniature Suntone cups and saucers. These were salesman samples from the 1950s to promote the line. Don't expect to find Skytone versions of these mini cups and saucers.

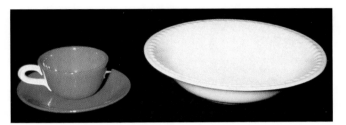

The Suntone mini cup and saucer was a salesman's sample. It is shown with a Kraft Blue 6" oatmeal for size comparison.

Suntone 7" plate, fruit cup, teacup and saucer.

Items marked with an asterisk have white handles and or finials. The small end of the double egg cup many also be white. As with Debutante, the Jubilee shape cereal/soup bowl was replaced by a lug soup. Skytone and Suntone have a piece not found in Jubilee: the 15" platter. (Note: covered butters with a blue lid and a white base are more than likely part of HLC's Orbit line. For more, see section on Orbit.)

Assortment and Values for Skytone & Suntone:

10" Plate	$6-8	Egg Cup	$12-15
9" Plate	$4-5	Gravy Fast Stand	$8-10
7" Plate	$2-3	Covd. Casserole	$15-20
6" Plate	$2-3	Covd. Sugar	$7-9
Teacup	$4-5	Creamer	$4-5
Coupe Soup	$4-5	15" Chop Plate	$8-10
Lug Soup	$4-5	Shakers, pair	$7-9
5½" Fruit	$2-3	Coffeepot	$20-25
11" Platter	$6-8	Teapot	$20-25
13" Platter	$6-8	AD cup	$18-20
15" Platter	$10-12	AD saucer	$8-10
7½" Nappy	$8-10	Mini Cup/Saucer	$75+ (rare)

There is an unusual purple/silver marbleized glaze showing up Skytone and Rhythm. This may be on individual pieces, but most of the time, it's found on tidbit trays that were assembled outside the factory. There is no information on this glaze (which has also been found on shapes from other potteries) and it may be the case that Skytone and Rhythm examples with this glaze are not official HLC products.

Swing

The development of Swing is unlike any other dinnerware line. The first piece created for this line was described as PLAIN PLATE, 7" NO MODELING, ROLLED BALL. This was noted on March 1937. The second piece was another plain plate and the sketches for both of these plates is very similar to the Swing we know today. A third very simply designed plate was modeled, but then development was put on hold for several months during which time attention shifted primarily to Kitchen Kraft.

What happens next is a little surprising. Work resumed on Swing in late September 1937 and the next plate modeled is described as, PLATE, PLAIN BUT WITH RAISED BAND ON RIM. The next fifteen plates modeled are variations of lines or rings, beads, lugs – both rounded and square. Next was the teacup. Eight different styles as diverse as the 7" plates were considered.

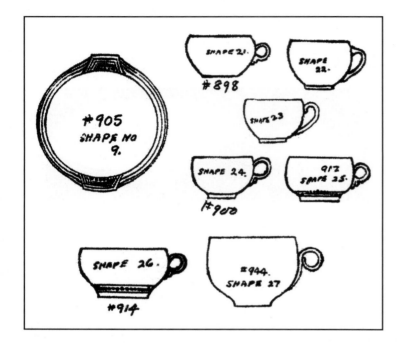

The plate, model 905, is just one of the many styles considered for the flatware for Swing. Its combination of beadwork, rings and lugs are a far cry from the plain round shape eventually decided upon. Also shown are the seven styles of teacups modeled during Swing's development. Like the prototype plates, none were ever released into production.

The covered casserole was the next item to be made and there are no surprises here. In all, six very similar casseroles were modeled by October 1937. Also modeled at this time was the saucer, oatmeal and the nappie.

Before development continued, it was finally decided that the first plate modeled would be the style for all other pieces of flatware. The eighth style teacup was also chosen. What started out as a very plain round shape and evolved into a collection of beaded and ringed embossed rims eventually became what it started out as: a plain round shape! The name given to this new shape was, "Convex."

After the basic style and name was chosen, all the other pieces were modeled; various sizes of plates, several different shapes of sugars, but all with the same style, and a fast stand (covered sauce dish).

By early November 1937, the name Convex was changed to "Swing" and more items followed; bakers, A.D. cup and saucer, cream soups, lug soups and creamers. It is also during this month that many items were released and production of Swing began. In December more items were modeled such as the gravy boat, various lug soups, celery tray, two shapes of shakers, and a coffeepot (26 oz.) In early 1938 more items were added to Swing; individual coffeepot (16 oz.), individual creamer, teapot and the handles on the sugar, sauceboat and casserole were made to be applied rather than cast on. The last major items added were the individual sugar and muffin cover in June 1938 and the only revision was when the spout on the teapot was restyled.

Official treatment numbers for Swing start off with an "S" but sometimes end in either a "P", "C" or "G". These suffixes were used to denote the colors of the handles and finials for some lines. The "P" was for pink bodied handles and finials and the "C" were for blue (Celadon) versions and "G" for green. If a treatment number is found in the form: S-105-C, then the hollowware for that line is going to have blue handles and finials. The pink, blue and green colors are in the body of the clay and are not applied colors.

The "Swing Eggshell" backstamp was only used for a few years and then dropped for the more generic "Eggshell" backstamp so that it could be used with both Swing and Andover which shared flatware.

Here is a comparison shot of the demitasse and regular cups and saucers found in Swing. The treatment on the regular cup and saucer is very common and popular on Swing: Colonial Kitchen. This decal also appears with red trim on Rhythm and Nautilus, and with gold trim on Virginia Rose and Liberty. In one vintage ad, the decal if referred to as, "Colonial Hearthside." The official number for Colonial Kitchen on Swing is S-179 and when it appears on Nautilus, N-1747.

The demitasse cup has small rose sprigs with gold trim.

This platter has two markings: the common "Eggshell" mark and "American Vogue" with the treatment name, "Belle Fleurs." The official number for this decal is VM-107 with the "VM" standing for "Vogue Mercantile," a company which sold glass and pottery in the 40s and 50s. Here the treatment is on Swing, but it can also be found on Nautilus Eggshell with the same type of special American Vogue backstamp.

The Swing regular sugar and creamer has the "Alameda" decoration. Its official number is S-131-C.

The Swing demitasse (A.D.) sugar and creamer has a Dogwood treatment. The A.D. sugar is the same as the A.D. cup without the handle.

The decal on this Swing 6" plate is called, "Conchita." When found on Kitchen Kraft shapes, the official number is KK-326.

The handles on Swing coffeepots and AD coffeepots were originally circular, but after a few months of production, the applied handles were restyled in an oval shape. Coffeepots (as shown) and AD coffeepots are very similar in appearance. Their major difference lies in their capacities.

The little daisy sprigs on this Swing demitasse cup and saucer are the same that are commonly found on Modern Farmer. It may be that the Swing A.D. cup and saucer was picked up by the rippled shape.

The creamer has no treatment except for the pink colored handle. The piece to the right is a gravy fast stand or covered sauce dish. It has the very popular Calirose decal. Sears sold this decal on the Swing shape – complete with pink border and pink handles – as "Moss Rose" in 1940.

"Calirose" is one of the most popular treatments on Swing. Here it is shown on a Swing 6" plage and an Eggshell Nautilus 6" bowl. Sears carried the Calirose treatment on Swing and called it, "Moss Rose." The decal can also be found with yellow trim on Eggshell Nautilus and with blue trim on Rhythm.

Andover

Andover Eggshell was made for Carson Pirie Scott & Co. of Chicago, Illinois. The first time Rhead mentions the line was on March 1, 1941: *Letter from Chicago office on Carson's Wishmaker. Make new hollowware for Swing flatware. Submitted sketches.* Two days later, Rhead notes the treatment for this line as, "Feather and Ribbon." This treatment would undergo many changes over the next few months.

Originally, the decal was to be a "Feather and Ribbon" design, however, on March 28, 1941, Rhead notes making: *a Star and Ribbon treatment with gray band and gold edge painted by Decal Products.* Soon after, on April 7, Rhead notes: *Its now a Feather plate with ribbon....*

On April 8, 1941, J.M. Wells approved sketches for the teacup, sugar, creamer, casserole, fast stand and cream soup. They were modeled from mid May to the beginning of June 1941. Rhead also noted that the "dish and baker" which he sketched for this line was not to be made. These pieces were unlike other HLC products in that each had a cylindrical pedestal with rings. The log notes that the line was released into production on June 26, 1941. Two more items were modeled at the end of June: the nappie and a "shallow" bowl.

In the middle of modeling the hollowware another change occurred with regard to the treatment:

5/21/41 *Joe Fenchlenger* [of the Chicago office] *& J.M.W. on Carson Wishmaker. Southern Potteries have copied Czech feather pattern. Consequently Carson's are switching over to the Ribbon & Star. Phoned Decal Products to find status of feather patterns. Just being proofed. Told them that we are changing to Ribbon pattern. Will delay delivery two weeks.*

With the treatments and shapes finally in place, it was time for a name for the new line. On June 27, the day after it was released into production, Rhead drew a new backstamp sporting the name, "Arcadia Eggshell" along with a note that a new generic "Eggshell" mark would be made for Swing so that the flatware and certain pieces of hollowware would be used with the new line. On the 30th of June, Rhead notes the name of the new line was changed to Andover Eggshell. On July 8, 1941, Rhead makes a sketch of the generic "Eggshell" backstamp which was used on both Swing and Andover.

All the flatware (saucers, plates, platters, bowls) for Andover is the Swing shape, but once in a while a set of "Ribbon and Star" can be found with the Swing shape teapot and the Swing shakers. Perhaps it may be revealed that other Swing hollowware was used such as demitasse sets.

"Ribbon & Star" low bowl with a cup and saucer. This treatment was often offered as "Gordon."

"Ribbon & Star" flatware. These pieces are marked simply "Eggshell" but since the decal was an exclusive, they can be identified as Andover and not as Swing.

Of all the Swing hollowware, only the teapot and shakers were used Andover. Here is the Swing shape teapot with the Ribbon & Star treatment. This is actually the second of two teapots modeled for Swing. The creamer is the Andover shape.

The modeling log sketch of the original Swing teapot is shown here. It's listed in the log as being modeled in March 1938 and as having a capacity of 37 ounces. Three months later, the teapot was remodeled. The original spout was too short and had an irregular opening. The second version was made with a longer spout and more conventional opening. Swing teapots are rather scarce. Of the ones found so far, all have been the second (longer spout) style.

This utility tray comes from Swing flatware. Only Fiesta, Swing (and consequently Andover) were given oblong utility trays intended for sugars and creamers.

A blank Andover cream soup cup.

Values for Swing and Andover:

Flatware:		Swing Hollowware:		Andover Hollowware:	
10" Plate	$8-10	Sugar	$10-12	Sugar	$6-8
9" Plate	$7-9	Creamer	$6-8	Creamer	$4-5
8" Plate	$8-10	Teacup	$4-5	Teacup	$2-3
7" Plate	$5-6	Casserole	$25-30	Casserole	$18-20
6" Plate	$3-4	Cream soup/liner	$12-15	Cream Soup	$10-12
5" Fruit Cup	$3-4	Fast Stand	$18-20	Fast Stand	$12-15
6" Oatmeal	$4-5	Teapot	$55+	Shallow Bowl	$4-5
15" Platter	$12-15	Shakers	$8-10	Nappie	$6-8
13" Platter	$10-12	Muffin Cover	$30-35		

Values for Swing and Andover Continued:

Flatware:		Swing Hollowware:	
11" Platter	$8-10	A.D. Pot (either handle)	$45+
Deep Plate	$5-6	A.D. Sugar	$12-15
Saucer	$1-2	A.D. Creamer	$12-15
Oval baker	$6-8	A.D. Cup	$6-8
Nappie	$6-8	Eggcup (Wells shape)	$8-10
Utility Tray	$10-12		

Tango

The basic shape for Tango flatware started out in several different forms. In July of 1936 two designs were considered which resemble the familiar Tango plate and were called, "Sweedish." For the next few months, work on Tango was put on hold while attention was given on developing Harlequin and other shapes. In late September of 1936, work resumed on Tango with the modeling of two sizes of teacups. Finally, in October, the flatware was put into place with a modification of the Swedish designs from July 1936 and the name "Tango" was applied.

Various sketches of Tango when it was under development.

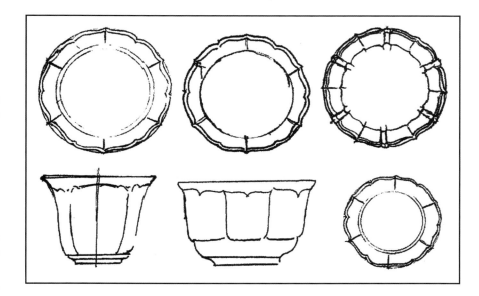

After a final design of flatware was decided upon, the other pieces were soon added. All the pieces a collector would expect are listed in the mold notes along with two unexpected entries. The first is of a Tango cream soup cup modeled in January of 1937. This is the only piece that was modeled that you won't find on the open market since there is no notation of this being released into production. The second concerns the teacup handle. The body of the teacup was settled on in October of 1936, but the curled teacup handle wasn't modeled until February of 1937. A second handle was modeled two months later – this time without the curled upper portion. Both styles of handles are found in today's collector market.

At one point some pieces of Tango were considered for Quaker Oats. During this time, the name Tango wasn't being used. Rhead states in his journals on September 21, 1936: *J.M.W. thought that Swedish type short set for colored glazes the right thing for Q.O.* There are also entries discussing making decaled Tango pieces for Quaker Oats, but to date, no evidence has been found that supports Tango was actually used by Quaker Oats – solid colored or decaled. However, a set of shapes called, "Italian" was developed similar to Tango. These were sold through Quaker Oats in the late 1930s as "Tea Rose."

Colors found with Tango are: maroon, spruce green, medium (mauve) blue, Harlequin yellow. In 1941, maroon was discontinued and red served as a replacement. Since the Century shape has no salt and pepper shakers, the Tango shakers were borrowed to be used with Riviera. If you find these in light green or ivory, then they belong to Riviera. In spruce green or maroon, the shakers are Tango. And finally, if they are in red, blue or Harlequin yellow, then they can be either Riviera or Tango since both lines share those three colors.

Tango casseroles and other hollowware forms are very hard to find and have risen dramatically in price over the past few years. Even the simplest of pieces, such as flatware, command high prices when placed on eBay. The hardest pieces to find are the demitasse cups and saucers which originated with the Republic shape, but were picked up by Tango. They can be found in red, yellow, blue and green. To date, none have been found in maroon.

There are some collectors who insist a double egg cup was made for Tango even though there is no evidence in the modeling log or in Rhead's journals that HLC ever made one.

This decaled teacup comes from the Homer Laughlin archives.

Plates in Harlequin yellow and spruce green.

Platter in maroon and oval baker in spruce green.

Tango cups can be found with two different handles as shown. On the left is the first version with the top of the handle curled. The second version on the right has handle with a plain top.

The regular Tango teacup with a Republic demitasse cup and saucer in red. Republic demitasse cups and saucers have been found in all the Tango colors except maroon, so it is most likely that they were picked up after the red glaze replaced maroon.

Tango deep plate in maroon, sugar and creamer in spruce green.

Shakers in blue and red. Since these colors overlap with Riviera, they could belong to either line. There's no shortage of Tango shakers. Overstock and their conjunction with Riviera account for their large numbers.

Tango Assortment and Values:

10" Plate	$18-20	11½" Platter	$18-20
9" Plate	$12-15	Fruit Cup	$5-6
7" Plate	$10-12	Coupe Soup	$12-15
6" Plate	$8-10	Baker	$18-20
Teacup (either handle)	$12-15	Nappy	$18-20
Saucer	$4-5	Shakers, pair	$8-10
AD Cup (Republic)	$45-50	Covered sugar	$18-20
AD Saucer (Republic)	$10-15	Creamer	$12-15
Casserole	$40-50		

Theme Eggshell

The original concept for Theme was taken directly from a very popular line of Jasperware made by Josiah Wedgwood & Sons of England. The new line was to have "slip decoration" which involves placing relief designs made from colored slip onto the surface of dinnerware. In this case, the slip decoration was made in the blue clay used for the handles and finials of certain Swing lines as well as the main body of Kraft Blue. The plate shown is on display at HLC and shows how the modeled fruit border was made in the blue clay, applied to a white Nautilus plate and then given a clear glaze.

Plates and cups with slip decoration were made in early October 1938 and are listed in the log as having, "Wedgwood embossed work." For the rest of the month and into December, more pieces of the new shape were made including nappies, various styles of teacups, plates, platters and saucers. The raised sprigs would also undergo several changes resulting in varying widths. By the end of November, Rhead was referring to the new line as "Theme."

Various Theme teacups under consideration in 1938.

From the end of December to the end of January, work was suspended on Theme while shapes were being created for Serenade. On January 29, 1939, with majority of Serenade modeled, Rhead makes several notes on Theme. He states that the line is "going out minus the blue slip treatment." From then on, shapes are modeled with the raised relief as part of the mold. All previous models and samples were shelved and development resumed the first week of March 1939. The embossing collectors know of today was chosen at this time and work would continue on creating new shapes based on this wide relief into the first week of June 1939.

There was a point when it wasn't certain if it was to be of regular body or in the eggshell weight which was new at the time. On March 24, 1939, Rhead notes in his journals: *G. Pittenger in. Asked if "Theme" is to be in "Eggshell." Price lists are made out for Eggshell. Told him to see J.M.W. who will be back today. Samples are in talc body and have been made light. Do no know definitely if the product is to be "Eggshell."* As collectors know, all vintage Theme was made in the eggshell weight.

A few late additions were made to the Theme shape. The teapot was created in the Fall of 1940 and would undergo a change in the shape of its spout in June 1942. The last standard piece added to Theme was the square plate which was released into production on May 7, 1941.

Theme Eggshell was discontinued in the late 1950s. Almost every decoration encountered will be floral decals, though there are some silver and gold band decorations and several rare examples in solid colored glazes. It was very common for outside decorators to use the Theme Eggshell dinner plates for church plates and other commemorative pieces. For more information on these items, see "Decorators" in the Appendix.

The wreath Theme marking is the most common type. It replaced the early and more deco styled marking around 1940.

The Sauceboat, stand (9" platter), and shakers all wear the same Apple Blossom decal used in the very early 1950s.

Theme cream soup cups are rather difficult to find. Here they are shown with the "Regency Theme" treatment. Not only did Theme have cream soup cups, but also lug soups and deep plates.

Sears sold this pattern as "Surrey" (TH-17). It must have been a very good seller since pieces with this treatment have date codes from 1940 to 1949. You may find this decal on other HLC shapes, such as Georgian Eggshell as G-3361, but it is more common on Theme.

The demitasse cup has no decal and isn't the easiest piece of Theme to find. As with almost every HLC cup, don't expect to find these marked.

Theme Eggshell covered sugar and creamer with colorful decals.

Both dinner plates are glazed in the same Spruce green used with Harlequin and Tango. Some collectors report other colors such as turquoise and cobalt. It's a shame Theme wasn't produced in solid colors in greater quantity since the embossing comes to life with colored glazes.

Vintage

In the 1980s, Theme shapes were again put to use. The flatware and teacup were made with new versions of a sugar, creamer, shakers and two new pieces; a coffeepot (as shown) and bud vase. The reissue hollowware is a teardrop shape with the modeled border low on the body. The new shape was named, "Vintage" and treatment numbers have the same "TH-" prefix as the older version. This doesn't cause a problem since the older decals start with TH-1 and reissue ones start with TH-100.

Vintage has been made in both a semi-porcelain and hotel bodies. There should be no problem in determining an older piece of Theme from the newer Vintage line since only the older line is marked with "Theme Eggshell" backstamps; Vintage almost always carries a general HLC marking.

Assortment and Values for Theme:

10" Plate	$10-12	Lug Soup	$8-10
9" Plate	$6-8	Cream Soup	$12-15
8" Square Plate	$10-12	Rim Soup	$6-8
7" Plate	$4-5	15" Platter	$15-18
6" Plate	$3-4	13" Platter	$8-10
Teacup	$6-8	11" Platter	$8-10
Saucer	$2-3	9" Platter	$10-12
Covered Sugar	$8-10	Fruit Cup	$3-4
Creamer	$6-8	Oatmeal	$5-6
Sauceboat	$8-10	Nappy	$6-8
Gravy Fast Stand	$15-18	Baker	$6-8
Shakers, pair	$12-15	Casserole	$25-28
Chop Plate	$12-15	Teapot	$45+
A.D. Cup	$10-12	Cream Soup Liner	$10-12
A.D. Saucer	$6-8		

Trellis

Trellis was first offered to the public in 1928. The flatware is basically the same as Newell but has periodic embossings on the rim of two different "trellis" designs. The hollowware has a "flat" look in contrast to the rounder Newell shapes.

The line was used as a basis for Quaker Oats promotions. Such pieces are marked simply, "Trellis." Otherwise, pieces will carry the general HLC backstamp. If a piece of Trellis has a single digit such as "1" or "2" as the year for the date code as in B1 N8 or D2 N8, then it is from 1931 or 1932. Many make the mistake that these pieces are from 1921 or 1922. For a more detailed explanation, see section on Markings at the beginning of the book.

Most treatments used on Trellis are stylized floral decals, but some solid colors such as green and yellow are also found. Another type of treatment which seems to be unique to Trellis involves the handles and finials with hand painted trim work in either green, orange, black, platinum and various combinations of the four on the light yellow glaze.

Trellis flatware isn't terribly difficult to locate, but the hollowware is a different story. The line was discontinued shortly after 1932 making its production run less than six years.

Embossing detail.

Shown are the 9" plate, 6" plate, coupe soup and fruit cup from Trellis. These are similar to Newell pieces with regard to the overall scalloped shape and gadroon embossing except these have trellis embossings on the rim. The glaze on these pieces is a rich yellow – not ivory – that was used on Trellis, Orleans, Old Roman and Wells during the very early 1930s. The yellow glaze tends to "pool" around the verge of flatware creating discolored areas. This transparent glaze is also subject to crazing.

The Trellis creamer and sugar shown has the rose decal which was used in the Quaker Oats promotions of the very late 1920s. They are marked simply, "Trellis."

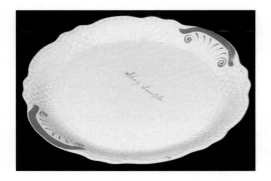

From the HLC factory is this Trellis handled tray which has one of the many types of hand-painted trim treatments often found on Trellis. In the center is written, "Shop Sample."

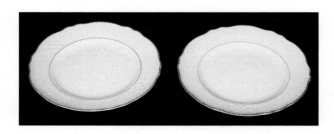

These 7" Trellis plates are on display at Homer Laughlin. They are marked on the reverse as being Quaker Oats samples.

This 6" plate is in the "Sea Green" glaze that was used during the late 20s and early 30s. This glaze was also used on Old Roman and Coronet.

Assortment and Values of Trellis:

10" Plate	$12-15	Milk Pitcher	$15-18
9" Plate	$8-10	Oatmeal	$5-6
7" Plate	$5-6	Fruit Cup	$4-5
6" Plate	$4-5	Rim Soup	$8-10
Teacup	$6-8	Coupe Soup	$10-12
Saucer	$2-3	Handled Tray	$15-18
Sugar	$10-12	Oval Baker	$10-12
Creamer	$6-8	Nappy	$12-15
Casserole	$30-35	Oval Platter	$12-15
Teapot	$75+		

Triumph

In the mid 1950s, the United States dinnerware market was flooded with Japanese imports. These lines were made in a true china (porcelain) body. Most American potteries produced semi-porcelain or pottery bodies. There are several differences between these two types of wares. The most obvious is that china is translucent – light can pass through the body of a piece. The new shapes being imported held a certain appeal. They were often offered in catalogs as "Fine China." The treatments were graceful and the shapes elegant.

In order to compete, many potteries started to experiment with China bodies. In the late 1950s, Homer Laughlin would create at least two "Fine China" lines. The Triumph shapes were first modeled in December of 1958. The line was released into production in the new year in late January 1959. There were several interesting shapes modeled for this line, such as a divided baker, footed cake stand, and a dinner bell. Based on vintage ads, none of these shapes were available.

The flatware for this line is typical of the late 1950s: plain, round and rimless. The hollowware has a conical form with a stretched look. When pieces have a backstamp, the treatment name is often included.

Here is what one vintage ad said about the then new Triumph shape: "TRIUMPH brings the graciousness of beautiful American china to today's informal living. Combining Old World charm with New World simplicity, the sculptural theme compliments both the traditional and contemporary setting. Featuring a swan-white background and simple gold or platinum bands, TRIUMPH durable china is available in many distinctive and decorative patterns."

There are some lines, especially the Hand-Decorated Serenade line of the early 1960s, that use the Triumph shapes in a semi-porcelain body. Most often they are the Triumph sugar and creamer with exterior solid colors.

You might not be able to find a diverse selection of decals on Triumph that you might encounter with other shapes. Shown is "Woodland" which seems to be the most common treatment on the Triumph shape.

Triumph coffeepot with the "Woodland" treatment.

Triumph sugar and creamer decorated with "Linda."

Ad from the 1960s featuring "Pastel Rose" on the Triumph shape. Its official treatment number is TR-21.

Triumph Snow White

In the early 1960s a line of HLC dinnerware was offered through Von's and Shopping Bag. Pieces could be purchased out right or with special coupons. The line was called, "Triumph Snow White" and should you find pieces, the backstamp will have the standard Triumph logo and the line name, Snow White.

The Snow White sugar, creamer and teacup have more rounder bodies compared to those from the standard Triumph line.

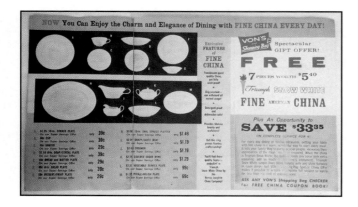

Triumph Snow White Brochures from 1963.

Triumph Snow White sugar and creamer.

Triumph Snow White cups and saucers.

This photo of a Snow White creamer with a light inside shows the translucent property of china.

On the right is the standard Triumph shape cup and saucer but to the left is the Triumph Snow White creamer with a rose decal. Almost every example of Triumph Snow White will be undecorated.

Assortment and Values of Triumph and Triumph Snow White:

13" Oval Platter	$7-9	8" Vegetable Dish	$5-6
11" Oval Platter	$7-9	7" Vegetable Dish	$5-6
Pickle/Relish	$5-6	8" Coupe Soup	$4-5
10" Dinner Plate	$6-7	Fruit Cup	$2-3
8" Salad Plate	$5-6	Covered Sugar	$5-6
6" Bread/Butter Plate	$4-5	Covered Casserole	$12-15
Teacup	$4-5	Sauceboat	$7-9
Tea Saucer	$1	Creamer	$2-3
A.D. Cup	$5-6	Coffeepot	$12-15
A.D. Saucer	$1-2	Shakers, pr.	$4-5

Victoria

Victoria was developed towards the end of 1964. There's a major problem surrounding this swirl shape: almost every piece is unmarked, including the large flatware (plates, platters). There is at least one exception: "Sheffield Bone White." As the name implies, the body has a white glaze with no trim or decal decoration.

The Bone White backstamp has mentioned that the ware is made in the USA, but there isn't any indication as to the maker, in this case, Homer Laughlin.

You may find Sheffield Bone White marks on another line of Swirl dinnerware that was made in Japan, but that line has nothing to do with Homer Laughlin. Royal China also made a line of Swirl dinnerware in the 40s and 50s, but it will generally be marked. For hollowware, HLC's Victoria will have a little "lump" towards the bottom of the handles. This can be found on the casserole, teapot, coffeepot, creamer and sugar. Also, Royal's version will have flattop handles. There should be little confusion between Victoria and other companies swirl shapes.

Victoria seems to have been made for a short period of time. Mold notes indicate some pieces were revised in 1965, but no new items were added. The assortment is straight forward with the most basic of serving pieces. Calendar plates were made using Victoria blanks for the years 1966, 1967 and 1968. The 1966 version is on a plain white blank while '67 and '68 examples have silver trim.

Note the stretched look to the Victoria shakers – this will help you differentiate them from other swirl shape dinnerware lines. The saucer has silver trim and no decal. It comes from a line called, "Silver Swirl" and its official number is V-110.

This casserole is from "Sheffield Bone White." Keep in mind that hollowware with handles will have the little lumps towards the base of the handles. You will also find a Sheffield Bone White handled tray (similar to the ones found in Sheffield Granada and Sheffield Amberstone).

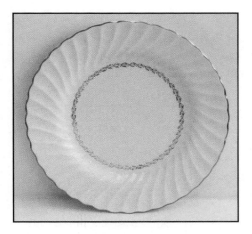

Victoria dinner plate with silver trim and verge treatment.

Covered sugar and creamer with a blue floral decal.

Victoria coffeepot with rose decal and a teacup with the "Star Flower" decal. This treatment can also be found on Georgian Eggshell and Cavalier.

Assortment and Values of Victoria:

Plates, any size	$2-3	Shakers, pr.	$3-4
Fruit Cup	$1	Casserole	$8-10
Lug Soup	$1-2	Coffeepot	$8-10
Teacup	$1-2	Teapot	$8-10
Saucer	$1	Butter	$3-4
Sugar	$3-4	Handled Tray	$3-4
Creamer	$2-3		

Virginia Rose

There is no pattern, decal, or treatment called, "Virginia Rose." The name Virginia Rose refers to a specific SHAPE of dinnerware. This shape has two very common decal treatments: VR-128 a.k.a. "Fluffy Rose" and JJ-59 a.k.a. "Moss Rose" and dealers and novices tend to think these two decals *are* Virginia Rose.

The confusion arises because of the backstamp. It is the same as the general backstamp HLC used for a great number of years, except the shape name, Virginia Rose, is included. Since VR-128 and JJ-59 are by far the most common treatments on this shape, people take it for granted that "Virginia Rose" in the backstamp refers to the treatment.

Two of the most common decorations on the Virginia Rose shape:

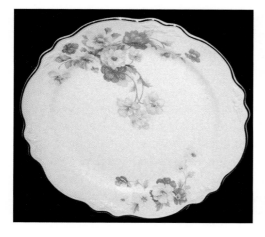

VR-128 "Fluffy Rose" Plate made for G.C. Murphy's

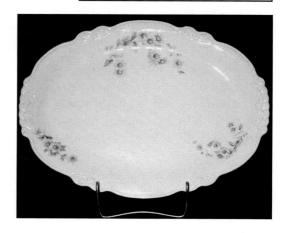

JJ-59 "Moss Rose" Platter made for J.J. Newberry's.

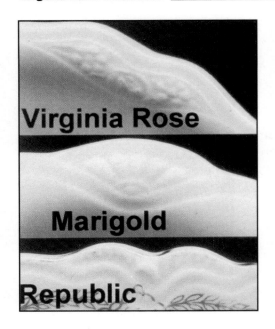

The shape is a round scalloped rimed form with periodic embossing. Marigold and Republic can be defined in these general terms and quite often they are confused with VR. To make matters worse, these other two HLC shapes wear floral decals which are either identical to those on VR or very similar.

Virginia Rose started out with one piece listed in Rhead's journals simply as a "modeled edge plate." Work began on the new shape on July 12, 1932. It would take two months and at least four revisions of the modeled edge plate before a final design was approved. Before a name was selected for the new line, Rhead often referred to it as "Rose Medallion" – an appropriate name for the small rose embossings. At first, work progressed slowly on Rose Medallion since the Art Department was creating shapes for Orleans, and Rhead was working on patterns for Jade and other existing shapes. During this time, several plates, bowls and a saucer were modeled, but it was on November 6, 1932 when Rhead notes, "Commenced modeling new shape." A week later on the 14th, he uses the Virginia Rose name for the first time. It has been well documented that this name was given in honor of Virginia Rose Wells – sister of J.M. Wells.

On November 22nd, one of the first Virginia Rose shapes, the 9" plate, was released into production. Others soon followed and by the end of December the following items were being made: casserole, teacup, saucer, oatmeal, gravy boat, fast stand, pickle, 10" plate, 11" platter, 13" platter, sugar, creamer and fruit cup. Only the teacup, sugar and creamer underwent revisions since the originals were, in Rhead's words, "thought to be too small."

On January 3, 1933, Rhead expressed enthusiasm for the new line in his journals stating: *Virginia Rose line selling favorably, promise of good business.* The line was expanded in January '33 with the 9" baker, 10" and 9" nappies, 6" plate, large cake plate, cream soup cup, cream soup liner, syrup, deep plate, 8" plate, and the 15" platter. More pieces would follow in the months ahead such as a batter jug in March, and the 8" baker, 9" platter, and 6" fruit bowl in April. The last piece added to Virginia Rose was the coupe soup on August 3, 1934 – almost two years after its original conception.

No new pieces were added to Virginia Rose after the fall of 1934, but it did "pick up" some generic pieces as well as some from existing lines. The cable egg cup and Jade butter dish are often found in Virginia Rose sets as is the Baltimore mug and Swing salt and pepper shakers. Once in a while a piece of Marigold shows up in a Virginia Rose line, but this is often a mistake. These two shapes were basically made side by side and are very similar with regard to size and style. Its not unheard of to find a Virginia Rose cup on a Marigold saucer or a stack of eight desert plates with seven being Marigold and one Virginia Rose.

Rhead's entry from January 3, 1933 about Virginia Rose promising "good business" was almost prophetic. The line was produced for 37 years from late 1932 until 1968. Since Virginia Rose was produced for such a long period of time, it was used as a basis for more decal treatments than any other shape. Besides the treatments made for the line, many decals which originated with preexisting shapes such as Wells and Yellowstone seem to have made their way on to Virginia Rose. The decals made for Rhythm, Cavalier and Debutante in the 1950s also were applied to Virginia Rose. Spanning four decades of varying styles of treatments makes for a diverse decal library for the Virginia Rose shape.

This 13" platter has a backstamp from 1947 and has an unusual petit point windmill treatment. Blue trim and silver stamps complete the decoration. One collector reports finding the same treatment on Virginia Rose plates but with red trim.

"Tulips in Basket" is the name of the colorful treatment on this VR platter. Shown with silver trim, it can also be found with gold, red, blue, yellow and black trim as well as none at all.

One of the many different "silver stamps" treatments, this was purchased from a set in which there was a baker with a proper ID number: VR-254. Shown is a 9" plate, sauceboat and covered sugar.

The teacup has the simple and very easy to find "Patrician" treatment. The cream soup has a decoration that is much harder to find. The 6" plate has "Garland" in silver. There is a variation of this treatment: the exact same garland treatment but with a center medallion. Garland treatments are also found on Century and Yellowstone.

"Colonial Kitchen" on a Virginia Rose fruit cup and a Swing 6" plate. Expect to find this treatment on Liberty, Rhythm and Nautilus as well.

The little rose buds on the cup and saucer are also found on Wells.

Silver stamp decoration on the verge. The official treatment number is VR-260.

Virginia Rose decorated with pink floral decals from 1941.

The 9" plate in the background has an odd silver stamp decoration from the mid 1930s. In the foreground is a 9" plate with a large yellow rose decal from the early 1950s.

Floral decal fruit cup and a 7" plate with a gold medallion decoration.

The 7½" jug and 5" jugs are often found without lids as shown. If you're lucky enough to find either with a lid, then its usually part of a batter set with the larger jug acting as a batter jug and the smaller as a syrup pitcher. The smaller jug has a treatment that was exclusive to Woolworth's. Its official number is W-137.

The cream soup cup has been given gold trim and is backstamped: WARRANTED 18K GOLD. This was a very simple and common type of decoration which was also applied to other HLC shapes such as Empress and Yellowstone.

The focus on this picture is on the very rare cream soup liner. It is basically the 7" plate with a saucer well for the cream soup cup – a piece which is almost as rare as the liner itself. The treatment shown is VR-108 and almost every piece I've seen with VR-108 has been crazed. Since crazing is a result of the body and clay expanding and contracting at different rates (and NOT necessarily a sign of age) its possible that HLC would set aside crazed pieces, apply a "bottom shelf" treatment like VR-108 and sell the pieces at a cheaper rate.

This "Red Water Lily" decal was used extensively by W.S. George and the Cronin China Co. It is not very common on HLC's Virginia Rose shape.

These blue medallion (VR-456) fruit cups came from the same set. Five of the six fruit cups have decals like that on the right: two large sprigs and two small ones. The remaining fruit cup is shown on the left: four large sprigs.

"Spring Wreath" Virginia Rose covered casserole.

Shown are two rim soups. On the left is "Spring Wreath" and to the right is a ring decal treatment with the official number, VR-104.

The official number for this rose decal on the coupe soup is VR-269 and originated on the Wells shape as W-7133. Expect to also find it on Yellowstone and Eggshell Nautilus. Unlike the rim soups, coupe soups are more continuous and "dish" like. Along side the coupe soup is a VR 7" plate wearing VR-118 - a floral decal common on the Century shape.

The Virginia Rose dinner plate with pink/gray floral decal from the very late 1940s was also used on Georgian Eggshell and Liberty.

"Louise" – a common treatment originally sold through Sears.

This single rose decal, shown on Virginia Rose, but commonly found on Century, has an unusual look. It has a unique depth which makes it look like it has been applied to glass rather than pottery.

The floral decal with its pink and lilac colors is shown on Virginia Rose, but was also used on Marigold.

This plate is marked with a 1934 backstamp and has a chrysanthemum decal common on Yellowstone. Though its not captured in the photo, the plate has a very rich ivory glaze.

Date codes for the decal with the hand-painted look indicate production from the mid 1950s. It would be interesting to see how this elongated treatment translates onto hollowware such as sauceboats and casseroles.

The smaller plate has verge decal. What's interesting is this treatment originated on the Kwaker shape as K-49 and appeared on the rim. On Virginia Rose, it is used on the verge.

This is one of the more colorful VR treatments with clusters of red, yellow and blue flowers and was made primarily in the mid 1930s. It also appears on Century.

The official number for this common rose decal is VR-233. It was also used on Marigold.

It may be safe to say that the VR-135 decal appears on more shapes than any other HLC treatment. It is shown on Virginia Rose, but also appears on Century, Liberty, Ravenna, Republic, Yellowstone and others.

The red pig decal has been found on pieces made by several different pottery companies. In HLC's case, it was used on Marigold and Virginia Rose. The 6" plate has an ornate medallion decal.

The tulip decals on this Virginia Rose plate were used mainly by W.S. George and Universal Potteries. HLC also decorated Kitchen Kraft with the colorful decals.

This 6" plate has unusual orange decals and trim. As you can see in the image, the decal is in great shape, but the trim is "chipping" away – characteristic of cold paint. "Cold paint" generally refers to colors which are applied over the glaze. Since they lack protection, they tend to wear away.

This 11" platter has a combination of roses and daisies and has colors which are similar to several other VR treatments. Its official number is VR-387 and records indicate this treatment was done for Neisner Bros.

Oval baker with VR-142 treatment.

This rim soup not only has a bold decal, but also a bold golden luster trim.

Two similar yet distinct VR floral treatments; the teacup has a decal which was also used by W.S. George. The soup bowl has the "Nosegay" decal.

Platter with three irises.

Oval baker with the VR-383 treatment.

The 6" plate at the top has a very common silver stamp decoration. At the bottom left is a decal commonly found on Newell and Yellowstone. It, along with the orange/green treatment on the right, is uncommon on the Virginia Rose shape.

The 10" plate has a long stem rose decal that was used on Georgian Eggshell and Liberty. On Virginia Rose, the decal is off center but on the other shapes, it is centered with small sprigs around the rim. The 8" plate is the rarest size among the plates. Shown is the cosmos decal commonly found on Republic.

Marked with a 1967 backstamp, the long stem rose decal on this round serving bowl may be among the last treatments used on the standard Virginia Rose shape.

Assortment and Values for Virginia Rose:

10" Plate	$10-12	Creamer	$5-6
9" Plate	$7-9	Sugar	$8-10
8" Plate	$15-18	Sauceboat	$8-10
7" Plate	$6-7	Gravy Faststand	$12-15
6" Plate	$4-5	Casserole	$25-30
Teacup	$5-6	15" Platter	$18-20
Saucer	$1-2	13" Platter	$12-15
Fruit Cup	$3-4	11" Platter	$10-12
Oatmeal	$6-7	9" Platter	$12-15
36s Bowl	$15-18	Coupe Soup	$12-15
Cream Soup	$45-50	Rim Soup	$8-10
Cream Soup Liner	$50-60	Baker, any size	$7-8
Batter Jug	$30-40		
Batter Jug lid	$20-30		
Syrup Jug	$25-30		
Syrup Jug lid	$20-25		

A VR-394 oval baker.

San Francisco treatment on the Virginia Rose shape. Los Angeles versions can also be found.

1950 Pink and grey floral treatment.

10" diner plate with stylized water lilies.

Pick Up Pieces

If a shape didn't have a particular item, then it could be taken from another rather than specially created. These are called, "pick up pieces" and Virginia Rose had them in abundance. The Baltimore mug, Jade butter, Cable eggcup, and Swing shakers are the most common of these pieces and usually have the JJ-59 or Moss Rose decal. Not every treatment on the Virginia Rose shape had the extensive assortment found with the popular patterns such as JJ-59 or VR-128 so trying to find egg cups for something like "Louise" on Virginia Rose may be an impossible task.

Values for Virginia Rose Pick-Up Pieces:

Onion Soup (Century/Coronet)	$50-60
Egg Cup (Cable)	$40-45
Butter (Jade)	$85-95
Round Butter (Republic)	$125+
Shakers (Swing)	$75-80
Mug (Baltimore)	$25-35

Sovereign Potteries

Rhead makes an interesting note in his journals on February 2, 1937: *VR molds for Sovereign Potteries, Canada.* Sovereign Potteries, or Sovereign Potters as it is also known, was a Canadian pottery located in Hamilton, Ontario. They began operations in 1933 and were known to import ware from American and British Potteries and decorate them. They also produced wares themselves including the Russel Wright Esquire line which was originally made by Knowles in the late 1950s.

So far, no Virginia Rose shapes have been found with a Sovereign Potteries mark. However, maybe someday examples of VR made in Canada may turn up. It would be interesting to have a whole new set of treatments on one of HLC's most popular shapes.

Wash Trims (a.k.a. Fade Away Trims)

The two pieces here make use of the Virginia Rose shapes, but they don't belong to any particular line of dinnerware. Starting in the 1920s, it was common for HLC to take serving pieces such as nappies, platters and trays and apply either a luster or wash trim along with a decal. In the Empress and Wells sections there are examples of pieces with luster trims.

Shown is a nappy and platter from Virginia Rose with wash trims and floral decals. Most of the time Virginia Rose is used, but some Marigold platters are showing up with the same textured wash trims. The lime green trim on the bowl is the most common, but there are varying shades of blue, yellow, browns and rose. There is a wide array of decals used – possibly overstock.

Expect most special pieces to be nappies and bowls, but sometimes other serving pieces such as bakers and sauceboats are found. Because these trims are not well protected, it is highly unlikely that wash trims will be found on the place setting pieces; cups, saucers or plates.

Sheffield Dresden

Sheffield Dresden is a line composed of standard Virginia Rose shapes such as plates, platters, cups, saucers, sugar, creamer and pieces made for the special line. These restyled and/or unique pieces received only the Dresden treatment: a blue onion design and are almost always unmarked. (For Fiesta collectors, Sheffield Dresden is similar to Sheffield Amberstone in that some pieces were restyled (mainly bowls) and others created (butter, pie plate, mug). For more on Sheffield, see section on Markings.)

The pieces created especially for the line were made from early May to late August 1963 and include: cereal bowl, chop plate, shakers, coffeepot, butter bottom and an ashtray. The cereal measures 7" and has a rim ("regular" VR small bowls are coupe shaped.) The butter bottom has the standard VR embossings and the top is a plain shape taken from Orbit. While older Virginia Rose picked up Swing shape shakers, the Dresden line had specially made shakers in the Virginia Rose style. Even the ashtray has the familiar embossings surrounding the cigarette rests.

A teapot was created in February 1967. When found, some collectors confuse it for a coffeepot. In May of the same year, a special mug was created for the Sheffield Amberstone line and was also used with Dresden along with a plain shape coaster. Since Dresden was discontinued shortly after 1967, the teapot, mug and coaster are rather hard to find today.

Dresden 7" cereal bowl.

Here are the standard VR shape sugar and creamer with the coffeepot created for Dresden all glazed in the same color used in Fiesta Ironstone. This photo was taken at the HLC plant, but

at least three sugars, a creamer and a teacup are known to exist outside the factory. This has led collectors to believe HLC officially made a tea set using the VR shapes and the antique gold glaze.

Special Dresden pieces:

Chop Plate	$10-12		Covered Butter	$12-15
Soup/Cereal	$3-4		Teapot	$40-45
Shakers	$18-20		Ashtray	$18-20
Mug	$4-6		A.D. Cup	UND
Coaster	$4-6		A.D. Saucer	UND
Coffeepot	$40-45			

Carolyn

According to the mold notes, this shape was first modeled in 1961. It is basically the Virginia Rose shape with the rose embossings removed resulting in a round scalloped shape. Carolyn has three qualities which further differentiate it from Virginia Rose.
1. Carolyn is hotel ware and has a much heavier body.
2. Carolyn is marked with a general HLC backstamp or "Best China."
3. Carolyn is limited in assortment.

Carolyn is still being produced for the restaurant trade today.

This Carolyn platter is glazed in mauve.

A comparison of Carolyn with Virginia Rose. Notice that both have the same general outline, but the Virginia Rose platter on top has embossing.

The teacup on the left is Virginia Rose. The custard on the right is from Carolyn which is just a restyled version of the VR teacup. There is no custard with the older Virginia Rose line.

Wells

Homer Laughlin introduced the Wells shape in 1930. Unfortunately, the first year Rhead kept a journal was 1931, so the development can't be traced. Hollowware was given applied finials and handles with little scroll decorations and the flatware consisted of plain round rim shapes. These flat pieces differed from HLC's other rim shapes Empress and Kwaker in that Wells' rim was much more concave and thinner. There is at least one creamer marked "Made In Japan" that is almost identical to the Wells creamer. Whether Rhead copied the design of Wells hollowware from an import or if it was the other way around isn't certain. Perhaps more MIJ "Wells" or vintage ads can be found and solve the mystery.

Wells started out in an ivory body with decals and in various solid colors. In early 1931, Rhead made notes in his journals about the Vellum glaze that was under development. In fact, numerous trials of Vellum were being made on the new Century shape as well as Wells and on April 27th, Rhead writes: .... *development in direction of Wells Vellum rather than Century Vellum.* Of course today collectors know that the Vellum glaze, while used on many shapes of the 1930s, was used much more heavily on Century than Wells.

Production for Wells was at a height in the early 1930s. It continued to be made into the mid 1940s, but on a much smaller scale. Originally the assortment was extensive with a demitasse set, cream soups, cream soup liners and muffin covers, but by the end of its run, Wells had been reduced to a simpler line with "standard" flatware and serving pieces.

Several pieces were picked up by other lines. The teapot was used with some Nautilus patterns and the eggcup was made in the eggshell body to be used with Swing. New lids were modeled for the casserole and teapot and they were used with the treatments, Blue Fantasy and Blue Willow, respectively.

Decaled Wells will be marked in one of several ways: a Vellum backstamp, a general HLC marking, or a Wells Peacock mark. Three different peacock marks exist: one as a multicolored decal, one as a gold stamp and the last as a silver stamp. This is also the case with Craftsman (Georgian) backstamps and it has been learned that with that line the multicolored mark was used for more "expensive" treatments and the silver stamp was revered for the cheaper patterns. Could this be the reason for the three peacock marks? If so, it doesn't seem to be of any concern to collectors today. What can be very confusing is the marks were used on Century and, to a lesser degree, Jade. Some argue that the peacock mark was used on anything with the Vellum glaze, but this isn't always the case as ivory (or white) pieces of Wells can be found with the Wells backstamp. Instead of being a Vellum mark, it seems more likely the marking was used for more "top shelf" treatments – regardless the glaze and regardless if it was Wells, Century or Jade. One thing does seem certain, it was no longer used after the mid 1930s.

"Clematis", W-8523, is a colorful stylized treatment that appears on many different HLC shapes. Here it is on Wells – its "parent shape." It can also be found on Jade, Virginia Rose, Oven-Serve and Royal OvenServe, as well as other shapes. This treatment will have different trims depending on the shape: Virginia Rose, OvenServe and Yellowstone – no trim; Wells and Jade – black trim; Kitchen Kraft – red trim.

"Pastel Tulip" is one of the more popular treatments on the Wells shape.

The covered sugar shown here has a floral treatment commonly found on Republic and in rare cases, Virginia Rose and Jade. The underside of the sugar lid identifies the treatment as: W-102.

This Wells handled platter is unmarked but it has the characteristic "open" tab handles. The yellow luster is uncommon on Wells items, but the colorful decal is often found on Wells and Yellowstone.

This piece is commonly called a "Square plate". It is sometimes confused with Yellowstone, an HLC octagonal shape. There is only one Wells "square" plate and the way to tell the difference from a Yellowstone plate lies in the sides: all the sides of Yellowstone plates will be of equal length; with the Wells plate, they alternate between sides measuring 2½" and 4¾". Decaled Wells "square" plates are easier to find than their solid colored counterparts.

Shown is a Wells covered casserole in Vellum with red bands, but green bands can also be found.

Here we see the "Black Tulip" decal on Wells demitasse sugars and creamers but the glazes are different. While it may be difficult to tell in the photo, the set to the left is done in the white/ivory glaze whereas the set on the right was done in the rich vellum glaze.

The marking on this Wells cup and saucer is "Tudor Rose." This mark was used on pieces of Wells intended as promotional items for Quaker Oats. A series of treatments were used so keep in mind Tudor Rose is the name of the line *not* a particular decal.

Wells Art Glazes

There's a lot of confusion generated by the Wells Art Glazes marking. It was subject to be used on any shape that received a solid color glaze – this includes, but is not limited to, the plain round Wells shape. The marking has been found on the following shapes: Wells, Old Roman, Orleans, OvenServe, Coronet and Empress. These unrelated shapes have the one thing in common; selected pieces were dipped in solid colors.

Art glazes are matte in texture and in many cases have very uneven glazes. These were HLC's first solid colors to be used. The following table lists shapes and various colors that have been confirmed on those shapes:

(Leaf) Green	Wells, OvenServe
Peach, a.k.a. Rose	Wells, OvenServe, Orleans
(Melon) Yellow	Wells, OvenServe, Old Roman, Coronet
Rust	Wells, Orleans
Sea Green	Old Roman, Coronet
Blue	Empress
Red	Wells

The first four colors listed above are considered by many to be the "standard" Art Glazes. Obviously from the list, Wells is the dominate shape, but other shapes of the day received the same glazes and in many cases, the same marks. Green and peach have been found on OvenServe casseroles and under plates. It isn't known if the art glazes are limited to those two pieces. Yellow was a standard OvenServe color (called, "Melon Yellow") so expect those to have the OvenServe backstamp and not WAG. Orleans in rust and Peach was sold as, "Antique Orleans" and may be marked as such or simply as "Antique."

The sea green color is a little more consistent than the leaf green commonly used on the Wells shape. In fact, sea green is rather close to Fiesta's green but slightly darker. Coronet and Old Roman can be found in sea green as well as yellow and may carry their own marks or WAG.

The blue color was only used on Empress shape teapots. These have also been found in yellow.

These Empress teapots were special order and not used with a dinnerware line. On December 15, 1932, Rhead notes making samples in blue: *Wells Art Glazes in blue. Samples sent in Century – medium blue 1226, Wells – light blue 895, gray blue 987, medium blue enamel 661, blue enamel 650, strong blue enamel 638.* Whether the Empress teapots were done in one of these blues is anyone's guess at this point. Rhead calls this color "Blue Vellum" on several occasions.

A memo to Rhead dated September 11, 1941 was found tucked in his journals and gives some indication as to when the Wells Art Glazes were finally retired: *As you know, we are discontinuing the art glazes in the four colors. It is suggested that you have the proper samples set aside for historical records.*

On the left is a pair of fruit cups in peach. These are from the Wells shape. The teapot is done in the "Blue Vellum" glaze. While the shape is Empress, the marking is "Wells Art Glazes."

The matte color on the 10" plate and covered sugar is called, "Rust." While it is a rather common color on Wells, it falls behind green, yellow and peach in popularity.

Unusual red glaze on a Wells teapot. This is the most difficult Art Glaze color to find and it is similar to Fiesta's red but lacks Fiesta's brightness and gloss.

Wells Assortment and Values:

10" Plate	$10-12	9" Nappy	$10-12
9" Plate	$7-9	8" Nappy	$8-10
8" Plate	$12-15	10" Baker	$10-12
Square Plate	$10-12	9" Baker	$10-12
7" Plate	$5-6	8" Baker	$8-10
6" Plate	$4-5	Bouillon Cup	$20-25
Handled Tray	$15-18	Bouillon Liner	$15-18
Covered Butter	$35-40	Fruit Cup	$4-5
15" Platter	$18-20	Oatmeal	$6-8
13" Platter	$12-15	36s Bowl	$20-25
11" Platter	$8-10	Muffin Cover	$30-40
Pickle	$12-15	Teapot	$65-75
Teacup	$6-8	Casserole	$50-60
Saucer	$1-2	Batter Jug	$65-75

Wells Assortment and Values Continued:

A.D. Cup	$18-20	Syrup Jug	$55-65
A.D. Saucer	$8-10	A.D. Coffeepot	$95+
Reg. Sugar	$12-15	Sauceboat	$10-12
A.D. Sugar	$20-25	Gravy Faststand	$30-35
Reg. Creamer	$8-10	Empress Butter Pat	$18-20
A.D. Creamer	$18-20	Double Eggcup	$20-25
Rim Soup	$8-10	Cream Soup	$18-20
		Cream Soup Liner	$10-12

White Dover (Colonial White)

The first pieces of White Dover were modeled in 1965 with each piece having sixteen panels. When this shape is found in a plain white glaze, its called, "Colonial White" and has the treatment number CW-100. Consequently, all treatments which appear on the White Dover shape will begin with "CW" and not "WD" as one might expect.

White Dover was produced until the early 1980s. It can be found with many decal treatments and solid colors. The most common solid colors are yellow, green (the same yellow and green used with the Harlequin reissue line of the late 1970s) and brown which is called, "Amberstone" or CW-200. There is also dark green and gold colored White Dover in which the flatware has black stamp decorations.

For the most part, only large flatware such as plates and platters will be marked, and then it will be with a generic HLC backstamp. Some pieces can be found marked, "Monticello."

Both of these plates come from the late 1970s/early 1980s. The backstamp reads: Homer Laughlin, Desert Stone II. It also notes that the dinnerware is dishwasher safe, detergent-proof, oven-proof, and has a USPA approved glaze. The specks in the glaze are lighter than the Desert Stone used in the Table Fair line produced at the same time.

The lug soup has the speckled "mustard" glaze which was also used on Challenger. The fruit cup is in the Desert Stone II glaze.

The covered sugar is decorated with the "Bay Berry" treatment. Its official number is CW-105. The creamer has a very common autumn theme floral decal.

"Amberstone" is the name for the line of brown White Dover. The brown is much lighter than what was used on Fiesta Amberstone and Hearthside and almost borders on a red. There are several different markings used on White Dover Amberstone, but the most common is: IRONSTONE DINNERWARE, General Housewares Corp., USA by Homer Laughlin.

The 7" plate is in the same green used with reissue Harlequin. White Dover in green is almost never marked.

White Dover sauce boat in Fiesta red. To date, this is the only known piece of White Dover in a Fiesta glaze.

A 7" plate with floral sprigs on the rim.

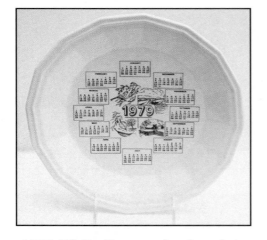

1979 White Dover calendar plate.

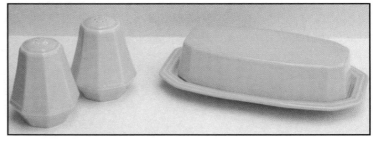

White Dover in the yellow glaze used with reissue Harlequin in the late 1970s is not at all uncommon. Shown are the shakers and covered butter.

1970s ad for White Dover in "Amberstone" (CW-200) and "Madrid" (CW-113).

Values for White Dover:

10" Plate	$3-4	Sauceboat	$6-7
7" Plate	$1-2	Shakers, pr.	$5-6
Chop Plate	$5-6	Soup Tureen	$15-20
Fruit Cup	$1	Tureen Ladle	$6-8
Lug Soup	$1-2	Casserole	$12-15
Tea Cup	$1-2	Coffeepot	$12-15
Saucer	$1	Teapot	$15-18
Sugar	$5-6	Butter	$5-6
Creamer	$4-5	Snack Plate	$7-9

Willow & Americana

In the early 1930s, several potteries in the United States were using "transfer-printing" methods as a means to decorate dinnerware. This process, originally developed in England, involved the use of a copper sheet with an engraved design. A thin layer of "color" or "ink" was then applied to the engraving. A special tissue paper was put over to the engraving. Rollers then transferred the design from the engraving to the special paper. This paper was then applied to a dish in a bisque state. The paper was removed, the dish given a clear glaze, fired and finished. The result was dinnerware with a one-color, all-over design.

Homer Laughlin started using this method heavily in 1934. It took some time to get the process to work properly. New machines had to be ordered and special rollers made. There were several times that HLC enlisted the advice of surrounding potteries, especially Taylor Smith & Taylor which had been using the process for several years prior, so that production of their Willow line could begin.

In April 1934, work began on creating Willow treatments. These were then turned over to the Arc Engraving Company of Youngstown, Ohio which made the special copper sheets. Several different Willow designs were considered until a "traditional" design was chosen. An excellent reference for Willow shapes and designs made by potteries all over the world is *Blue Willow, An Identification and Value Guide* by Mary Frank Gaston.

Kwaker flatware was always considered to be used for the new line from the beginning, but there were several options for the hollowware. Wells and Kwaker were the top contenders - at one time Rhead mentions the possibility of using some OvenServe shapes. It was decided in June 1934 that special shapes would be made for most of the hollowware. This included a sugar, creamer, sauceboat, lug soup, cream soup and 36s jug.

In July, Rhead notes the following regarding Willow:

07.13.34 The last shape for Willow commenced – sauceboat
07.15.34 Completed Willow curves [designs]
07.20.34 To make a design for mark for printed Willow
07.30.34 J.M. Wells O.K.'d boat mark for Willow

Production of Willow began soon after and for the next year, there were minor changes to the design and the engravings in order to make manufacturing more efficient. Pieces were added later such as modified Nautilus pickle for a sauceboat stand. The casserole was picked up from Empress and a special teapot was made using the Wells base and a lid made to match the Willow shape sugar lid.

In the mid 1950s, a jumbo cup and saucer was made with the Blue Willow treatment. The cup comes from Epicure and the saucer is the 67/8" saucer used with jumbo cups. (See section on Speciality Items for more on Jumbo cups and saucers.)

Several retailers carried Blue Willow (as well as pink version made in the very late 30s and early 40s) including Woolworth's, Marshal Fields and Sears. The Willow "boat mark" wasn't used very long and was replaced with the general HLC backstamp. Pink Willow was not made too long after 1942 and Blue Willow was discontinued around 1965.

After HLC was successful with the Willow line, they started using the transfer-printing process on other shapes. Coronet, Century and Orleans are just a few that make use of different one-color transfer designs. There was one instance in early 1936 where Fiesta compartment plates were being considered with the Willow treatment for Woolworth's. Rhead notes making samples on March 27 of the same year, but these must not have gone any further than the planning stage. In 1942, the Liberty shape was developed along with a special "Historical America" transfer design.

On May 25, 1939, J.M. Wells informed Rhead that Montgomery Wards wanted a special line with "printed American patterns." Two weeks later, Rhead went to Chicago, Illinois to meet with Montgomery Wards on the new line and other HLC wares. Later that day, he notes going to the Chicago Art Museum, Chicago Public Library, and bookstores to "hunt for Currier and Ives subjects."

On June 11th and 12th, Rhead worked on Currier and Ives (C&I) treatments to be used on the same shapes as Willow. After meeting with Ed Fry, buyer for Montgomery Wards, and shapes and patterns were decided upon, work began on the new line on June 19, 1939. Wards offered the line called, Americana, from 1940 until 1956. Each piece has a special C&I scene and in most cases, the name is printed along with the backstamp in red.

There were some special shapes made for Americana at the request of Wards, all of which were released into production on March 29, 1940. A complete breakdown of the Americana line is given here:

Flatware – Kwaker
Square Plate – Century and later Nautilus
Sugar, Creamer, Sauceboat, Cup, Saucer – come from Willow
Sauceboat Stand – modified Nautilus Pickle
Teapot, Cream Soup Cup, Cream Soup Liner, Demitasse Cup,
    Demi Saucer – designed *for* Americana
Casserole – Brittany (second style with solid finial)

Another transfer design in red is Early American Homes and was produced for J.C. Penney in the early 1940s. Rhead notes working on different designs in late December 1940 and the finial selection is given below. The 9" plate and platter are the easiest to find. Each piece has a specific treatment and are marked appropriately.

9" Plate	Mount Vernon
Platter	Independence Hall
Teacup	Paul Revere Home
Saucer	Robert E. Lee Home
Fruit Cup	Thomas Jefferson Home
Nappy	Betsy Ross Home
6" Plate	Abraham Lincoln Home

1940s Sears ad showing HLC's Blue Willow.

Willow creamer and covered sugar.

1950s Montgomery Wards ad featuring Americana with matching frosted tumblers.

Americana Creamer

Americana bowl; "Fox Hunting"

Americana marking.

Early American Homes backstamp.

Early American Homes 9" plate.

Blue Fantasy is a blue transfer floral design made in the late 1930s. Shown are the Willow shape sugar and creamer and Kwaker flatware.

Assortment and Values for Willow/Americana and related treatments:

Shapes common to all treatments:

10" Plate	$8-10
9" Plate	$7-8
7" Plate	$5-6
6" Plate	$4-5
Teacup	$7-8
Saucer	$1-2
15" Platter	$18-20
13" Platter	$12-15
11" Platter	$10-12
Sugar	$12-15
Creamer	$7-9
Sauceboat	$12-15
Sauceboat Liner	$8-10
Egg Cup (Cable)	$15-18

Americana only:

Teapot	$40-45
Chop Plate	$18-20
Casserole (Brittany)	$50-55
Square Plate (Century or Nautilus)	$10-12
Cream Soup	$10-12
Cream Soup Liner	$7-9
A.D. Cup	$12-15
A.D. Saucer	$6-8

Willow only:

Teapot (modified Wells)	$45-50
Casserole (Empress)	$20-25
Jug	$35-40
Jumbo Cup (several styles)	$8-10
Jumbo Saucer	$4-5

Blue or Rose Fantasy only:

Casserole (modified Wells)	$50-60

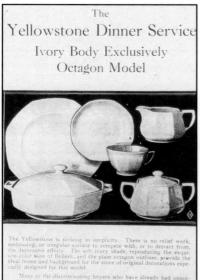

Yellowstone

Yellowstone was introduced in 1926. A trade ad dated August 5, 1926 best describes the design.

The ad reads:

> *The Yellowstone is striking in simplicity. There is no relief work, embossing or irregular surface to compete with, or to detract from, the decorative effects. The soft ivory shade, reproducing the exquisite color tone of Belleek, and the plain octagon outlines, provide the ideal frame and background for the score of original decorations especially designed for this model.*
>
> *Many of the discriminating buyers who have already had opportunity to inspect the Yellowstone have been good enough to pronounce it the outstanding creation of the year, one destined for unrivaled popularity.*

The confident tone of the ad was well founded as the Yellowstone shape would go on to be among HLC's best selling lines for the next ten years. It would continue to be made into the late 1940s, but not in the same quantities as its peak years in the 1930s. For most of its production run, it was made in ivory and the rich vellum glaze originally developed for Century. Many stylistic floral decals popular in the late 1920s are found on Yellowstone as well as a wide array of gold stamps.

Rhead joined HLC as art director in 1927 and made no significant changes to Yellowstone. There are at least two sugar and casserole types: one where the lid fits "into" the base and the other where the lid extends over the base's opening. These changes occurred several years after Yellowstone was introduced so Rhead oversaw the remodeling. This was probably done so the sugars and casseroles could be sold as "open" pieces as well as with lids.

Most pieces are marked with a general HLC backstamp. The octagonal body and flat top handles as well as the stylized treatments are usually not confused with other companies products. Most of the earliest pieces of Yellowstone are often found crazed, however, Yellowstone Vellum is often found with perfect glazes.

This is just one of several black/yellow treatments you may encounter on Yellowstone.

One of the most sought after treatments on Yellowstone is this one which was sold through Woolworth's. Its often referred to by different names such as, "Briar Rose" or "Pastel Rose." Its treatment number is W-132.

Another yellow/black treatment.

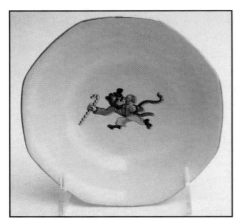

The 6" oatmeal bowl shown here has the "monkey on skates" decal and gold trim. It is dated 1944. (See also child's sets.)

This Mexican theme decal is common on Yellowstone. Shown is a coupe soup which comes from the late 1930s. Huxford's call this, "Max-i-cana."

This Yellowstone piece was listed in vintage ads as a relish tray. It measures just under 9" from handle to handle.

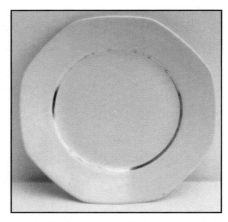

A Yellowstone 9" plate with gold trim on the verge.

Yellowstone open jug.

This pattern on a cup and saucer originated on Yellowstone as Y-137, but it would eventually be used on Century, Virginia Rose with several different trims, Marigold as M-118, Republic, Liberty and several others.

This egg cup is actually from Yellowstone, but it lacks the familiar paneled sides found with other hollowware. It was sometimes used as a pick-up piece with other decaled shapes. It's very similar in size to the Fiesta egg cup.

The lid on the regular sugar fits into the base and is part of the original design. Within three years of its introduction, the sugar was remodeled with the inner lip removed from the base and the lid made to fit on top of the opening. The resulting lid extends over the base. This was also done with the covered casserole. It may be that both pieces were changed with the lip removed so that they could be sold as either "open" or "covered."

"Raymond," or Y-12, is the name of the treatment on this Yellowstone covered butter.

Assortment and Values for Yellowstone:

10" Plate	$10-12	Egg Cup	$20-25
9" Plate	$7-9	Platter, any size	$12-15
8" Plate	$10-12	Nappy, any size	$8-10
7" Plate	$6-7	Baker, any size	$7-9
6" Plate	$3-4	Coupe Soup, any size	$6-8
Fruit Cup	$3-4	Rim Soup	$8-10
Oatmeal	$5-6	Cream Soup	$18-20
Teacup	$6-7	Cream Soup Liner	$8-10
Saucer	$1-2	Covered Butter	$20-25
Covered Sugar	$12-15	Casserole	$25-30
A.D. Sugar	$18-20	Teapot	$35-40
Creamer	$6-8	Open Jug	$20-25
A.D. Creamer	$10-12	Jug with Cover	$40-45
Sauceboat	$8-10	Bouillon	$10-12
Gravy Faststand	$15-18	Bouillon Liner	$7-9

Kitchenware

The first pieces of kitchenware HLC produced in the late 1800s were a loose collection of generic shapes such as mixing bowls, various sizes of jugs, bakers and other utilitarian items. It wasn't until the mid 1930s that Homer Laughlin and other pottery companies started to make oven proof wares with specific decorations. In HLC's case, the two major lines were embossed OvenServe and Kitchen Kraft OvenServe.

Two sizes of generic shape jugs produced by Homer Laughlin circa 1910.

In the early 1930s, HLC made two sets of mixing bowls that don't belong to a specific line of dinnerware or kitchenware. The Apple Tree bowls were made in 1931. A year later another set was made based on a very simple design. Rhead referred to this set several times as simply, "Kitchen Bowls" or "Nappy Bowls."

Apple Tree Bowls

From late September to mid December 1931, the Apple Tree bowls were developed. The first time Rhead mentions the set in his journals is on September 21, 1931:

> *J.M. Wells asked for Colgate Bowl, tree design 91/4 by 4 inches.*
> *The best height for practical use and appearance. Sample needed*
> *in 8 days . . . to see AV on* [glazes] *blue and yellow mattes also*
> *look up green.*

Later that same day he writes:

> *Commenced work on bowls. Model to Al Kraft and Bill* [Berrisford] *to*
> *model tree pattern in wax for shipping. Saw AV on yellow and blue*
> *mattes and gave him samples of green.*

For the next several days, the Art Department worked solely on samples of the 9¼" Apple Tree bowl. The log entries reveal the work that went into creating the piece so that samples could be reviewed on time:

09.24.31	*Worked all day on bowls* [and] *at night until 10 pm*
09.25.31	*Finished modeling bowls – being blocked and cased*
09.26.31	*Three of each in three colors in glost kilns – Placed in kiln ourselves*
09.27.31	*More bowls modeled and put in glost kilns*
09.28.31	*Six bowls out satisfying. Six more out, chipped at bottoms but glaze satisfactory*
09.30.31	*J.M. Wells to NY with Colgate bowls and Woolworth samples*

The hard work paid off since on October 2, 1931, Rhead notes that five sizes were ordered and that they were to nest. The original design must have been very different from the set collectors know of today as the shape of the bowls had to be changed so that they could nest properly. On October 6, J.M. Wells reviewed all five sizes of the Apple Tree bowls and Rhead had to explain *"the difference in appearance and capacity due to change in shape for clay fit."* On the 7th, modeling of the bowls was complete and an HLC marking was made on the 9th.

Another design was made on November 30th. Rhead calls this the "B" models and notes the sizes as 9¼", 8⅝", 7⅝", 6½" and 5½". Finally, on December 16, 1931, Rhead notes: *J.M. Wells phoned from NY . . . Colgate bowls O.K.*

The Apple Tree bowls would continue to be made until the mid 1940s. The most common color is the matte blue glaze (called green in vintage ads) followed by melon yellow and ivory. Some sets are found in ivory with different colored trim and decals, but these are rare. The larger size is found in orange (pumpkin) only and is often marked with a generic HLC marking. Some collectors believe the orange bowls were made to go with orange OvenServe.

What some collectors find confusing is that there are two sizes of the largest bowl resulting in six sizes total. While Rhead commonly called the large bowls "9¼" bowl" they actually measure 9¾" and 9½". Both 9¾" and 9½" bowls are known in blue, melon yellow and ivory. Rhead's notes don't reveal if one size replaced the other or if they were made simultaneously. In ads that feature the bowls only five sizes are ever mentioned so it is probably the case that one replaced the other at some point during production.

All six sizes of nesting Apple Tree bowls in blue.

Appletree bowls in orange, melon yellow and blue.

Values are for Appletree bowls in solid colors. Ivory bowls with colored trim or decals may be priced higher.

5"	$40-45	8"	$25-30
6"	$18-20	9½"	$30-35
7"	$20-25	9¾"	$30-35

Nappy Bowls

Almost exactly a year since work began on the Apple Tree bowls, a new set was developed. On September 26, 1932, Rhead notes the specifications on the new mixing bowls: *nappy sets, width as present apple tree bowls but low. Small size is the Premium bowl. To nest low and level at the top. Desired kitchen bowls.* In October the five sizes of nappy bowls were made. The Premium bowl mentioned in the journal entry is the small Ralston Purina bowl (see section on Children's dishes). Each size was patterned after this piece with a beaded edge and convex sides.

The easiest of the nappy bowls to find is the largest size – 9½". These are almost always glazed in vellum and decorated with floral or exotic bird decals. This size was also used for Tom & Jerry sets along with the Little Orphan Annie shape mugs into the 1950s.

It's not clear if the full set went into production. A few 8" bowls have surfaced, but the other sizes have not yet been confirmed. Those which have been found carry a general HLC backstamp and date code.

"Nappy Bowl" mixing bowl with blue band and gold decoration.

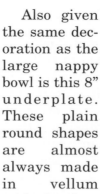

Also given the same decoration as the large nappy bowl is this 8" underplate. These plain round shapes are almost always made in vellum with decals and sometimes have gold stamp advertisements of various businesses ranging from banks to furniture stores.

Values: 9" Nappy Bowl $15-20
              Underplate $10-12

OvenServe

In the early 1930s, most pottery companies started to produce kitchenware. A brief list of potteries and their special kitchenware lines include: Paden City–Bak Serve, Harker–Bakerite, Cronin–Bake Oven, Crooksville–Pantry Ware. In 1933 Homer Laughlin introduced an extensive assortment of embossed kitchenware called, "OvenServe." This line included various sizes of bowls, bakers, platters as well as some dinnerware pieces; plates, teacups and saucers.

On January 23, 1933, Frederick Rhead writes in his journals about a "cooking and kitchenware program." After collecting samples of kitchenware lines from other companies, Rhead set out making sketches of various items. By February 6th, the drawings were "made into a folio and turned over to J.M. Wells." However, for the rest of the month, the Art Department worked on Chelsea for Quaker Oats and adding new items to the recently released and very successful Virginia Rose shape.

Rhead notes making a couple "Thermo" custard cups in brown, pink and white glazes on the last week of March. We can assume these first oven ware pieces were plain shapes. The first time Rhead notes any type of embossed work is on March 30, 1933. The next day, on the 31st, representatives from Woolworth visited HLC to view various samples. After reviewing the "Thermo" custards, a line of kitchenware with the following items was suggested:

1. small custards
2. individual casserole
3. bakers
4. pie plates/Welsh rabbits
5. large casserole
6. bowls for sauce
7. jug
8. salt and pepper
9. mixing or measuring bowl
10. 8", 7", 6" & 4" Plates*
11. teacup
12. St. Dennis cup and saucer
13. bowl for soup
14. 4" 5" soup
15. 36s oatmeal
16. nappy
17. sugar/creamer
18. restaurant individual creamer
19. baked apple
20. ashtray

* The 20 items listed above are as Rhead wrote them. Remember he used *trade* sizes so the 8", 7", 6" and 4" plates would have actual measurements close to: 10", 9", 8" and 6".

Several trials of clays with various decorations were made to see which could withstand oven temperatures. On April 4, 1933, Rhead notes the new oven ware glaze samples were not good. More patterns, specifications and trials were conducted for the next two weeks and on the 17th, J.M. Wells approved the first nine items from the March 31st listing. It was during this time that Kaufman's became interested in the oven ware.

More buyers became interested in the oven ware, but only a few pieces had been modeled at the time and nothing had yet been released into production. It became apparent to many at HLC that the new oven ware was going to be a success even though it wasn't anywhere near completion. On April 25, 1933, J.M. Wells advised Rhead that the Art Department was to "concentrate on oven ware." From May to August 1933 the new oven proof line was developed.

The first items modeled were made in two styles: plain and with the familiar floral embossing. Some of the items from the March 31st list were dropped and new items such as the French casseroles and Shirred Egg dishes were added. On June 9, 1933, Rhead notes producing several trial glazes for the cooking ware:

Pink – 1383	Turquoise Green – 1425
Light Blue – 841	Deep Ivory – 1434
Fawn – 1423	Melon Yellow – 1436
Golden Green – 1427	Vellum Yellow – 1432
Orange – 1428	

Eventually, OvenServe was made primarily in Orange (a.k.a. pumpkin), Melon Yellow and Ivory. The ivory glaze was developed especially for this shape and would go on to be used with Kitchen Kraft, Virginia Rose, Marigold and others. At some point, it was decided that the Art Glazes would be used. Casseroles and under plates have been found in green and peach complete with a Wells Art Glazes backstamp. Small OvenServe in other solid colors was made by HLC and Taylor Smith & Taylor for Quaker Oats.

On June 9, 1933, names were being considered for the oven ware. One option was, "OvenDrive," but "OvenServe" was selected. Two days later backstamps and labels were being made with the new OvenServe logo. By the end of the month, dozens of decorations were tested on OvenServe. On July 7, Polychrome, the hand-painted treatment consisting of yellow, blue, green and pink, was being used and variations would be considered in the weeks ahead.

With the majority of OvenServe pieces modeled and in production, the Art Department started to develop other wares, namely Georgian/Craftsman. More pieces would be revised and added to OvenServe for the next year including pie plates, casseroles and jugs. In August 1934 three new items were modeled: the (long) spoon, pie server (listed as a "cake knife" in the modeling log) and a 40 oz. teapot. In April 1935, an open sugar and creamer were made for OvenServe. A sugar lid was modeled in January 1936 and released in February. It was also during this time that two more teapots were modeled. Both had capacities of 16oz., but they were listed as "low" and "tall" teapots.

Rhead was not in the habit of noting when items were released into production until 1937. While there are four OvenServe teapots listed in the log, all were modeled before Rhead started penciling in release dates. To date none have been reported and there are no vintage ads showing any of the OvenServe teapots. It may be the case they never went into production. This is also true of the shakers. Several embossed OS sets were modeled over the years, but none have been found.

The last piece of OvenServe modeled was the salad fork in June 1937. This was done during the development of the plain kitchenware line, Kitchen Kraft. The embossed salad fork, pie lifter and short spoon were used in both OvenServe and Kitchen Kraft.

The treatments on OvenServe vary just as they do on dinnerware lines. Solid colors, decals, trim, silver stamps and hand-painted work can be found on almost every piece. The more exotic items, such as batter jugs, measuring cups, the long spoon and others are generally found with very simple treatments such as trim or hand-painted embossing. Several retailers carried OvenServe with green hand-painted embossing including Woolworth's. This is without a doubt the most common OvenServe treatment. Decals and silver stamps are generally found on more common pieces like pie plates and casseroles.

Almost every piece of OvenServe is marked with a backstamp. The only exceptions are the four utensils which will have no markings. It should be pointed out that three of the utensils; the cake lifter, fork and small spoon are currently being made in various solid colored glazes and sold through a company called China Specialties. These are marked with a small embossed, "C.S." initials on the upper part of the reverse of the handles.

OvenServe was mass produced from 1933 until late 1937. It was made after 1937, but was overshadowed by the plain shapes of Kitchen Kraft. By this time, many of the OvenServe pieces had been discontinued and are very hard to find today. These "key" pieces are the measuring cup, long handled spoon, batter jug, both styles of sugars and the creamer. The most common pieces are five items which were produced for Quaker Oats. The baker, cereal, custard, ramekin and smaller French casserole were produced by both Homer Laughlin and Taylor Smith and Taylor in various solid colors until the mid 1950s.

Embossed OvenServe

Backstamp

5½" and 4½" covered leftovers with various decorations: from left to right; Polychrome, green and orange trim.

The original label on this 9" plate reads: "Guaranteed to Withstand Changes of Oven and Refrigerator Temperature. OvenServe. The Oven Ware for Table Service."

OvenServe cups and saucers are not too hard to find in pumpkin, ivory and various decorations, but are scarce in melon yellow as shown.

This covered casserole is decorated with black trim. Its official treatment number is OS-52.

The small baker to the left is a common piece, but it has the unusual and hard to find greenish-ivory Clair de Lune glaze that was meant to be used on Jade. Several OvenServe Clair de lune pieces have been accounted for in different parts of the country, so they must have been special order. Shown alongside the baker is a baked apple in ivory for color comparison.

Shown along with a 6" plate is the very hard to find "long" OvenServe spoon. This was the first version to be modeled. It was later replaced by the more common "short" spoon.

The 6" plate has the same type of hand-painted embossing, but note the dramatic differences in the green color between these two pieces. The lighter color on the spoon is found more often on embossed OvenServe and other HLC embossed lines.

Generally, OvenServe utensils are found in Fiesta colors or with decals. They are uncommon in pumpkin and very rare in melon yellow which is much paler than Fiesta's yellow.

The smaller of two sizes of Shirred egg dishes is glazed in pumpkin. The little brown cup is the ramekin and the yellow piece is the custard.

Various sizes of embossed plates in pumpkin (orange).

OvenServe creamer in ivory and open sugar with green hand-painted embossing.

The OvenServe creamer is shown with a measuring cup that has a rose silver stamp decoration. The inside of the measuring cup has raised lines measuring quarters of a cup.

Batter jug with green embossing.

The small casserole, shown with a custard for size comparison, has an original OvenServe sticker and an unusual ivory speckled glaze.

Batter jugs are almost always found in ivory. This particular example was decorated with green trim around the opening and on the handle. To the left of the jug is a measuring cup with the Polychrome decoration.

This OvenServe pie plate has two unusual features. It lacks the familiar rose embossing and its glazed in the same pastel blue color used with the Serenade dinnerware line.

One of several sizes of embossed OvenServe mixing bowls.

Small platter in melon yellow a.k.a. "fish platter."

Here are two of the "small" OS pieces used for Quaker Oats. These were made by both HLC and Taylor Smith and Taylor, but the colors shown are unique to TS&T. On the left is the French casserole in a gray-green glaze. The TS&T French casserole differs from HLC's in that the handle and bowl are one piece. HLC's has an applied handle.

Though its probably not visible in the picture, the turquoise oval baker has a speckled glaze - this is from TS&T's Pebbleford line which was produced in the mid 50s to the mid 60s.

All TS&T and HLC OvenServe pieces will be marked appropriately. With TS&T, the items are marked with a cast mold mark as shown; HLC's will generally have a backstamp, but there are some HLC examples found with a mold mark.

This group of ramekins and custards was made for Quaker Oats by Taylor Smith and Taylor and Homer Laughlin.

Assortment and Values for Embossed OvenServe:

10" Plate	$10-12	Cereal, 5"	$3-4
9" Plate	$7-9	Custard	$2-3
7" Plate	$7-9	Ramekin	$2-3
6" Plate	$10-12	Small Oval Baker	$4-5
Teacup	$6-8	Medium Oval Baker	$8-12
Saucer	$2-3	Large Oval Baker	$18-20
Shirred Egg, small	$18-20	Batter Jug	$75-95
Shirred Egg, lg.	$20-25	4" Leftover	$30-35
Creamer	$75+	5" Leftover	$35-40
Open Sugar	$75+	Baked Apple	$12-15
Covered Sugar	$150+	11" Platter	$15-18
French Casserole, small	$4-5	13" Platter	$12-15
French Casserole, lg.	$7-9	9" Platter	$12-15
Measuring Cup	$95+	6" covered Casserole	$18-20
9" Pie Plate	$10-12	9" covered Casserole	$15-18
10" Pie Plate	$12-15	Cake Lifter	$50-60
6" Bowl	$15-18	Fork	$60-70
8" Bowl	$18-20	Small Spoon	$50-60
9" Bowl	$20-22	Long Spoon	$125+
10" Bowl	$20-25		

At least five sizes of mixing bowls were modeled and they were noted in the log by their trade size numbers, from largest to smallest: 6s, 9s, 12s, 18s, 24s. Most often, but not always, these will have a special "NOT FOR OVEN USE" backstamp.

7¾"	$35-40	11"	$30-35
8⅞"	$25-30	12¼"	$35-40
9¾"	$25-30		

There is a major problem with pieces of OvenServe that were heavily used whether they are in a solid color, plain ivory or with decorative treatments. Many pieces have dark spots that developed from being placed in the oven over and over and its almost impossible to get these "baked-in" stains off. While this is not typical damage such as a chip or crack, the appearance of a piece is greatly affected. Fortunately, this staining occurs on very common items such as casseroles, pie plates and bakers. Stained pieces can be passed up for better examples.

Royal OvenServe & Royal Metal

In 1934 the Royal Metal Company of Chicago, Illinois approached Homer Laughlin on producing ware to be sold in metal frames. On October 22, 1934 the Art Department began work on creating special items based on the new OvenServe heat resistant body. By December 1st, all the new pieces were modeled and released into production. Rhead lists these in his journals as:

- Pie Plate
- Cake Plate
- Casserole
- Deep Platter
- Mixing Bowl Casserole
- Relish Dish

The relish dish was a one-piece round tray with five compartments. It would have to be modified twice to properly fit the metal frame. The Royal OvenServe pieces are very plain with no type of embossing. A special backstamp was made adding the word "Royal" to the OvenServe name. All six pieces were given the ivory OvenServe glaze and decorated with decals. The relish plate was discontinued early, but the others continued into the very late 1930s.

It should be noted that the six items listed are not the only pieces made for Royal Metal. They also used embossed OvenServe casseroles and bakers with various decals for metal frames. Such pieces will have the standard OvenServe mark and the special Royal OvenServe silver stamp. A Fiesta cake plate and mustard were developed especially for Royal Metal. The mustard, sold through Royal Metal with the shakers as a special condiment set, became a standard Fiesta item, but the cake plate did not. Another special item made for Royal Metal is the "promotional casserole" in 1937. These have been found in red, light green, spruce green, mauve blue, Harlequin yellow and cobalt.

This 10⅝" cake plate, like all Royal O.S. cake plates, is unmarked. Of all R.O.S. pieces this seems to be the most common. You will find a whole family of decals on this shape. The regular cake plate in Kitchen Kraft, which is also generally unmarked, has a slight curvature to its body. The R.O.S. cake

Royal OvenServe marking.

plate is completely flat and its base has a double foot ring.

Underside of the R.O.S. cake plate: notice the triple ring pattern – common to almost every piece of OvenServe and Kitchen Kraft.

This large and very heavy R.O.S. platter/baker is sometimes called an oval pie plate. It got that name due to the large pie plate-like lip. Like all R.O.S. pieces, this was sold with a metal frame. It has a completely glazed underside with no rings and may or may not be marked.

The Red Clover decal can be found on other R.O.S. shapes as well as Swing shapes. The oval baker, pie plate and straight sided casserole are rather easy to find with red clover. Rhead made notes on this treatment several times in his journals giving us an idea as to when the decal was in use:

06.15.35   Stafford here proofing shamrock sheets for Royal Metal
06.26.35   Stafford submitted second series of red shamrock decal for Royal Metal
07.02.35   Royal Metal red clover tests out of kilns. 5033 D and B are best colors . . . commencing on D until we hear by wire from Royal Metal
07.08.35   D confirmed and lighter green if possible using B green.

This Royal O.S. casserole is commonly called the "straight sided casserole." Note the lid has a steam hole. Like the R.O.S. cake plate, these will generally be unmarked but can be identified by the same triple ring pattern on the underside. When marked, the backstamp is usually found on the underside of the lid.

Dimensions:
> height: 3"
> base opening diameter: 7⅝"
> lid diameter: 7¼"

The second R.O.S. casserole has a curved bottom and when found without the lid, they are usually misidentified as mixing bowls. Like the straight sided casserole, the "curved base" casserole will not be marked on the underside of the base. You will find a set of two rings instead of the triple set found on the straight sided casserole and cake plate. If there is a marking, it will be on the underside of the lid.

The floral decal on the curved base casserole shown is rather common on all R.O.S. and since most pieces lack backstamps, most are mislabeled as Harker which used similar decals on their kitchenware. While the lids on the straight sided and curved base casseroles look similar, they are not interchangeable. Don't be surprised to find deep marks on the sides of the base. They are sagger pin marks – the same kind that are often found on the undersides of vintage HLC flatware.

Dimensions: height: 4"   base opening diameter: 8⅛"   lid diameter: 7¼"

Other than the cake plate with the Fiesta rings, this divided relish is the most difficult Royal OvenServe item to find. Like many other R.O.S. pieces, it has a well pronounced lip so that it can be placed in a metal frame. This piece has a diameter of 10½: and is almost 1¼" tall.

216

The decaled R.O.S. pie plates will usually be marked as such. The R.O.S. pie plates will have a set of three rings on the underside.

Pie plates glazed in the Harlequin colors: mauve blue (as shown), spruce green and Harlequin yellow were made for Royal Metal and were sold with metal frames. These are PLAIN with no decoration. There are some who maintain that there is a true Harlequin pie plate with a band of rings on the inner wall, but these are actually made by Cronin China. The Royal Metal pie plates in Harlequin colors will not have any rings and will be unmarked. The underside will not have the typical rings often found on OvenServe pieces.

The oval platters were made in red, Fiesta yellow, Harlequin yellow, cobalt, light green, spruce green, mauve blue and with decals to be sold with metal frames. Shown is the Royal Metal oval platter in light green.

Sometimes found with a "Royal Chrome" sticker, the Royal Metal casseroles were made in light green, spruce green, mauve blue, Harlequin yellow, cobalt and red (as shown). They aren't marked, but the distinctive pie crust motif on the underside of the rim is unmistakable. While these may have been included in various Fiesta promotions, they are not part of the standard Fiesta line.

Caption on following page

In June 1939, HLC made the medium size Kitchen Kraft casserole in Serenade glazes for the west coast distributor, M. Sellers Company and for Royal Metal. These special casseroles have the same mold marking as Fiesta Kitchen Kraft casseroles except the name "Fiesta" was replaced with "Serenade." The casserole is the only piece of Serenade Kitchen Kraft put into production, even though a pie plate and Royal Metal oval platter in the pastel glazes were also under consideration.

The bases made for both companies are identical, but Sellers sold theirs with a standard Kitchen Kraft lid whereas Royal Metal used at least two different glass lids along with a metal frame. Royal Metal had a large stock of oven proof glassware since they sold metal frames for various sizes of glass casseroles, custards, etc. Rhead always referred to the glass lids as Pyrex, but most of the original lids found on Serenade casseroles are marked, "Glassbake."

The standard KK lids in pastel glazes are very hard to find which implies the Royal Metal promotion was much more successful than Seller's. Casserole bases with the Serenade KK mark can be found in all four pastel colors along with light green from Fiesta and the Swing (white) glaze.

Values for Royal OvenServe & Royal Metal:

Pie Plate	$10-12	10" Pie Plate:	
Casserole	$18-20	Fiesta colors	$45-55
Mixing Bowl Casserole	$12-15	Harlequin colors	$150+
Cake Plate	$10-12	Oval Platter:	
Deep Platter	$12-15	Fiesta colors	$40-55
Relish Dish	$20-25	Harlequin colors	$150+
Serenade Casserole base	$40-45	Promotional Casserole:	
Serenade Casserole lid	$100+	Lid	$20-25
Glass lid	$20-25	Base	$55-65
Metal Frames, any size	$15-25		

Special OvenServe Items

Handy Andy

The Handy Andy casserole comes in three parts: a ceramic bowl made by Homer Laughlin, a metal lid and metal base – both of which were made by an outside company (probably Royal Metal). The bowl was made in June of 1936, but had to be adjusted. On June 19, Rhead makes the following journal entry regarding the Handy Andy casserole: *Body of the casserole to be adjusted. Overall diameter to be 8 1/8" and body adjusted to permit framing. Don't forget* [OvenServe] *trademark is to be used including the addition* [of] *Handy Andy.* By the 24th, a new body had been modeled and approved for production.

About a dozen or so decals and special trim decorations have been found on Handy Andy casseroles. The one shown seems to be the most common.
Values: $30-35

Many times the bowl of the Handy Andy casserole is found alone. Here is what it looks like without its metal pieces. Though they should all be marked, the rings under the rim can help you identify it as Handy Andy. It has an opening diameter of 8" and stands 3" tall.

Daisy Chain

There are only two shapes made with the Daisy Chain embossing; the pie plate and the covered casserole. Many popular decals such as Deco Leaf, Mexicana and others have been found on both shapes. According to the modeling log, they were crafted in May and June of 1935 with the notation that they were to be made with metal frames. Both were produced until the very early 1940s and have the general HLC OvenServe backstamp.

Regular OvenServe marking found on the Daisy Chain pie plate.

Daisy Chain pie plate. This treatment has been documented on the Virginia Rose and Theme Eggshell shapes.

The daisy chain casserole will have the daisy embossing along the rim of the lid and the lip of the base. The lid has a very pronounced finial and sometimes it can be found on Handy Andy OvenServe bases. Shown is the very popular "Deco Leaf" treatment which was used on embossed OvenServe, Kitchen Kraft OvenServe, and Nautilus dinnerware. As with the Daisy Chain pie plate, the casseroles will have the regular OvenServe backstamp.

Values for Daisy Chain OvenServe:

Pie Plate $18-25   Casserole $30-35

Georgian

Georgian kitchenware is the most difficult to locate. According to the modeling log there were only a few items made for this line starting in May of 1934; casserole, divided baker, pie plates (10³/4" and 9³/4" diameters), the 10" dish (platter), and the French Casserole.

Each piece has the familiar Georgian type dot-dash rim embossing and has the very heavy kitchenware weight. Most pieces will have a generic HLC or OvenServe backstamp, but some are found marked, "Georgian." If you're lucky enough to find pieces from this line, expect them to either be plain ivory or with floral decals.

Georgian OvenServe casserole minus the lid.
Value: UND

Libby Pig Bean Pot

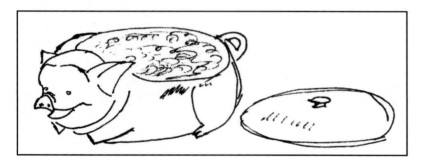

Stuck in Rhead's journals was this sketch of a pig bean pot along with the note dated May 24, 1934 (not in Rhead's handwriting): *Bean pot individual or Family size. Design copyrighted – not to be copied, manufactured or used unless permission given by Libby, McNeil & Libby.* Apparently, Libby approached HLC on making the special item in the then one year old oven proof body.

For the next two months, work proceeded on developing a pig bean pot. The first pot, a round version, was modeled in the beginning of June. After samples were made and reviewed, the following specifications were recommended for a second model on June 20, 1934:

1. more oval in shape
2. same height as now
3. about same capacity slightly larger O.K.
4. more pronounced legs and features
Note: outside dimensions 4" x 3¹/2"

5. Libby's OvenServe HLC [marking]
6. Two orange [pumpkin] three ivory
7. Outline in black. Features – legs and tail are orange and ivory
8. Outline in red and ivory

On the 21st, Rhead notes: *Oval not right. Capacity too small. Have increased height and width to 4¹/4" x 3⁵/8".* Finally on July 7, the new oval Libby pig bean pots were made with the decorative trims and in the OvenServe colors; ivory, melon yellow and orange.

Rhead never mentions any more revisions to the pig bean pot and makes no notes about them being released into production.

Kitchen Kraft OvenServe

On October 6, 1936, Rhead makes the first mention of what would become known as Kitchen Kraft OvenServe: *making designs for streamline OvenServe casserole for 1937.*

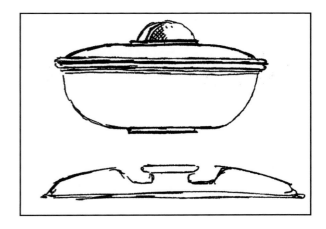

At the end of March 1937, an item is recorded in the modeling log as, "Casserole for new line of ovenware." Shown is the sketch of the new casserole with two versions of lids; one with a semicircular finial and the other with a recessed knob.

From April to mid June 1937, the Kitchen Kraft line was developed, though during this time, it was referred to as simply, "new ovenware line." The casserole would undergo several changes with regard to the lid. It was modified to fit "inside" the base and the little foot from the March prototype was eliminated. The large covered jar that we know of today has no handles, but there were versions with two types of lug handles that never went into production. Even the stacking refrigerator bowls were made with and without lugs, but only the handleless versions were released into production. The covered jug started out as an open jug and without a cover. The salad fork, which didn't exist in the previous OvenServe line, was made so that the embossings matched the cake lifter and "small" spoon.

There are some items that didn't make it into the final assortment. One was the salad nappie listed as 11¼" x 3". While it wasn't used in Kitchen Kraft, it was given interior rings and became part of the standard Fiesta line. There is also a "s/s onion soup" or short size onion soup listed in the log. Unfortunately, there is no sketch of this piece. Two styles of shakers were made for Kitchen Kraft. The first pair is listed simply as "Salt and Pepper, new ovenware" in early June 1937. The second set is listed as, "Salt & Pepper, same as OvenServe but without modeled embossed sprig." Only the first set went into production. There are no sketches of the second set which would have given collectors some insight into what the embossed OvenServe shakers might look like.

All of the Kitchen Kraft items were released into production by the end of June 1937. There was one revision in July when the covered jug was "made smaller" and is listed as a 24s. The shapes are rather plain with only a double band decoration at the rim. Unlike embossed OvenServe, KK doesn't have any dinnerware shapes such as plates, teacups and saucers. Though it seems that Kitchen Kraft was designed to supplement other dinnerware shapes since it is found with decals and solid colors used primarily with dinnerware lines. There aren't very many decals that are found on KK and *not* on dinnerware shapes. Virginia Rose's Fluffy Rose and Moss Rose decals are common on KK. The Mexican theme decals Mexicana and Conchita are very popular as is Sunporch.

From 1939 until circa 1942, The Kitchen Kraft shapes were made in the Fiesta glazes, red, yellow, cobalt and light green. Once in a while an example in ivory is found but more often than not, it is simply an untreated blank that should have received a decal treatment. Plain round rim shape plates called, "under plates" were offered with the casseroles. In the case of Kitchen Kraft in Fiesta glazes, it has recently been learned that standard Fiesta shape 9" and 6" plates with Fiesta Kitchen Kraft stickers were used as under plates.

Most kitchenware lines made by potteries were discontinued in the early 1950s. Heat resistant Pyrex and other glassware were becoming more popular at the time. While KK was produced in the 50s, the line was cut back. Covered jars, utensils the smaller casseroles and stacking jars were phased out. Mixing bowls, the large casserole, pie plates and jug continued to be produced with decals in use at the time; Rhythm Rose and Priscilla most notably. By the early 1960s, almost all of the kitchen shapes were no longer in production.

The KK backstamp perserves the OvenServe name. In the early 1950s, the KK/OS marking was no longer used. Instead many surviving shapes such as mixing bowls, casseroles and pie plates are marked with a generic HLC backstamp.

This is the smallest of three sizes of covered jars. Shown is the Mexicana decal with blue trim. Mexicana Kitchen Kraft has been found with blue trim, red trim and no trim at all.

The tulip decoration on this 6" mixing bowl is common on Kitchen Kraft shapes but can also be found on Georgian Eggshell dinnerware. The official treatment number is KK-308.

This 9" KK pie plate has a rose floral decal treatment which was used on many HLC shapes of the 30s and 40s. Not only was it used on KK, but also embossed OvenServe.

The KK coffeepot was a late addition. It was modeled in April of 1951 and was produced with decal treatments only.

Flat rim covered casserole with a black/red/yellow treatment complete with red trim. Casseroles commonly come in two versions which involves the edge of the base. There are some which have sloped or "dropped edges" and others, which are more common, will have flat rims. You may also find KK platters to have similar rim variations.

On display at Homer Laughlin are these two pieces: a Kitchen Kraft small casserole (a.k.a. bean pot) and an ivory Fiesta marmalade with the Black Tulip decal.

Fiesta Kitchen Kraft mixing bowl in yellow.

The embossed OvenServe utensils were the only pieces to be picked up by the Kitchen Kraft line. Here we see all four – cake lifter, fork, long spoon, and short spoon – in solid colors. The fork and long spoon in turquoise are thought to be unique since turquoise was never used with Kitchen Kraft. In fact, don't expect to find the long spoon in any solid colors. They come plain or with hand-painted embossing.

"Rhythm Rose" Cake Plate.

Kitchen Kraft Shakers with the KK-300 treatment.

Assortment and Values for Kitchen Kraft OvenServe:

10" Mixing Bowl	$15-18	Large Covered Jar	$55-65
8" Mixing Bowl	$15-18	Medium Covered Jar	$60-70
6" Mixing Bowl	$12-15	Small Covered Jar	$60-70
8" Casserole	$18-20	Stacking Unit	$18-20
7" Casserole	$18-20	Stacking Lid	$18-20
Indiv. Casserole	$45-50	Cake Plate	$15-18
Under Plate	$12-15	9" Pie Plate	$12-15
Shakers	$20-25	10" Pie Plate	$15-18
Coffee Pot	$20-25	Lidded Jug	$35-40

Assortment and Values for Fiesta Kitchen Kraft:

10" Mixing Bowl	$90-125	Large Covered Jar	$275+
8" Mixing Bowl	$75-100	Medium Covered Jar	$200-225
6" Mixing Bowl	$70-85	Small Covered Jar	$275+
8" Casserole	$100-125	Stacking Unit	$45-55
7" Casserole	$95-115	Stacking Lid	$55-65
Indiv. Casserole	$125-155	Cake Plate	$45-55
Skakers	$85-95	9" Pie Plate	$60+
Spoon	$100-115	10" Pie Plate	$45-55
Fork	$110-120	Lidded Jug	$225-250
Cake Lifter	$125-135		

Before closing the section on OvenServe and Kitchen Kraft, it should be pointed out that the divisions between the various shapes are not as clear as they are with dinnerware lines. For example, a retailer would never offer a line mixed with pieces from Swing and Theme or Fiesta and Epicure, but with the OS/KK lines, it was common for a retailer to choose a decal and then offer a combination of shapes.

The ad shown comes from a late 1930s catalog. It shows the same Deco Leaf decal on a *Daisy Chain* casserole and pie plate, a *Royal Metal* straight sided casserole, *embossed OvenServe* mixing bowl, casserole, under plate and *Kitchen Kraft* under plate, cake plate, covered jar. The utensils actually belong to both embossed OvenServe and Kitchen Kraft.

Speciality Items

Not every item HLC has made belongs to a specific line of dinnerware and kitchenware. Ever since they started production, there have been specialty pieces. These may have been created as generic shapes to be used when needed or to fill a special order put forth by a distributor or other company not specializing with dinnerware such as Quaker Oats, Kraft Cheese, etc. This section has a sample of collectible HLC speciality items.

Breakfast Sets

From the early 1900s until the 1960s, Homer Laughlin produced wares for the Quaker Oats Company. In the 1920s, breakfast sets were made consisting of tea cups, saucers, 6" plates, oatmeal bowls, and fruit cups. There are basically two sets of shapes; those coming from a standard line of dinnerware and those specially created for the promotion.

Two examples of shapes used from an existing line are Trellis and Wells. The dinnerware line Trellis is often found with a general HLC backstamp, but pieces used in the promotion are marked simply, "Trellis." The same is true for Wells except promotional pieces are marked, "Tudor Rose." It was very common for other pottery companies to share production of these small pieces which was necessary in some cases to fill the large orders put forth by Quaker Oats. Ivora (a shape based on Kwaker/Empress flatware) is another small breakfast set made for Colgate in the early 1930s. In the 1950s, HLC made use of Rhythm coupe shapes in making sets along with area potteries with various treatments. One such pattern not shown here is "Golden Wheat" which was made by HLC, French-Saxon and Scio. These small breakfast pieces were sold in boxes of DUZ soap and are very easy to find today.

Ivory Color & Trellis

Ivory Color was a name used on one of the first breakfast sets in the mid 1920s. Sebring Potteries' Barbara Jane shape was used for this set which is a round rim shape with a wide fluted verge. Several potteries made Ivory Color including Sebring, Homer Laughlin and Knowles. When marked, pieces will have an "Ivory Color" backstamp with the initial of the maker. In Homer Laughlin's case, a capital letter, "L" is located under the Ivory Color name.

Soon after the use of Sebring's Barbara Jane shape, HLC started to make sets with the Trellis shape. Initially, pieces were marked with the same "Ivory Color" marking before a new Trellis backstamp was made. Like the Barbara Jane shape, multiple companies made Trellis and often pieces are marked with an initial to signify the pottery. With both shapes, larger serving pieces could be purchased to make sets of dinnerware.

6" Plate	$2-3	Fruit Cup	$2-3
Teacup	$2-3	Oatmeal Bowl	$2-3
Saucer	$1		

Chelsea

When the Virginia Rose shape was first being offered in late 1932, Quaker Oats decided they would like to pick up the necessary pieces for a breakfast set. In late January 1933 several samples were made, but Quaker Oats changed their minds and by late February 1933 had decided on Taylor Smith and Taylor's embossed shape, Marvel. This shape was similar to Virginia Rose, but had heavier embossings. Rhead noted the treatment was to consist of "6 sprays and a center." The name "Garland" was applied to this new small line, but it was changed to "Chelsea" after it was realized that TST had another embossed shape called Garland.

Chelsea can be found with the simple colorful sprigs used for the promotion, but once in a while, pieces can be found with familiar HLC decals. The dinnerware version made by Taylor Smith and Taylor is extensive and will be marked with a general TS & T backstamp.

Chelsea cup and saucer.

Whenever a new dinnerware line was modeled, samples were always made for Quaker Oats, but many ended up rejected. This was the case with Virginia Rose, Ravenna and several others. The main reason was Quaker Oats wanted their own shape. It was viewed that the promotions would be much more successful if Quaker Oats could offer pieces that couldn't be purchased through retail.

Plate	$5-7	Oatmeal Bowl	$5-6
Teacup	$6-8	9" Plate	$10-12
Saucer	$1-2	Platter	$12-15
Fruit Cup	$3-4	Nappy	$10-12

Peachtree

As early as 1934, Homer Laughlin started designing exclusives for Quaker Oats. Most of these shapes never made it into mass production. There is one major exception: "Peachtree." This heavily embossed cup and saucer set is rather difficult to find and is simply marked "Peachtree" in the same fashion as other breakfast sets such as Chelsea and Tudor Rose. The cup and saucer were modeled in July 1936, but records indicate a backstamp wasn't made for this shape until early 1937. Peachtree was shelved for approximately eight months before being put into production.

Original sketches for the Peachtree cup and saucer.

Teacup	$8-10
Saucer	$1-2

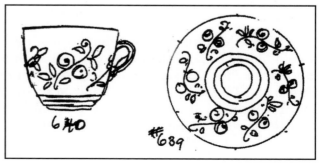

Tea Rose

In the fall of 1936, a new shape was modeled called, "Italian." This scalloped/petal design mimicked other popular petal shapes of the day such as "Toulon" by Mt. Clemens Pottery Co., and "Rainbow" by W.S. George. The new line was being developed during the same time as the Tango dinnerware so the similarity between the two shapes is not too surprising. However, in October 1936, only an Italian 7" plate was modeled. Attention was given to developing Tango as a dinnerware line and eventually Tango pieces were selected to be made for Quaker Oats' breakfast sets. But, as with Ravenna and Virginia Rose, the Tango shape was rejected.

In 1937, pieces were added to the singleton "Italian" set. The Oatmeal and fruit cup in January and in February, a teacup and saucer. By March, the original Italian plate was reduced in size to 6⅝". The name, "Tea Rose" was given to the line and a new backstamp was made by mid-April.

As with Chelsea, Tea Rose is rather easy to find with small floral sprigs or with familiar decals used on other HLC shapes. Larger pieces of Tea Rose could be purchased and the buyer could create dinnerware sets. These additional pieces are much harder to find than the smaller breakfast sets and may or may not be marked with a general HLC backstamp. Three "larger pieces" were added to Tea Rose: 9" plate, 9" round serving bowl, and the 11½" oval platter.

Tea Rose marking.

Tea Rose fruit cup, oatmeal and 6" plate.

This Tea Rose shape oval platter marked with a general HLC backstamp.

6" Plate	$3-4	Oatmeal Bowl	$10-12
Teacup	$6-7	9" Plate	$12-15
Saucer	$1-2	Nappy	$12-15
Fruit Cup	$2-3	Platter	$10-12

Carnival

With the success of Fiesta and other solid colored dinnerware lines, Quaker Oats decided upon brightly colored breakfast sets. In early November of 1937 development began on what would make use of the Fiesta glazes. Two styles of cups, saucers and 6" plates were modeled. With regard to the cups and saucers, both versions are very similar in shape, but had different decorative elements. The first set had rings at the base of the cup and on the rim of the saucer. The second version had small blunt "flutes" at the base of the cup and surrounding the well of the saucer. The same is true with the 6" plates: rings towards the edge versus flutes at the verge.

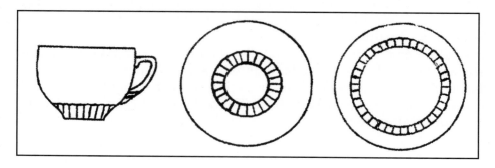

Fluted style version of Carnival that was passed over in favor of the ringed pattern.

Before the end of November, the fluted style was no longer under consideration and the ringed version fruit cup and oatmeal were made. At the end of January 1938, all five ringed pieces – teacup, saucer, 6" plate, fruit cup and oatmeal – were put into production and were sold by Quaker Oats as, "Carnival."

The Carnival sets came in colors from the 30s: cobalt, red, (Fiesta) yellow, light green and ivory as well as colors used in the 50s: dark green, gray, Harlequin yellow and turquoise. Some of the colors from the "30s" sets are hard to find in some cases. Collectors note having difficulty locating light green, red and cobalt teacups, but find other items such as light green and yellow 6" plates very common. With the "50s" Carnival sets, the five shapes in all colors are found with very little difficulty.

There is no record that any "larger" pieces were made to go with Carnival. In very rare instances, Carnival in the 50s colors will have a backstamp.

This original Carnival Oats box featuring plates, cups and saucers on the front, is from the 1950s based on the color assortment: yellow, gray, turquoise and dark green.

Here are all the shapes used for Carnival, though many insist that there are larger pieces such as dinner plates, platters and serving pieces.

Knowles produced a line of dinnerware called, "Deanna" which was made in solid colors and with decals. Shown is a rust colored Deanna saucer with a Homer Laughlin Carnival saucer in light green. The shapes are similar, but Knowles' has three raised rings and Carnival has an indented pair.

To the left are Carnival cups in standard colors: ivory and Harlequin yellow. The third cup is in a glaze similar to melon yellow.

6" Plate	$3-4	Fruit Cup	$3-4
Teacup	$5-6	Oatmeal Bowl	$3-4
Saucer	$1		

Harvest

In September 1941, Homer Laughlin modeled five new shapes for Quaker Oats. These are listed in the modeling log as "Q.O. MODELED BORDER" shapes and include the cup, saucer, fruit, oatmeal and a 6" plate. All five were released into production in the same month. These shapes would be used with three different one-color treatments over a period of over fifteen years.

The first of these patterns was "Harvest" – a red treatment of a basket with fruit. The project of making Harvest was shared by Homer Laughlin and Taylor Smith and Taylor (TS & T). Before production began, both HLC and TS&T had to have consistent treatments. On October 16, 1941, Rhead notes some problems with getting HLC's Harvest to match TS&T's: . . . *Miller from TS&T here on Q.O. pattern. Having trouble with the printing . . . Saw J.M. Wells who said there is to be no production until TS&T and our products were checked.*

Harvest was produced until the very late 1940s when it was replaced by Wild Rose.

Harvest marking.

6" Plate	$2-3
Teacup	$4-5
Saucer	$1-2
Fruit Cup	$2-3
Oatmeal Bowl	$2-3

Harvest oatmeal bowl.

Wild Rose

The second treatment to be put on the "modeled border" shape was "Wild Rose" – a one-color blue print of roses and leaves. Unlike the five-piece set for Harvest, Wild Rose had extra serving pieces. Notes from 1946 indicate that a creamer with "rose relief modeling" was made in April. Another was made in May of the same year along with a matching covered sugar. Other pieces of Wild Rose have been found such as a dinner plate, sauceboat, sauceboat liner, nappie, chop plate, a handled serving tray and deep plate. Royal China of Sebring, Ohio produced most of these larger pieces. Six different offerings were printed on the reverse of Quick Mother's Oats boxes. Each instructed the comsumer to send in $1.00 and a "trademark from Mother's Oats" to an address in Sebring, Ohio in order to obtain the extra pieces. The extras, or "units" as they were called, consisted of the following: Unit A – Sugar and Creamer, Unit B – Gravy Boat and Utility Dish, Unit C – 9" Vegetable Dish and Lugged Meat Platter, Unit D – 12" Round Chop Plate, Unite E – 3 Dinner Plates, Unit F – 3 Soup Plates.

According to the modeling log, HLC produced the 9" plate, sugar and creamer. There is no evidence they made the other larger pieces. There are two styles of 9" plates and are shown in the following pictures:

HLC's example (right) will have the same light embossing that was developed for Harvest. The second type (left) made by Royal China, has sharper and more detailed embossings.

The HLC plate has the same size blue treatment found on the small items; the sharper modeled plate by Royal China has a larger treatment to correspond with the size of the plate.

Backstamps can be helpful in determining if a piece of Wild Rose was made at HLC or Royal China. If the marking has the familiar generic date code with month, year and plant number, such as "M52N6", then it was made by HLC. If the word UNDERGLAZE is in the marking, then its Royal China. They often promoted their wares, which used transfer design treatments, as being underglaze. Sometimes they would ad a date code consisting of a letter and a two digit number such as F52.

Wild Rose sugars and creamers were made at both HLC and Royal China.

Shown here in the three pictures at the right are the vegetable bowl, sauceboat fast-stand and liner, and the handled tray – all of which have the Royal China Wild Rose UNDERGLAZE backstamp. Not shown are the soup bowls and chop plate.

Breakfast set pieces: cup, saucer, fruit cup, oatmeal and 6" plate.

Wild Rose by Homer Laughlin		Wild Rose by Royal China		Both HLC and Royal China	
6" Plate	$2-3	9" Plate	$18-20	Creamer	$20-25
Teacup	$4-5	Chop Plate	$20-25	Covered Sugar	$25-30
Saucer	$1-2	Handled Tray	$20-25		
Fruit Cup	$2-3	Sauceboat	$20-25		
Oatmeal Bowl	$3-4	Sauceboat Liner	$15-18		
HLC 9" Plate	$18-20	Nappy	$18-20		
		Rim Soup	$12-18		

Pastoral

"Pastoral" was the last decoration to grace the five modeled border shapes. Unlike Harvest and Wild Rose, Pastoral had a different scene for each piece. All in green, the theme for each print is a farm scene. This was produced mainly in the mid 1950s and to date, the only "large" item found is the dinner plate. Taylor Smith and Taylor shared production of Pastoral with Homer Laughlin. All items will be marked with the appropriate potters' name. Pastoral is the easiest to find followed by Wild Rose and finally, Harvest.

6" Plate	$2-3	Fruit Cup	$2-3
Teacup	$4-5	Oatmeal Bowl	$2-3
Saucer	$1-2	9" Plate	$18-20

Pastoral was not produced much longer after 1957 when emphasis was placed on small embossed OvenServe shapes which were made by both HLC and TST. For more on this small set, see section on OvenServe.

This pink and blue floral treatment was produced by Homer Laughlin and Taylor Smith & Taylor in the late 1950s. Pieces are marked, "Fortune" with either the initials HLC or TST.

6" Plate	$1-2	Fruit Cup	$1
Teacup	$2-3	Oatmeal Bowl	$1-2
Saucer	$1		

Mayfair

The "Mayfair" set comes from the early 1960s. It was shared by Royal China, Stetson China and HLC. The only pieces made by HLC are the generic coupe shape 6" plate and fruit cup. Royal China and Stetson made the other two under the name, "Royal Stetson." Notice the unusual handle on the teacup – this is a common shape used by Stetson.

6" Plate	$1-2	Fruit Cup	$1
Teacup	$2-3	Oatmeal Bowl	$1-2
Saucer	$1		

Chateau Buffet

In the 1960s, Taylor Smith and Taylor introduced a new line of kitchen/dinnerware called, Chateau Buffet. The body of this line was made of a brown clay composed primarily of Nickel Oxide. The specially formulated body resulted in a line that was perfect for going from the refrigerator to the oven to the dinner table. TST produced an extensive assortment of Chateau Buffet. Most pieces were given a turquoise application on either the interior or exterior. The brown you see is actually the clay with a clear glaze.

Homer Laughlin produced four pieces of Chateau Buffet; the cereal (as shown,) French casserole, custard and ramekin. The relationship between HLC and TS & T with respect to Chateau Buffet is the reverse of that with respect to embossed OvenServe. With OvenServe, it was HLC which made the extensive line and TS & T was the one that assisted in production of the smaller items.

With HLC's Chateau Buffet, expect the colored interiors to be turquoise, but with TS & T, they can be any color and some dinnerware items may be found with decal decorations. All of HLC's pieces will be found with a cast mold marking.

Values for pieces marked HLC:

Cereal	$4-5	Custard	$2-3
French Casserole	$6-7	Ramekin	$2-3

Child's Sets

Homer Laughlin has produced children's dishes almost since they began operations in the 1870s. Various staple pieces (items not belonging to a particular line) were made with treatments that would appeal to children and in the 1920s. The Empress shape was used rather heavily with "Tiny Todkins" decals. Even the very popular Art China line was used as a basis for treatments with child themes. While the art ware probably wasn't intended for children's use, today many people enjoy adding these pieces to "juvenile ware" collections.

In the 1930s, Homer Laughlin started producing special shapes and treatments directed towards children. The first was the Little Orphan Annie mug made for The Wonder Co. of Chicago, Illinois. On April 23, 1931, Frederick Rhead made four sketches of mugs that he referred to as, "Ovaltine Mugs." By May 1st, the fourth version was selected and the "Ovaltine Mugs" went into production. This generic shape mug would end up being used in several child's sets as well as Tom & Jerry sets. Once in a while, an Ovaltine mug can be found with a Fiesta glaze.

The examples shown are not common. Ordinarily the handles and rim don't have the reddish brown coloring. Instead, they are trimmed in green and Annie is usually saying, "DID JA EVER TASTE ANYTHING SO GOOD AS OVALTINE? AND IT'S GOOD FOR YAH, TOO."

Values: Little Orphan Annie mugs $40-45   in Fiesta glazes $60+

There are several special child's sets that were planned and modeled, but were never produced. Rhead describes some of these sets in his journals. One such set, described as an "Elephant" set, was modeled in June and July of 1931. This set had a bowl, mug, and even a cream. Elephant sets were to have been made with "Jungle Sam" decals. Rhead even notes making a special Jungle Sam box to market the set. After working on this for two months, he never mentions them again. While examples can be found at the factory, none have surfaced on the open market so one can only assume Jungle Sam sets never went into production.

In late July 1931, another specialty item was made: a "Purina" bowl. Purina bowls are small promotional bowls made for the Ralston Purina Company and packed in boxes of Ralston's whole wheat cereal. An ad from the early 30s states:

Little folks get a thrill eating from the "Find the Bottom of the Bowl." Just to find the happy bunny at the bottom of the bowl, they eat on and on until the cereal is all gone.

Unlike other small size premiums offered in boxes of oats, soap, etc., the Purina bowl could be obtained by sending, "25 cents with one Ralston package top."

Value: $20-25

The Purina bowl, like the Ovaltine mug, would become a general item in various child's sets as well as a basis for mixing bowls. One of the first child's sets that use the Ovaltine mugs and Purina bowls is the Tom Thumb set. A plate was selected from the Wells line and in 1932 the three pieces were glazed in vellum and given a series of Tom Thumb decals. Each decal depicts Tom Thumb with a different animal such as a frog, butterfly and others.

Another set made in the late 1930s to early 1940s made use of the same shapes from Tom Thumb, but treatments are the "Circus Animals" or "Comic Animals" decals. A pig (riding a goose), elephant, monkey and hippo are found in various positions on the child's sets. If you find an unmarked piece with one or more of the animal decals, then it doesn't automatically mean its an HLC product since they were used by other potteries such as Crown Potteries, Knowles China and several others.

The animal decals: monkey on skates, hippo on skates, elephant on skates and pig on goose, were used by at least five pottery companies: HLC, Edwin M. Knowles, W.S. George, Crown Potteries, and Syracuse. To date, they have been found on the following HLC shapes: the "generic" child's shapes, Swing, Yellowstone, and Fiesta.

There is actually a fifth decal: a combination of the elephant and the pig on goose. This treatment has the elephant holding onto the goose's tail feathers. The pig comes in two forms. In the picture the pig on the cup has a blue coat and blue interior to his cap. In the bowl, the blue is replaced by gray. When I first noticed this variation in a picture, I thought the gray version might be the result of the blue color fading. But when I saw them in person, it became clear that the gray suited pig is a distinct treatment.

Plate: $35-40   Bowl: $18-20   Mug: $18-20

The Dick Tracy child's sets makes use of the Purina bowl and Ovaltine mug, but unlike other sets, uses a Century plate. A series of decals depicting characters from the popular comic strip grace the three items which were glazed in ivory vellum. The set with the original box is the standard Dick Tracy set. The other set was photographed at HLC.

Plate: $50-60   Bowl: $20-25   Mug: $20-25

You may find other child's sets produced by HLC. Throughout the years, various treatments and shapes have been used. Those discussed here are the most sought after and, as a result, have the most value. Homer Laughlin is still making child's sets on hotel body shapes today and in 1999, a special Fiesta child's tea set was released with an individual teapot, demi cups and saucers, sugar, creamer and 7" plates.

"I go here plates" were made in the 1950s by at least two potteries: Salem China Company of Salem, Ohio and Homer Laughlin. They were produced for International Silver which distributed these pieces with specially made forks and spoons. *"I go here" says the Fork* and *"I go here" says the Spoon* are lettered in gold on the lugs. Several retailers carried these plates (or bowls as some prefer to call them). The example in the center has a treatment that was offered by Montgomery Wards in the early 1950s.

Plates are marked with a gold backstamp which also includes the name of the pottery. Due to the popularity of children's dishes, these rather common plates sometimes go for higher than normal prices.

Values: HLC or Salem example: $15-20

Specialty Bowls

Though most "salad" specialty bowls will date from the 1940s and 50s, the Swirl or Pennsylvania shape bowl was produced as early as the mid 1920s. The trim on early Pennsylvania bowls are light and softer than the green, blue and tan trims used in the 50s. The decal shown is the most common, but you will find others. In some cases, especially with those from the 20s, there are no decals at all.

In 1939, Rhead notes the Pennsylvania salads were to be made in Harlequin yellow, Harlequin blue (mauve blue) and Fiesta green (light green). There is no evidence these solid colored PA bowls ever became standard items offered by HLC.

Value: $5-6

This fluted specialty bowl (note it is not swirled) was first made in the early 1920s. The decal and trim combination in the picture seems to be the most common on this shape, but you will also find this shape with pale green trim and no decal.

Value: $5-6

The New York shape salad bowl is not as common as the Pennsylvania. The embossing along the rim is of oak leaves which are brought out by the wash trim. The decal on this particular example is the same that is shown on the Pennsylvania bowl.

Value: $8-10

Of the 9" specialty bowls, this seems to be one of the harder shapes to find. It is called the "Boston" bowl and this particular example has a gold luster trim.

Value: $8-10

Stenciled designs generally occur on two shapes: plain round and Virginia Rose. Virginia Rose is by far more common than the round version and there are at least three variations. Shown is a "medallion" type stencil. Stencils can come in several colors: green, red and blue.

The round 9" salad bowl with a blue stencil decoration.

Values: Virginia Rose shape - $10-12
Plain Round shape - $7-9

In March and April 1935, the Art Department at HLC worked on several types of salad bowls. Four versions are listed in the log as Orange border, Orange border and center, scale design, and scale design with modeled center. Those with modeled centers were not released into production. Instead, the two that were, the orange border and scale design, have plain centers which are decorated with decals. Both versions are rather easy to find. Most often they have light green wash trims, but examples with blue, yellow, tan and pink wash trims have also been found.

Both bowls are identical except for the embossed designs. They are listed in the log as having diameters of 9¾" but they're closer to 10" even. Expect examples to have a general HLC backstamp.

Orange border bowl in front of a scale bowl.

Scale Bowl

Values: Orange border - $10-12
Scale bowl   - $15-18

This plain round shape specialty bowl is from the late 1940s.

Value: $7-9

The Betty Crocker bowls were made in 1940. Several versions were modeled, but this is the only one that went into production. They were also made by Red Wing and Gladding McBean with minor differences and similar markings. Homer Laughlin's versions have an opening diameter of 8½" and stands 2¾" tall. Expect to find these in turquoise and Harlequin yellow only.

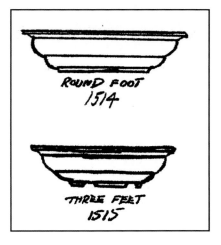

From the modeling log are two sketches of proposed Betty Crocker bowls which were also called, "open casseroles" at the time. The top sketch, model 1514, is the style that was chosen over model 1515, a similar bowl but with three feet.

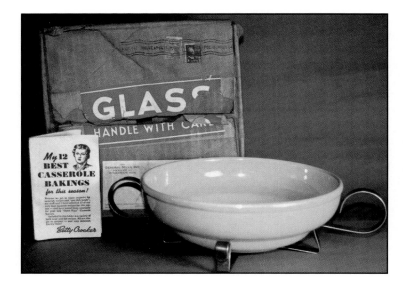

Glazed in Harlequin yellow, this Betty Crocker bowl comes complete with a collapsing metal frame, small casserole cook book and original box.

Value: HLC bowl only, turquoise or yellow - $12-15

These large salad bowls in dark green were originally sold as parts of salad sets which included small Rhythm shape bowls in chartreuse and plastic salad spoon and fork. Interestingly a glass version exists in the same shapes and colors and marked Pyrex. HLC's versions are unmarked and were also used with HLC's buffet line, Kenilworth. The jumbo salad was also used with several Duratone lines as well. None from any line have been found marked.

Value: Jumbo Salad, diameter 9", height 4¼"
Dark Green or Turquoise - $20-25
Other colors - $45-50
Decaled - $12-15

Divided bakers, like the ones shown, have been found in rose, chartreuse, dark green, Harlequin yellow and turquoise. They are not marked, but the few collectors who have found these

believe them to be Homer Laughlin products. An entry in the modeling log dated April 11, 1956 lists a divided baker, but gives no size or capacity specifications. There is also a note off to the side indicating the bakers were released into production on June 20th – presumably the same year. In a recent interview conducted by

Steve Sfakis, Don Schreckengost revealed the divided bakers were made as a generic shape on the same order as the jumbo salad bowl and spoon rest. They were meant to be used with multiple lines – both solid colored and decaled. Those shown were made for Woolworth's to go with Harlequin.

According to the backstamp, this bowl was made in 1984 for FTDA. It has rings on the outside which makes it look as if it was hand thrown, but the interior rings are identical to Fiesta. The trim for this bowl is purple, but other colors can be found. They will all have the same yellow-ivory color with speckles, and glaze is a matte texture so it scratches very easily. These were made in at least four different sizes.   **Value:** $5-8

Mugs

Baltimore mugs were commonly used with decaled wares, especially Yellowstone and Virginia Rose.

Values for Baltimore Mugs:
    with the Virginia Rose, JJ-59 "Moss Rose" treatment – $50-55
    with any other treatment – $15-18

In mid 1938, HLC worked on several versions of handled mugs in various shapes ranging from straight sided, to conical, to curved bodies. The handles were also diverse in shape. Some were rather plain while others were picked up from existing dinnerware lines, especially Swing. These mugs were very similar with regards to capacity holding an average of 9½ fluid ounces.

The mugs started out as being called simply, "mug" with no reference to a retailer or decoration so HLC's intention on how to use these mugs is unclear. Later versions are referred to as "SKI" mugs.

In late 1938 two more ski mugs were made, this time holding 11 ounces each. After that no more mention is made of ski mugs. Fifteen distinct mugs in all were modeled, but there are no notations that any were released into production. Shown are sketches from the modeling log of nine of these "ski mugs."

The handled mug was made in 1933. The entries in Rhead's journals tell the story behind this piece:

03.17.33	*Modeled Beer Stein – grape border*
04.01.33	*Barrel shape stein, molded borders. Quantity three dozen only. Advise when made in clay. Purpose: Beer mug possibility.*
04.15.33	*Clay Stein – fruit border out*
04.20.33	*First modeled stein out in Art Glazes. Ordered bisque out today in Rust and Vellum.*

Shown is the beer stein in the green art glaze. It was even marked with the Wells Art Glazes backstamp. To date, no others have been reported, though based on Rhead's notes, there must be some to be found in rust and ivory.

241

While there is substantial background information on the stein, the same cannot be said for the "deco" tumbler. This piece is glazed in a golden color similar to OvenServe's orange (pumpkin) glaze and its marking is similar to the HLC impressed logo found on the Apple Tree bowls.

Values: Either Mug: UND

On the left in ivory is the Ovaltine shape mug produced from the 1930s until the 1960s. This utilitarian mug has been found with child's sets, Tom & Jerry sets, advertisements, and even in the Fiesta glazes; turquoise and light green. To the right is the heavier Best China version that has been decorated by an outside company.

Values: Best China Mug – $2-3

The FDR mugs were developed from July to October 1933 in at least two different heights and capacities. The 43/4" versions were made in ivory and yellow and collectors have found both colors. Interestingly, an "Al Smith Mug" was also made at the same time but none have been found on the open market. Al Smith was originally a supporter of FDR, but in 1933, Smith openly opposed FDR's New Deal policy.

FDR mugs don't have any HLC markings, but they will say "Franklin D. Roosevelt" along the side. **Value:** $200+

The Tom and Jerry sets were made in ivory with gold lettering from the late 1930s into the 1950s. The mug designed for the Little Orphan Annie Promotion was originally used, but a second version was modeled (shown on the left) in the 1950s.

The bowl is the large size made for the "nappy bowl" mixing set of 1932.

Both styles of mugs are easy to find as is the bowl. The same style lettering was used on Fiesta shapes – the footed salad bowl and Tom & Jerry mug. Fiesta examples are much more costly than the generic shapes shown here.

Values:

        Tom & Jerry Bowl
                nappy shape – $10-15
                Fiesta footed salad shape – $150-200

        Tom & Jerry Mug
                L.O.A. shape – $4-5
                50s shape – $6-8
                Fiesta shape – $20-25

In the early 1950s, Homer Laughlin started to produce specialty oversized 18-ounce coffee cups and saucers with "Mother" and "Father" treatments. The saucers are oversized to match the cups. They are plain round coupe shapes similar to the smaller Rhythm saucers and have a diameter of 6⅞". There are two styles of cups which have identical bodies but different applied handles. The ones shown have a rounded handle and are the most common of the two versions. The saucers used for both styles of cups are the same. Don't expect the cups to be marked, but saucers will often have the general HLC backstamp. The particular examples shown are marked with the HLC backstamp and the date code: E52 N 5 (May 1952, plant 5).

This is the second style cup which is harder to find than the ones with the curved handle. This version was produced in the mid 1950s.

In 1955, Homer Laughlin started to produce jumbo coffee cups for the Harlequin line which were sold through Woolworth's. The body for these jumbo cups comes from Epicure and the handle was specially modeled to fit the Harlequin line. However, the saucers used with these cups were already in production for the specialty "Mother" and "Father" jumbo coffee mugs. Recently, several of these sets were offered on eBay in chartreuse and rose with their original Woolworth's price stickers. The jumbo Harlequin saucers are always found unmarked.

Values: Jumbo Cup, either style – $5-7
Jumbo Saucer, white with trim - $1-2
Jumbo Saucer, solid colors (sold with Harlequin large cups in the 1950s) – $50-60

This mug was produced for many years. Most will be marked, "Best China." They have the familiar Fiesta ring handle that was used on the Fiesta Tom and Jerry mugs. Sometimes they have a solid color exterior glaze.

Value: $3-5

Troy mug with a "Market Street" shape cup glazed in cobalt from the new Fiesta line.

The shape name of this decaled mug is "Troy Mug." Still in production, they have been made for over 20 years.

River mug in turquoise, bouillon cup and Shakespeare mug.

The generic shaped mugs shown here are listed by Homer Laughlin as: shape 0300, Mug Coffee, 8¾oz. Here they are seen glazed in the new Fiesta colors, rose and turquoise and have special Looney Tunes treatments. They were made for The Warner Bros. Studio Stores in 1994 to go with the popular Looney Tunes treatments used on new Fiesta shapes.

Value: $5-8

Marquis shape mug and plain 4¼" coaster with Chester High School treatments. Coasters were first made in November of 1961. They can be found with advertising treatments, colored exteriors, decals and plain and were almost always unmarked.

Other Specialty Items

The "deco ashtrays" were first made in 1931. They didn't originate with any particular dinnerware line and examples have been found with at least three different backstamps: Wells Art Glazes, OvenServe, and the general HLC backstamp with date code. When the first pieces of OvenServe were being modeled, an ashtray was under consideration. Instead of creating an ashtray with the embossed OvenServe design, the "deco" ashtray was used. Most of the ashtrays found with the OvenServe marking are in pumpkin or ivory.

The original center ring design mimicked the partial rings found on the rim: small with wide spacing between them. Within two years, these small center rings were replaced by the larger and more narrowly spaced type shown.

Values: Any color, any mark – $95+

First produced in 1952, "square ashtrays" are very easy to find. Most are unmarked, but some will carry a general HLC backstamp from the early 1950s. Pearl China decorated square ashtrays with a series of dogs playing poker and the United States Post Office used specially decorated square ashtrays to promote the use of Zip Codes in the 1970s.

Values: Blank – $1-2   Decorated – $5-8

Homer Laughlin produced dinnerware as movie theater premiums starting in the early 1930s. The Century plate with the blue medallion treatment is by far the most common. It's believed sugars from this set don't have lids since it was easier to hand out one piece of pottery instead of the two that would be needed to make up a covered sugar.

Values: any shape with a movie house promotion – $10-15

At the end of February 1933, six drawings were made for a muffin plate for General Mills. Only two designs were modeled and are listed in the log at the beginning of March 1933. The first is noted as a "scroll" muffin plate and the second is "shell." On the 16th, Rhead notes the "new modeled plate out in Art Glazes." He never mentions these plates again.

Shown is the shell muffin plate in the peach art glaze. It is marked with a generic HLC backstamp and the date code indicates April 1933 production.

Value: $200+

The 7" Snack Plate or "Leaf Saucer" was made in Fiesta red and light green for the Kraft Cheese in 1938. They could be purchased for 25 cents and two Kraft Cheese jar labels. It's sown in green along with Kraft swanky swigs and an original metal cap with the leaf saucer promotional offer.

Value: $75-85

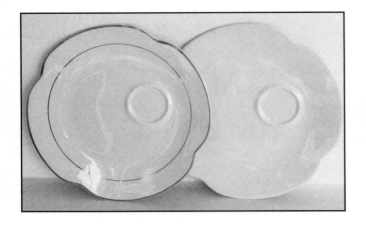

T.V. plates, as they were commonly called in the 1950s and 60s, were modeled at the end of November 1962 and are still offered by HLC today. There was no cup made for this plate and through the years, different shape cups have been used. Orbit cups are often found with T.V. plates which isn't too surprising since the Orbit shape was crafted soon after the T.V. plate.

Examples are often found plain or with trim, though once in a while, a decaled version from the 60s and 70s show up on the collector market.

Value: $3-4

In 1939, HLC made a special teacup and saucer for the M. Seller's, a west coast distributor of HLC wares. Though the Sellers' body might look like the same as Carnival, it isn't. The Seller's cup, shown in red with a turquoise Carnival cup for comparison, was made with a different ring configuration and a new handle. Also shown is a coupe shape saucer with rings towards the center.

Neither the cups nor the saucers have been found with any markings and come in red, light green, Harlequin yellow and mauve blue.

Value: Sellers cup – $65-70   Sellers saucer – $25-30

For the 1939-1940 Worlds Fair held in New York, several potteries – HLC, Knowles China, Cronin China, Hall China and Paden City Pottery – made wares as souvenirs for a special exhibit on the pottery industry. HLC made several items which have become collectible not only to Homer Laughlin collectors, but also to World's Fair (W.F.) collectors. This crossover has driven up the prices for many of the harder to find items.

There were different styles and sizes of hand thrown vases made at the Fair, but there were also machine made pieces made at Homer Laughlin in a bisque state (undecorated and unglazed) then transported to New York where they were finished with solid colors at the special exhibit. Shown in this picture are various hand thrown and machine made pieces. On the far left and lined up in front are ashtrays which were modeled in April of 1940. A set of four depicts each of the four seasons; green for spring, turquoise for summer, red for autumn and yellow or ivory for winter.

Behind the season ashtrays is the zodiac cup and saucer. These are found only in turquoise and have embossings of the twelve signs of the zodiac. Like the season ashtrays, these were also made in the spring of 1940. There's evidence the zodiac cups and saucers were also made at the Cronin China Company of Minerva, Ohio.

In the center are George and Martha Washington pitchers. The Washington jug is the first W.F. piece Rhead notes in his journals. On February 21, 1939, he wrote: *Washington Jug, Medium size, Size of Roosevelt mug.* The Roosevelt mug he was referring to was the FDR mug produced several years prior in 1933. A month later, he noted finishing a model of the Washington mug and on April 12, 1939 trails were made in ivory vellum and what Rhead called a, "glossy rose." He also wrote that Vellum was, "more appropriate." The Martha Washington jug would have to wait another year. It was modeled in April of 1940 and released into production in May. The smaller jugs are also of George and Martha.

To the right is a stack of Potters Plaques. Two versions were made and they are listed in the log as, "Thrower at Wheel" and "Artist at Wheel." They were modeled at the same time as the Washington jug in April 1939.

Note the three vases in ivory, turquoise, and cobalt. These are three examples of hand thrown pieces made at the World's Fair.

The W.F. plate in the back and to the left is very desirable to W.F. collectors. Shown is 1939, but a 1940 version was also made. The plate and ashtray on the far right were made for the 1939 San Francisco Exposition.

Values for World's Fair items:

Seasonal Ashtrays	$40-50 ea.
Potters Plates	$18-20

Jugs in Ivory:

George Washington Jug	$40-50
Martha Washington Jug	$50-60
Mini George Washington Jug	$25-30
Mini Martha Washington Jug	$25-30
1939 W.F. Plate	$85-95
1940 W.F. Plate	$100-125
Zodiac Cup and Saucer	$60-75
Hand-Thrown Vases	$50-70

Close up of the Spring W.F. ashtray in light green.

Potter's Plates are rather common and measure 7¼" in diameter.

Shown are two items made for the San Francisco Exposition of 1939. The plate, which is a Georgian plate without the embossed rim, was modeled on October 1938 and was listed as *Plate 8" Plain "Georgian" Shape* and written off to the side was "Exposition." The 6¼" ashtray with the same SF Exposition treatment was made in early November 1938. Both pieces were released into production in November 1938 (the plate on the 12th and the ashtray on the 16th) so expect to find examples with generic HLC marks, many of which have date codes of "L38N6" and "M38N6", along with a special SF Exposition mark.

There must have been an overstock of ashtrays as many are found in pearlized glazes and with different decals complete with the SF mark.

Values:

10" Plate with SF treatment (1939 or 1940)	$60-70
Ashtray with SF treatment	$40-50
Ashtray with other treatments	$15-18

According to records, between March and July of 1937, there were three versions of a "Jewel Tea" vase. The one shown here is the final version. You may find these with a general HLC marking.

The decal on this vase was also used on Kitchen Kraft.

Height: 5¾"   Opening: 3¾"

Value: $20-25

The shell plate shown is in Fiesta red. The modeling log and Rhead's journals tell the full story of this plate. Two entries in Rhead's journals discusses the shell plate to be made for Proctor & Gamble:

02.10.39 Model shell plate – actual over all 10½" samples in all 4 colors. Green, turquoise, yellow and red.
02.27.39 Large shell trays for Proctor & Gamble back from glost kiln. Sent off this morning. J.D.T. made out shipping notice. One each in Fiesta red, yellow, green and turquoise.

Here are three of the four sketches of shell plates under consideration. Their listings in the modeling log are as follows with the description, date:

1123	PLATE, 7" SHELL DESIGN	AUG 38
1127	PLATE, 7" SHELL DESIGN	SEPT 38
1128	PLATE, 7" SHELL DESIGN (1/8" deeper than 1123)	SEPT 38
1203	PLATE, SHELL 10½" DIA	FEB 39

The last entry, model 1203, is the only one with a notation that it was released into production. Several of this version have been found in Fiesta red (as shown) and light green. Perhaps yellow and turquoise examples will show up. If you are lucky enough to find a Proctor and Gamble shell plate, expect it to be unmarked.

Value: $100-150

Pottery Festival Doorknobs. These are listed in the mold notes as being created in 1985. The Pottery Festival was an event held in the East Liverpool area for a number of years. These were made as commemorative items and for the doorknob toss – a game held during the pottery festival.

These pieces are still being produced. They are commonly found in white, but can be found in brown and some of the new Fiesta colors. Shown are examples in seamist and apricot. Doorknobs in lilac and sapphire are known to exist.

Values: $3-4

These two contemporary pieces, the "Ornate Salad" plate and soup bowl, are in the cobalt glaze from the current Fiesta line.

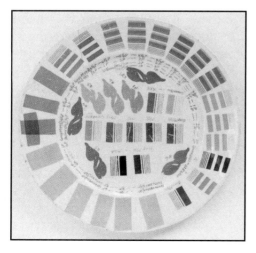

Vintage HLC test plates such as this one – complete with backstamp – are very hard to find.

HLC Color Chart Plate, circa 1980.

Calendar Plates

Calendar plates were produced from the early 1900s until about 1925 with gold stamp promotions of a particular store, bank or other business. Many potteries produced such plates with elaborate gold filigree and large floral decals. In Homer Laughlin's case, The Angelus was a popular blank for calendar plates and they aren't particularly hard to find today.

Starting in the 1950s, many area potteries such as HLC, Taylor Smith & Taylor and Knowles China produced calendar plates, but this time, without advertising. The decoration usually involves the twelve signs of the zodiac or a simple farm scene and is most often applied to a 10" plate, but 9" plates exist as well. The first known HLC examples are from 1953 and make use of Jubilee (as shown), Debutante and Skytone.

For the rest of the 1950s and into the 70s, HLC used different shapes as a basis for calendar plates. Below is a brief list of the HLC shapes that had calendar plates. Other years and shapes can be found.

1953	Jubilee, Debutante, Skytone	1959	Rhythm
1954	Jubilee, Fiesta	1963	Palette Ware
1955	Fiesta	1966	Triumph Snow White, Victoria
1956	Nautilus	1967	Victoria
1957	Cavalier, Skytone	1968	Victoria
1958	Rhythm	1979	White Dover

The 1953 plates are the most common. If a plate is marked, the year in the date code almost always differs from the calendar on the face of the plate by two to three years. For example, 1959 Rhythm calendar plates almost always have a backstamp with the year '56 as part of the date code. This would imply that HLC made use of overstock to create these special plates.

Fiesta plates were usually done in ivory for 1954 (more common year) and 1955 in green, yellow and ivory. Jubilee plates have been found in Shell Pink, Celadon Green and Creme Beige.

Values: Fiesta calendar plates: any color, any year $40-50
            Shapes other than Fiesta: $8-10

Turkey Plates/Platters

The turkey decal shown on this Fiesta 9" plate was used by Homer Laughlin (and other potteries) on dozens of shapes from the very late 40s to the mid 1950s. Most of the time, it's featured on a platter, but on Fiesta, its been found on the 10", 9" plates as well as the round chop plates. On Rhythm, it has appeared on the three platters as well as the 10" plate.

For other shapes, expect the turkey on oval platters. Marigold, Republic, Virginia Rose and Cavalier are just a few of the decalware shapes to be decorated with the turkey decal. The treatment can be on a simple blank with no further decoration or with gold trim, filigree or, in Cavalier's and Fiesta's cases, with a thick colored border. Kraft Blue and Skytone turkey platters aren't all that uncommon, but the same can't be said for the Kraft Pink versions.

As with the calendar plates, expect turkey plates and platters to come from different lines and vary in size.

Turkey Plates/Platters: Fiesta Shapes – $65-95   Shapes other than Fiesta – $20-35

Appendices

Best China

Homer Laughlin had been producing hotel and restaurant ware as early as 1900 using, as vintage ads describe it, "Semi-Vitreous Hotel Wares, Double Thick." This collection of shapes included dozens of sizes and styles of mugs, sugars, covered jars, platters and bowls.

These "restaurant sugars" are two examples of early Laughlin Hotel Ware.

In 1960, Homer Laughlin started to use the name, "Best China" to describe their hotel and restaurant ware. These heavy dishes make use of a date code where the first letter or double letter signifies the year.

A – 1960	X – 1983
B – 1961	Y – 1984
C – 1962	Z – 1985
•	AA – 1986
•	BB – 1987
•	etc.

The backstamps HLC uses today on its restaurant ware, Fiesta and other products make use of the date code which originated with Best China.

Treatments used on Best China are usually simple rim decorations. Sometimes pieces are found with special logos or advertisements of a restaurant or hotel. Shown are just a few of the many Best China shapes and treatments.

Best China marking with Z A II – a 1985 marking.

EEC - a 1990 mark.

Best China dinner plate with green decoration and platter with yellow decoration.

Navy teacup. This treatment was used on various pieces such as dinner plates and soup bowls. Expect to find the same treatment on pieces by other companies, namely Shenango and Sterling China.

Soup/cereal bowls

Test plates with red floral treatments. Their official numbers are given at the top rim with dates at the bottom rim: left: BC-1230, 10-14-86; right: BC-517, 10-10-86.

Test Plate: BC-1121, 11-24-86

The BC-1055 treatment in use on various sizes of plates.

Best China sauceboat. The slightly scalloped embossing on the rim makes this perfect for Carolyn – a modified version of Virginia Rose used in the restaurant trade. See the section on Virginia Rose for more on Carolyn.

Test Plate: BC-1055, 11-14-86

Four Best China saucers marked: SAMPLE, H.L.C. CO.

Today, most of HLC's production is geared towards the restaurant trade, however, the Best China name is no longer in use. Various contemporary shapes and patterns can be seen on their web site: http://www.hlchina.com/

Decorators & Combination Sets

"Combination Sets" are special sets of dinnerware which are combinations of shapes and decorated by an outside company such as Pearl China, Pacific China, Atlas, et. al. Blanks were assembled together, decorated and sold as a set.

Shown in the photo are four pieces from such a set. The flatware: platter, dinner plates, 6" plates and saucers are all marked (Swing) Eggshell by Homer Laughlin. The remaining pieces are unmarked, but their shapes are easily recognizable: HLC Brittany covered sugar; teacup and creamer by Harker Pottery Co. In general, pieces from a combination set will have a double backstamp: one of the company which produced the blank, and one of the company that decorated it. In this case, there is no double marking so the decorator may remain a mystery.

Since neither Harker nor HLC applied the treatments to these pieces, chances are very good that there are no official decoration numbers or special names. This presents a problem when trying to identify a piece that gets separated from a combination set and lacks a double marking. Lets say the Brittany covered sugar shown had gotten separated from its combination set, it would be extremely difficult to trace it down since it has a "non-standard" treatment. Because of combination sets, there may be pieces that can never be properly identified.

Virginia Rose and Marigold pieces were brought together to make up a set with a series of Colonial couple decals and ornate gold trim. These were decorated and backstamped by Pacific China.

The name of the decal on this platter is, "Deco Tulip." It was used extensively by the Harker Pottery Co. on their dinnerware and kitchenware shapes. This platter has a double backstamp: the general HLC marking with L39N5 as a date code and a gold BAKERITE mark. The Bakerite mark was used by Harker on their kitchenware. (The name Bakerite is to Harker as Kitchen Kraft is to HLC.) We can conclude from the markings that HLC produced the platter or blank when it received the HLC

mark and then Harker decorated it with their decal and gold trim. Harker's Bakerite gold markings was then applied over the glaze.

This cake set is a combination of HLC Trellis shape 6" plates and an unidentified handled tray. The tray is not a Homer Laughlin product (there is a series of numbers, but no makers mark) but these pieces have been brought together to form a cake set. the ornate gold decoration is over the glaze and can easily wear off.

Nautilus Eggshell salad bowl with serving spoon and fork. The utensils are from Harker Pottery and the set was decorated by the Maryland China Co. of Baltimore, Maryland. It is also marked, "MARCHICO Warranted 22KT. Gold."

"Oakwood" is the name of the decoration on these pieces of early HLC ware. They were made by the Oakwood China Company of East Liverpool and Sebring, Ohio which used wares from surrounding potteries. Pieces were treated with a special wood grained decoration.

During the 1950s there were several small decorating companies which would purchase dinner plate blanks and put special treatments with churches. These blanks include Harker Pottery's Gadroon, Steubenville's Adam Antique and Mt. Clemen's Vogue. Most of the blanks came from the Homer Laughlin shapes Theme Eggshell, Georgian Eggshell, Rhythm and Nautilus. The Theme Eggshell church plates are by far the most common with Georgian next and Rhythm and Nautilus being a little harder to find.

The churches featured are from all over the United States with no region being more common than any other. Church plates have been found from almost every one of the 48 contiguous states with several different denominations such as Presbyterian, Methodist, Church of Christ, Nazarene, Episcopal, Lutheran, Baptist and Catholic.

The treatments themselves are very simple: a single color and sometimes with gold or silver trim. The most common colors are: black, brown, red, blue and purple. The name of the church and its location are also featured on the front of the plate, and many times a brief history of the church is given on the reverse.

More often than not, a church plate will have the added marking of the decorator. The vast majority of church plate treatments were made by World Wide Art Studios of Covington, Tennessee. Others include: "Decorated Ceramics" of Cincinnati, OH, "China & Glass Decorators" of DuBois, PA and "Delano Studios" of Long Island, NY.

While most of the plates by these companies featured churches, some show other buildings such as courthouses, college buildings, hospitals and schools. Some companies also used the blanks to make souvenir plates for cities and states.

Church Plates using the Theme Eggshell shape.

This Theme Eggshell plate was decorated by World Wide Art Studios and shows the "Odd Fellows Historical Building" located in Caldwell, Idaho.

Another World Wide Art Studios treated plate, this time featuring "Old Harrisburg" the "Capital of Republic of Texas." This is much more elaborate than the single color treatments found on church plates. The plate has been hand-painted with pink and green shadowing and the embossing comes to life with purple grapes and dark green leaves. The back has Homer Laughlin's Theme Eggshell marking and World Wide Art Studio's stamp along with "Special tint by Mimi."

Values for Church plates and similar items: $3-5

Trade Sizes

In the early days of dinnerware production, a series of measurements called, "trade sizes" was often used. In the late 1940s, most of these became obsolete and potters opted for more practical and actual measurements. One of the most common for flatware involved measuring from the verge (where the well or flat portion curves into the rim) to the opposite edge of the plate. An actual measurement would go from rim to rim. The difference between the actual and trade sizes is approximately 2 inches. Thus, in the early 1900s, a plate advertised as 8" would be closer to 10" in reality.

Hollowware was given a special set of measurements. A number was assigned to a particular piece that indicated how much would fit into a barrel. (In the late 1800s and even into the early 1900s, it was customary to ship pottery in barrels packed with straw.) The larger the piece, the less that could fit into a barrel and thus a number was given to reflect that property. Conversely, the smaller the piece, the more that could fit into a barrel. A creamer, a rather small piece of hollowware, was generally considered a "48s" and something larger such as a batter jug, was around a "24s."

The only problem with this system is there was no standard. Each pottery had their own conversions from the special numbers to actual capacities. To make matters worse, potteries would often change their *own* standards. A bowl made by Homer Laughlin in the early 1900s may be listed as a "30s" bowl, but years later, the same shape but from a different line may be listed as a "36s."

Below are two lists of trade sizes for jugs from the 1930s. The list on the left is from Homer Laughlin and the one on the right is from the W.S. George Pottery Company. Notice the different standards and conversions to liquid measure.

HLC	WSG
48s – 3/4 pint	42s – 3/4 pint
42s – 1 pint	36s – 1 pint
36s – 1 3/4 pint	30s – 2 pints
30s – 2 1/2 pint	24s – 3 pints
24s – 4 pints	12s – 4 pints

Trade sizes follow no exact science and unless the collector encounters vintage ads (mainly those from before the early 1930s) then there should be no real need to know various trade sizes. Most collectors and reference guides don't list the trade sizes except in one case; the 36s bowl. For some reason, this name stuck! This may seem confusing, but many dinnerware lines have two 36s; the *36s bowl* and the *36s oatmeal*. The 36s bowl is sometimes called a deep bowl and generally has a capacity of 16oz. The 36s oatmeal is a low shallow bowl which is a larger version of a fruit cup. 36s oatmeals are approximately 6" in diameter. Virginia Rose, Marigold, Harlequin and several others had both a 36s bowl and a 36s oatmeal.

The Internet

Below is just a sample of the many websites on the Internet. The list is accurate as of this writing but please note that domain names may change or a site may disappear entirely. Visit a search engine such as Google at http://www.google.com/ and type in key words such as *Homer Laughlin* or your favorite line such as *Homer Laughlin Tango*. New sites are added all the time, so you never know what you'll find.

Visit the various for sale sites as well as eBay. They contain a wealth of information and can be very helpful when trying to identify a treatment or shape.

Title: fiestafanatic@work
URL: http://www.fiestafanatic.com/
Description: A collector site featuring vintage ephemera, advertisements and examples of Homer Laughlin dinnerware with emphasis on Fiesta.

Title: GOFIESTA!
URL: http://www.tc.umn.edu/~mutc0003/INDEX.htm
Description: Collector site with pieces of Homer Laughlin from toilet sets to decaled and solid color dinnerware.

Title: HLC Factory Tour
URL: http://www.fiestapottery.com/
Description: An on-line tour that shows the various manufacturing methods used by Homer Laughlin in recent years. Great photos and detailed descriptions.

Title: The Homer Laughlin China Company Home Page
URL: http://www.hlchina.com/
Description: The official HLC website which features shapes currently in production. Many assortments are shown in line drawing form. New developments with the ever popular Fiesta line are often posted.

Title: MediumGreen.com
URL: http://www.mediumgreen.com/
Description: A Fiesta, Harlequin and Epicure site for collectors. From here you can find information on the HLCCA – Homer Laughlin China Collectors Association – a club devoted to the promotion of Homer Laughlin's products throughout the years.

Title: The Missing Piece
URL: http://www.missing-piece.com/
Description: An online shop which sells mainly Homer Laughlin decal ware.

Title: OhioRiverPottery.com
URL: http://www.ohioriverpottery.com/
Description: A site run by the author of this book giving general information on American dinnerware manufactures, primarily those along the Ohio River Valley including Homer Laughlin, Taylor Smith & Taylor, Knowles, Hall and many others.

Title: Robbins Nest
URL: http://www.robbinsnest.com/
Description: An online shop specializing in American dinnerware with great emphasis on Homer Laughlin.

Title: 1site4all
URL: http://www.geocities.com/oregunn/
Description: A collector site with tables of links to dinnerware collectors, repair, and how-to-sites.

One Last Shape . . .

In late March 1938, four special pieces of hollowware were created. Rhead noted these as being for Woolworth's in an "all-over" decoration. The first piece created was the sauceboat followed by the teacup body. The cup was made with a tapered foot and two different styles of handles. Of the four shapes, the teacup is the only one that isn't listed as going into production. The last two pieces were modeled in the beginning of April; the covered sugar and creamer.

This is how the plain shapes were sketched in the modeling log. The sauceboat, sugar and creamer were noted as being released into production on April 14, 1938.

Rhead's journals don't provide an official name for this shape. In general, after a line was put into production, he would go on to refer to it with a proper shape name. However, in this case, he continued to call it "plain" or "all-over decoration shape." On May 16, 1938, he mentions a Woolworth's "all-over" teapot and casserole, but those pieces never got any further than the planning stage.

Exactly what was the official name for this line? Also, what was the special "all-over" treatment? Could it have been a silk screen or transfer design? At least three plain shape sugar and creamer sets have been found with a pearlized glaze. Perhaps this is the "all-over" decoration Rhead mentions. Some collectors speculate the special treatment was a Chintz-like pattern.

This is one of the few plain shape pieces found so far. It's marked with a general HLC backstamp and date code: F38N8 or July 1938, Plant 8. This would imply the shape had a run of at least three months. We can also infer that the shapes were used for more than an "all-over" decoration since this has a simple floral decal with gold trim.

One last question surrounding this shape is with regard to the flatware. None was specially created so pieces must have been picked up from an already existing line. Brittany and Kwaker – two plain round shapes – were available at this time and would have made perfect candidates for flatware. Perhaps a collector has more of these plain shapes within a set and can clear up the mystery of the Woolworth's "all-over" shapes!

Bibliography

Cunningham, Jo: *Homer Laughlin A Giant Among Dishes.* Schiffer Publishing, 1998.

Duke, Harvey: *The Official Price Guide to Pottery and Porcelain,* 8th Edition.
House of Collectibles, 1995.

Gillespie, Karen: *Home Furnishings.* Prentice-Hall, Inc. 1951.

Huxford, Sharon and Bob: *The Collector's Encyclopedia of Fiesta,* 8th Edition.
Collector Books, 1998.

Jasper, Joanne: *The Collector's Encyclopedia of Homer Laughlin China,* Collector Books, 1993.

Lehner, Lois: *Lehner's Encyclopedia of U.S. Marks on Pottery, Porcelain & Clay.*
Collector Books, 1988.

Racheter, Richard G.: *Collector's Guide to Homer Laughlin's Virginia Rose.* Collector Books, 1997.

Spargo, John: *Early American Pottery and China.* The Century Co. 1926.

The Homer Laughlin China Collectors Association: *Fiesta, Harlequin, Kitchen Kraft Dinnerwares.*
The Homer Laughlin China Collectors Association Guide. Schiffer Publishing 2000.